# Translation and Multilingual Natural Language Processing

Editors: Oliver Czulo (Universität Leipzig), Silvia Hansen-Schirra (Johannes Gutenberg-Universität Mainz), Stella Neumann (RWTH Aachen), Reinhard Rapp (Johannes Gutenberg-Universität Mainz)

In this series:

1. Fantinuoli, Claudio & Federico Zanettin (eds.). New directions in corpus-based translation studies.

2. Hansen-Schirra, Silvia & Sambor Grucza (eds.). Eyetracking and Applied Linguistics.

3. Neumann, Stella, Oliver Čulo & Silvia Hansen-Schirra (eds.). Annotation, exploitation and evaluation of parallel corpora: TC3 I.

4. Czulo, Oliver & Silvia Hansen-Schirra (eds.). Crossroads between Contrastive Linguistics, Translation Studies and Machine Translation: TC3 II.

5. Rehm, Georg, Felix Sasaki, Daniel Stein & Andreas Witt (eds.). Language technologies for a multilingual Europe: TC3 III.

6. Menzel, Katrin, Ekaterina Lapshinova-Koltunski & Kerstin Anna Kunz (eds.). New perspectives on cohesion and coherence: Implications for translation.

7. Hansen-Schirra, Silvia, Oliver Czulo & Sascha Hofmann (eds). Empirical modelling of translation and interpreting.

8. Svoboda, Tomáš, Łucja Biel & Krzysztof Łoboda (eds.). Quality aspects in institutional translation.

9. Fox, Wendy. Can integrated titles improve the viewing experience? Investigating the impact of subtitling on the reception and enjoyment of film using eye tracking and questionnaire data.

ISSN: 2364-8899

# Can integrated titles improve the viewing experience?

Investigating the impact of subtitling
on the reception and enjoyment
of film using eye tracking and
questionnaire data

Wendy Fox

language
science
press

Wendy Fox. 2018. *Can integrated titles improve the viewing experience?: Investigating the impact of subtitling on the reception and enjoyment of film using eye tracking and questionnaire data* (Translation and Multilingual Natural Language Processing 9). Berlin: Language Science Press.

ISBN: 978-3-96110-065-1 (Digital)
       978-3-96110-066-8 (Hardcover)

ISSN: 2364-8899
DOI:10.5281/zenodo.1180721
Source code available from www.github.com/langsci/187
Collaborative reading: paperhive.org/documents/remote?type=langsci&id=187

Cover and concept of design: Ulrike Harbort
Typesetting: Sebastian Nordhoff
Proofreading: Ahmet Bilal Özdemir, Amr Zawawy, Andreas Hölzl, Brett Reynolds, Claudia Marzi, Ezekiel Bolaji, Felix Hoberg, Gerald Delahunty, Ikmi Nur Oktavianti, Jean Nitzke, Jeroen van de Weijer, Plinio Barbosa, Selçuk Eryatmaz, Teresa Proto, Umesh Patil, Vadim Kimmelman,
Fonts: Linux Libertine, Arimo, DejaVu Sans Mono
Typesetting software: XƎLATEX

Language Science Press
Unter den Linden 6
10099 Berlin, Germany
langsci-press.org

Storage and cataloguing done by FU Berlin

Freie Universität Berlin

# Contents

Contents

# Introduction

While translation has long been an integral part of film production, beginning with the intertitles and title cards for silent films, it slowly shifted towards the post-production process where it remains until today. It therefore has become highly unlikely that any consultation takes place between translator and film-makers, pre-existing text elements are often not editable, and the potential for translation errors and layout challenges has continuously risen – regarding both the dubbing and subtitling process. Historically a dubbing country,[1] Germany is not well-known for subtitled productions. But while dubbing is obviously pre-dominant in Germany and other neighbouring countries with a similar language-related history and a sufficiently large target audience, more and more German viewers prefer the original versions of English film productions.[2] Fans of series such as *Game of Thrones* (USA/UK 2011-)[3] or *The Big Bang Theory* (USA 2007-) yearn for each new episode and many do not want to wait for the German dubbed version. Combined with the desire for a more authentic film experience, many German viewers prefer original and subtitled versions of their favourite show.[4]

Traditional subtitling, however, can be seen as a strong intrusion into the original image composition that can not only disrupt but also destroy the director's intended shot composition and focal points. But is the carefully composed interplay of image and sound not what makes film "the most popular art form"

---

[1] For the history of dubbing in Germany, refer to http://www.sprechersprecher.de/blog/die-geschichte-der-film-synchronisation-in-deutschland [2014-12-30, in German].

[2] This is reflected in the increasing number of screenings of original versions in German cinemas (see for example http://www.koeln.de/kino/ov-filme [2014-12-16, in German] and http://against-dubbing.com/de/ovkinos/ [2014-12-16, in German]), especially since the introduction of digital film, changing from 35 mm film to digital projection. This allowed for a considerably easier and more cost-efficient process for film distributors (see http://www.dw.de/der-35mm-film-stirbt-aus-kino-wird-digital/a-17013764 [2014-12-16, in German]).

[3] For better readability, film credits (year and country of origin) will only be stated the first time a film is mentioned. The full credits for all mentioned films are listed in Appendix B.

[4] This assumption is supported by the increasing number of German internet forums that centre around creating and providing fansubs – subtitles created by fans – for download: subcentral.de with approximately 134 new posts per day, as well as subtitles.de, tv4user.de, and opensubtitles.org [2014-12-30].

(Mercado 2010: 35) of today's entertainment landscape? Long eye movements between focal points and subtitles decrease the viewer's information intake, and especially German audiences, who are often not used to subtitles, seem to prefer to wait for the next subtitle instead of looking back up again. Furthermore, not only the placement, but also the overall design of traditional subtitles can disturb the image composition – for instance titles with a weak contrast, inappropriate typeface or irritating colour system. So should it not, despite the translation process, be possible to preserve both image and sound as far as possible? Especially given today's numerous artistic and technical possibilities and the huge amount of work that goes into the visual aspects of a film, taking into account not only special effects, but also typefaces, opening credits and text-image compositions. A further development of existing subtitling guidelines would not only express respect towards the original film version but also the translator's work.

Nowadays, audiovisual translation, i.e. subtitling, is only part of the main production process in the case of multilingual films. And a few of these mainly English production use individually placed titles to translation an additional language in the film – for instance *Man on Fire* (USA/UK 2004), *Heroes* (USA 2006-2010), and *Slumdog Millionaire* (UK/FR/USA 2008). These new concepts of subtitles are seen as "radical, popular re-conception of the subtitle's status" (Kofoed 2011) that "have been redirected from their customarily subsidiary, external position to become a central aspect of the filmic mise-en-scene" (Kofoed 2011). The idea therefore explored in this thesis is to retain the audio track – as usually done in traditional subtitling – but to place the "sub-"titles in a way that is based on the original image composition. These titles are to be integrated into the image in such a way as to create the best possible contrast and indicate speaking direction and speaker position. There are already several terms that attempt to grasp these new subtitling concepts and designs: the term of "abusive subtitles" (Nornes 1999: 17ff.) describes the experimental use of subtitles in regard to both graphical and linguistic aspects while the terms "hybrid" (Díaz Cintas & Muñoz Sánchez 2006: 51) and "creative" (McClarty 2012: 133ff.) subtitles focus on the overall presentation and are presented in opposition to traditionally placed and designed subtitles. Even though they do cover most of the differences between traditional subtitles and more recent concepts, these terms do not seem to apply to the titles used in the pilot study in Fox (2012) and the present study as they might still refer to subtitles being automatically placed in the bottom (or top) area of the screen. Therefore, the term "integrated titles" (Fox 2012: 1ff.) was used, referring to titles being integrated[5] into the shot composition. Nowadays,

---

[5]Inspired by Bayram and Bayraktar who described "text information [that is placed] directly into the picture" (2012: 82) as "integrated formats" (2012: 82).

audiovisual translation, i.e. subtitling, is only part of the main production process in the case of multilingual films. And a few of these mainly English production use individually placed titles to translate an additional language in the film – for instance *Man on Fire* (USA/UK 2004), *Heroes* (USA 2006-2010), and *Slumdog Millionaire* (UK/FR/USA 2008). These new concepts of subtitles are seen as "radical, popular re-conception of the subtitle's status" (Kofoed 2011) that "have been redirected from their customarily subsidiary, external position to become a central aspect of the filmic mise-en-scene" (Kofoed 2011). The idea therefore explored in this thesis is to retain the audio track – as usually done in traditional subtitling – but to place the "sub-"titles in a way that is based on the original image composition. These titles are to be integrated into the image in such a way as to create the best possible contrast and indicate speaker direction and position. There are already several terms that attempt to grasp these new subtitling concepts and designs: the term "abusive subtitles" (Nornes 1999: 17ff.) describes the experimental use of subtitles in regard to both graphical and linguistic aspects while the terms "hybrid" (Díaz Cintas & Muñoz Sánchez 2006: 51) and "creative" (McClarty 2012: 133ff.) subtitles focus on the overall presentation and are presented in opposition to traditionally placed and designed subtitles. Even though they do cover most of the differences between traditional subtitles and more recent concepts, these terms do not seem to apply to the titles used in the pilot study in Fox (2012) and the present study as they might still refer to subtitles being automatically placed in the bottom (or top) area of the screen. Therefore, the term "integrated titles" (Fox 2012: 1ff.) was used, referring to titles being integrated[6] into the shot composition.

So far, there has been no eye tracking analysis of German integrated titles except for the first basic pilot study in Fox (2012). Additionally, no eye tracking study has been conducted on the aesthetics and perception of subtitles combined with attempts to draft a new, updated set of guidelines for more recent subtitling concepts.

The present eye tracking study addressed whether the individual placement and design of (sub)titles can increase the viewer's reading time, the time spent exploring the image (rather than waiting for the next title), shorten the eye movements between titles and focus points as well as improve the overall viewing experience. Additional thought was given to indicate speech direction and rate as well as speaker position. Pablo Romero-Fresco gave his permission to use his short documentary *Joining the Dots* (UK 2012) and agreed to discuss his image

---

[6]Inspired by Bayram and Bayraktar who described "text information [that is placed] directly into the picture" (2012: 82) as "integrated formats" (2012: 82).

system and shot compositions as a first step to creating the integrated titles. A total of 14 English native speakers watched the film without subtitles to define the natural focus[7] points and provide reference data. Fifteen native speakers of German with little or no knowledge of English watched the film with traditional subtitles and 16 additional German native speakers with little or no knowledge of English watched the film with integrated titles. The gaze behaviour of the German participants was analysed in regard to reaction times, reading times, and the general visual attention distribution.

Expected results are decreased reading times and a more natural gaze behaviour with integrated titles. It is to be assumed that the reaction time for integrated titles is slightly longer than for traditional titles. Due to the individual placement of the titles, the distance between focal point and title is on average smaller and the viewer would therefore gain more time to explore the image and focus on the focal points. Overall, expectations are that integrated titles will have a positive effect on both the aesthetic viewing experience of the audience and the split attention between image and title, as integrated titles appear to motivate the viewer to return to the main focal point faster and spend more time exploring the image in between titles. Based on the study described in the present thesis, the advantages and disadvantages of integrated titles will be discussed and the question answered whether these titles can improve the viewing experience. The study aims to prove that consciously placed titles do a better job of maintaining the original image composition and reduce the necessary eye movements between title and main focus thus giving the viewer more time to explore the image. Additionally, integrated titles should have a positive effect on the aesthetic viewing experience.

The relevance of this research is seen not only in the increasing use of integrated titles in English film productions but in the fact that "even though these translation and accessibility services only account for 0.1 % – 1 % of the budget of an average film production (Lambourne 2012), over half of the revenue of, for example, both top-grossing and award-winning Hollywood films comes from foreign territories" (Romero-Fresco 2013: 202). Therefore, it is only in the interest of film producers to take a critical look at the perception of the translated version of their film and studies on more content- and image-related ways of audiovisual translation might be helpful in motivating this shift. And as a huge amount of work is invested nowadays in creating breath-taking effects from fonts to the image composition to the special effects, both of technical and artistic nature, why not also invest in the translation of the film and uphold the same standard and respect through the last steps of the production process. Implementing efforts

---

[7]The term 'natural' is used to describe the baseline data collected from the English native speakers as their eye movements were not affected by subtitles.

concerning audiovisual translation strategies and practices would mean a step closer to the original film and be indicative of the requisite respect to both the film material and the translation.

Chapter 1 of this thesis provides an overview of the fundamentals of audiovisual translation in general and subtitling in particular. It focuses on the relevant theoretical aspects, the different kinds of subtitling as well as traditional guidelines, specific challenges, and conventional solution strategies.

Chapter 2 discusses text elements in film and their graphical translation. Concerning film aesthetics and design, the way the text elements are treated is one of the more obvious indicators for changes made during the translation process. Not only do subtitles change films due to their additive character, but also the translation of already existing text elements such as captions, displays, inserts etc. can influence the reception of a film. Thus, the individual text elements and conventional graphical translation strategies are presented. Furthermore, a first concept of typographic film identity is introduced.

Chapter 3 then introduces the concept of integrated titles. This includes a historical overview, a discussion of existing similar terms, and the reasoning for the used term of 'integrated titles'. Further fields of study such as communication design and film studies are used to create a concept of required characteristics of integrated titles and the skills needed to create them. As there are already some examples of similar concepts, these are analysed with regard to the used placement strategies in Chapter 4.

Chapter 5 puts together the theoretical framework discussed and created in the previous chapters and introduces a first workflow for the creation of integrated titles. The proposed three main steps of film material analysis, creation of placement and layout strategies, and the application process are presented.

Chapter 6 introduces eye tracking as the main tool in this study. The general relevant functions of the eye are explained and, based on eye tracking studies in reading, usability research, and conventional subtitling, relevant eye movement measures are defined. Furthermore, relevant studies that served as inspiration for the experiment design are presented.

Chapter 7 then gives an overview over the method and experiment design. This includes the used eye tracking setup, software, insights from the pilot study, and the resulting hypotheses. The main study is introduced in Chapter 7.5 including the participant groups, film material, and individual adjustments to conventional subtitling strategies.

Chapter 8, the recorded eye tracking data and questionnaire data is presented and discussed. Chapter 9 then presents the conclusion, discusses the limitations of the study, and gives an outlook on future work and studies.

# 1 Audiovisual translation

Audiovisual Translation comprises all those modes of translation that are applied with multimodal texts based on both auditory and visual channels (cf. Jüngst 2010: 1). It provides "access to [...] audiences who are either excluded from one or more of the auditory or visual codes, or who only have partial access to these codes" (Kruger n.d.), including various kinds of subtitling and synchronisation, it also includes game localisation and the translation of other modern multimedia products. Four communication channels can be differentiated according to Gottlieb (1998: 245):

- *Verbal auditory channel*: This channel includes all auditory elements produced by speech, thus not only dialogues etc. but also background voices or song lyrics.

- *Non-verbal auditory channel*: This channel includes non-verbal music elements as well as all background noises.

- *Verbal visual channel*: This channel covers all written texts in the film material such as subtitles, displays, and captions.[1]

- *Non-verbal visual channel*: Here, all the elements that create the overall image are summarized.

Based on these channels, a number of common shifts between these channels can be defined:

- *Diasemiotic translation*: In this type of translation, a shift from channel a) to c) takes place (Leißner 2009: 24), which means a conversion from spoken elements to written text. Accordingly, diasemiotic translation describes the subtitling process. As text not included in the original version is added, this change is of an "additive" (Leißner 2009: 25) nature.

---

[1]More details on the various types of text elements are to be found in §2.4.

- *Isosemiotic translation*: With this form of translation, the verbal auditory channel is retained. It describes different types of dubbing: synchronisation, commentary, voice-over, etc. In general, they are usually considered to be "replacing" (Leißner 2009: 25) elements, although they are sometimes better characterized as additive, for example when an additional sound track is added, e.g. during the voice-over.

- *Intersemiotic translation*: In addition to the common types of translation, Jüngst describes this change of channel which she also refers to as "transmutation" (2010: 5). This term defines a change in the sign system, so a shift from d) to a) (picture to spoken elements) or vice versa – for example verbal to non-verbal or auditory to visual. This includes, among others, the description of the picture for the blind.

The following Table 1.1 lists the main forms of audiovisual translation that can be distinguished.

Synchronisation or 'dubbing' is a substituting form of translation and should be as synchronous as possible with regard to lexis, syntax, semantics, etc. This means that the audiovisual translation has to match lip movements as well as gestures and facial expression in the film material (Herbst 1994: 87, Leißner 2009: 23). For a long time, synchronisation aimed to convince the viewer of watching the

Table 1.1: Forms of Audiovisual Translation

| Form | Professional | Non-professional |
|---|---|---|
| Subtitling | Conventional subtitling[a] (Semi-)live subtitling Subtitles for the deaf and hard-of-hearing (SDH) | Fan subs |
| Synchronisation | dubbing Voice-over Commentary Audio description | Fan dubs |

[a]This work makes use of both the terms 'traditional subtitles' as it was used in the underlying pilot study and the term 'conventional subtitles' (Foerster 2010: 81). They are considered interchangeable.

original version of the film. In Germany, it is the main form of translation used for film material and games. Regarding the dominance of synchronisation in comparison to subtitling still being prevalent, Jüngst (2010: 5) assumes that because of the numerous jobs related to it as well as of the habituation of the audience, "countries of synchronization [...] will presumably stay countries of synchronization" (2010: 5). However, Jüngst admits that due to DVDs no clear prediction can be made "since DVDs have massively changed the habits of watching and the young generation might be already completely used to watch subtitled versions" (2010: 5), including subtitled videos on the internet and fan-produced subtitles.

The voice-over aims at a true translation as synchronous as possible to the original text (OT). In addition to the OT, a translation is put "over" it, while reducing the volume of the original to a minimum (Luyken 1991: 80; Leißner 2009: 21). The translation begins a little later and ends a bit earlier (Herbst 1994: 19). Complete synchronisation is not the objective and the voice-over is mainly used for newscasts and interviews, but can also be found in fiction films in America and Eastern Europe (cf. Szarkowska 2009). Moreover, narration is also counted as voice-over. In narration however, the text is shortened and altered, therefore the translation is an entirely different lingual process. This more formal result is usually used for documentary productions (Luyken 1991: 80; De Linde & Kay 1999: 2; Gambier 1994: 276).

Similar to narration, dubbing for commentaries does not aim for a true translation. A modification of the foreign language film material for the target language and culture takes place. Due to deletions, additions, etc., a "new" original is produced (Luyken 1991: 82; Leißner 2009: 22).

Furthermore, so-called audio described films are produced for the blind and visually impaired who cannot, or only partially, access the visually channels. They are equipped with an "audio description" (Jüngst 2010: 3) that describes what can be seen in the film. They therefore offer access to the visual channels by describing elements relevant to the story as well as the overall atmosphere visible in the image. While the various audiences include a range of needs from people who are born blind to partially visually impaired people and those who became blind later in their life, the goal is usually the same: to provide understanding and enjoyment.

Another rather rare and very specific form is the live interpretation, which is only used at festivals (Jüngst 2010: 3). This interpretation can be simultaneously heard through headphones or loudspeakers while the original is playing. It is used less and less often.

While the audience for synchronisation is one of the least heterogeneous, targeting exclusively hearing viewers that cannot understand the language in the original film, subtitling has a wide range of target groups: deaf audiences,[2] hard-of-hearing audiences, viewers with cognitive disorders, language learners, and those who need interlingual translation. The following section will give an overview over the various kinds of subtitles, challenges, and strategic solutions.

## 1.1 Subtitling

Intertitles, or title cards (Díaz Cintas & Remael 2007:25), are often seen as the "origin of subtitles" (Díaz Cintas & Remael 2007: 26) and accompanied the first silent films. Modern subtitling is defined as "diamesic translation in polysemiotic media (including films, TV, video, and DVD) in the form of one or more lines of written text presented on the screen in sync with the original verbal content" (Gottlieb 2012: 37). Nowadays, there are at least three types of text that can be found in a film: subtitles, captions, and displays. These can be accompanied by additional text elements such as the film title, inserts, prologues and epilogues, opening and closing credits or other elements that do not always require a translation. While a subtitle is a written intralingual or interlingual translation of the spoken content, the other text elements might already exist in the original film and might or might not require translation. Captions are types of information which are important for a plot of a film, and which are inserted on a separate layer in the foreground. Typical captions are, for example, people's names and indications of places or time. Displays, however, are an essential component of the picture such as street names, letters, and newspaper headlines. They are additionally mentioned in the subtitle according to their relevance whereas captions usually appear in the subtitle (unless they are comprehensible without subtitling as it is usually the case for people's names and indications of places). As significant progress has been made and there seems to be more liberty in the creative handling of these additional written information than with subtitles, §2.4 gives an overview of the various text elements in film and their visual translation.

Most challenges and shortcomings in subtitle production arise due to the overt character of subtitles: They are superimposed on the original and co-exist with the source text in an interlinear way, and therefore are constantly open to comparison and criticism if the audience has at least basic knowledge of the source language. While the term 'captions' is often used to describe additional text ele-

---

[2]This includes both viewers that were born deaf or became deaf before spoken language acquisition and after.

ments such as name and place indicators, in the United States they refer to the subtitles for the deaf and hard-of-hearing – either simply as "captions" or "closed captions" (CC, Díaz Cintas & Remael 2007: 14).

Gottlieb describes five types of subtitles (2012: 43–44):

- I normally visible (= *open*) subtitles for special cinema screenings,

- II open TV subtitles broadcast as part of an analogue transmission signal,

- III optional (= *closed*) TV subtitles, transmitted via teletext (Santiago 2007),

- IV closed TV subtitles broadcast digitally, and

- V optional DVD subtitles selected via the on screen menu.

As is visible from this classification, subtitles are technically divided into 'open' and 'closed' (Díaz Cintas & Remael 2007: 21). Open subtitles are always visible, including not only the mentioned analogue broadcast or special screenings but also subtitles that are part of the original version of a film, e.g. as translation of an additional language (see Chapter 2 for examples). Closed subtitles, on the other hand, can be switched on optionally, including intralingual and interlingual subtitles in television, video-on-demand and DVDs respectively Blu-rays. Digitally extracted professional subtitles and fan-produced subtitles ("Fansubs", O'Hagan 2009: 94) can also often be downloaded and then added to a film or programme. Gottlieb also defines at least nine forms of interlingual subtitles (2012: 45). Multilingual subtitling that includes more than one language[3] and "pivot subtitling" (Leißner 2009: 27), which works indirectly through a more common language when "movie material from an exotic language has to be subtitled" (Leißner 2009: 27) can be seen as special forms of subtitling. Another specialised group of subtitles are those displayed during live performances such as conferences, in the theatre, at the opera or at concerts – called super-, supra- or surtitles (Díaz Cintas & Remael 2007: 25). Since these variations are rather rare, too specialised and not especially relevant for this book, they will not be discussed in the following.

---

[3]Bilingual or multilingual subtitles are often used in countries that have more than one official language such as Belgium (Dutch, French, and German) and Finland (Finish, Swedish, and Sami). In these countries, each language takes up one or even two line(s) in the subtitle. Additional disadvantages arise, such as the image always being covered by at least two lines of text, a reduced display time and the general disadvantage of speakers of the language subtitled in the second row as they might intuitively read the previous line first.

Intralingual subtitling works exclusively with the language of the original film, with the hearing-impaired usually being the main target group. However, intralingual subtitles are also very useful for a better understanding of foreign language films or dialects and accents and are widely used by language learners, studies including Danan (2004), Bianchi & Ciabattoni (2007), and Remael et al. (2008). Intralingual subtitles do not only provide access for entertainment reasons but also to daily information and target an audience far from homogeneous. Concerning hearing-impaired audiences, four major groups are usually distinguished here: Hard-of-hearing, people who became deaf postlingually, people who were born deaf, and those who wear Cochlear implants (CI).[4] While the hard-of-hearing and postlingually deaf feel as part of the hearing society, an independent Deaf culture emerged (Jüngst 2010: 125), and while the first group usually develops the language of their country as their native language, people who became deaf prelingually communicate with the sign language of their country or region that has its own grammar and distinctive features. The challenge for someone creating intralingual subtitles is that of not only understanding the target audiences and their culture but also the physical and psychological implications of being deaf or hard-of-hearing (Remael 2007: 44). Additional decisions have to be made concerning the presentation of information, its density, and the amount of supplementary information. While redundancies of auditory and visual information make it easier for a hearing audience to follow the plot presented as an polysemiotic audiovisual text, SDH also has to provide access to relevant noises and music, etc. (Neves 2009: 156). Professionals have to be literate in the film code and image composition to be able to understand and communicate various effects (Neves 2009: 157) as well as understand the variety "in terms of literacy, hearing loss and socio-economic factors" (ITC 1999: 4).

Relatively young subgroups of SDH are semi-live and live subtitles. They provide real-time access to live film material such as sport events, news programmes or political debates and are displayed with a delay of a few seconds. Also called "simultaneous subtitling" (Luyken 1991: 80) and "real-time subtitling" (Orero 2006), it is prone to mistakes (Jüngst 2010: 138). Live subtitles are a live broadcasted written form of spoken language in television that is produced during the broadcast (see Kraus 2010: 12) and normally offered as closed captions that can be added manually. Semi-live subtitles are pre-prepared subtitles (Jüngst 2010: 138–139) for live programmes that have a relatively dense script. The goal is to minimise the

---

[4]For an overview and impression of the difference in frequency range of Cochlear implants, see http://www.telegraph.co.uk/news/health/10848586/What-the-world-sounds-like-with-a-cochlear-implant.html [2016–05–01].

risk of mistakes, which is relatively high for live subtitling. Live subtitling and semi-live subtitling are often combined and produced with speech recognition software such as that offered by Nuance.[5] Traditional guidelines for intralingual subtitles are discussed in the following chapter.

Interlingual translation accounts for the largest part of audiovisual translation as this mode describes translations from one language to another (Díaz Cintas & Remael 2007: 13). While Germany is historically and traditionally a dubbing country, inter- and intralingual subtitles are becoming more and more attractive, not only offering more access for hearing-impaired audiences but also catering to audiences that value the original audio channel of a film but do not (fully) understand the source language. Costing less than 10 % of lip-sync dubbing (Media Consulting Group 2007: 38), subtitles generally allow for a higher number of films translated, more access for both hearing-impaired and hearing viewers as well as a faster overall process while adding an additional text layer instead of replacing the verbal audio track.

However, subtitles are seen as a "necessary evil" (Foerster 2010: 82; cf. Marleau 1982) and cannot fulfil the often voiced demand of "transparency of the target text and [...] invisibility of the translator" (Foerster 2010: 83) that "still dominate[s] the commercial world" (Foerster 2010: 83). Norms and guidelines demand "invisibility" (Ivarsson & Carroll 1998: 157–159) and that subtitles "blend in with the film in such a way that the viewer doesn't notice them" (Subtitling International UK 1994: 3). While dubbing sometimes might be able to "provide the illusion of the original" (Subtitling International UK 1994: 3), "this industry does not pay much attention to the actual process of translation, and tends to adhere overwhelmingly to domesticating translation theories and to producing the illusion of transparency" (Subtitling International UK 1994: 83–84). Díaz Cintas and Remael describe this predicament the following way:

> However, the general opinion is that the best subtitles are those that the viewer does not notice. From this perspective, the subtitler's task seems to be a contradiction in terms: to provide a translation that is written a posteriori on the original programme, flashes in and out at the bottom of the screen but pretends not to be there. (2007: 40)

This "attempt at invisibility [...] tends to have a negative impact on the social recognition of subtitlers" (Díaz Cintas & Remael 2007: 40), even though they have the same copyright as writers (Ivarsson 1992: 106).

---

[5] An overview of the *Dragon* speech recognition software offered by Nuance can be found here: http://www.nuance.com/dragon/index.htm [2016–05–01].

The skopos of the source text should determine the approach (Stolze 1997: 155) and even though Benjamin speaks of the content of translation, his demand for transparency (1972: 18) seems to apply to subtitling, considering its interlinear character. Source and target texts are available at the same time and "aiming for invisibility becomes a paradox verging on the absurd" (Foerster 2010: 83): "Subtitles have never been and will never be invisible" (Foerster 2010: 83) – so we should try to make the best out of their presence instead of denying it.

Due to this simultaneity of source and target text and their combination with the moving image, viewers have to split their visual attention between reading the subtitles and processing the image (Bayram & Bayraktar 2012). This and other characteristics of subtitles such as time and space constraints lead to several challenges subtitle professionals and viewers are confronted with. Common strategic solutions to these challenges and a basic set of guidelines are summarised in the following section.

## 1.2 Strategic solutions for subtitles

Subtitling and its various subgroups have lacked binding norms ever since. However, there are basic guidelines concerning both interlingual and intralingual subtitles most subtitle professionals agree on. These are reflected in articles such as the "Code of Good Subtitling Practice" (Ivarsson & Carroll 1998: 157–159) and "A Proposed Set of Subtitling Standards in Europe" (Karamitroglou 1998), various books and book chapters (e.g. Leißner 2009; Díaz Cintas & Remael 2007; Díaz Cintas et al. 2007), as well as official guidelines by companies such as the "ITC Guidance on Standards for Subtitling" (Independent Television Commission, ITC 1999) and the "BBC Online Subtitling Editorial Guidelines" (Ford Williams 2009).[6] While the lack of standardised norms can be criticised (Leißner 2009: 30), it also provides – at least theoretically – creative freedom and room for adjustments for individual applications, just as with any other multimedia form of translation. Most authors of guidelines point out that "good subtitling is a complex balancing act" (Ford Williams 2009: 3) and that "it will never be possible to apply all of the guidelines all of the time" (Ford Williams 2009: 3) as they are sometimes "mutually exclusive" (Ford Williams 2009: 3). It is therefore a "question of deciding which elements in the soundtrack merit reporting" (eAccess+ 2016). Additionally, the focus of a set of guidelines might be on language, appearance, or a mixture

---

[6]More information on British guidelines can be found here: http://hub.eaccessplus.eu/wiki/ Standards_and_Guidelines_for_accessible_audio-visual_media_in_the_United_Kingdom [2016-02-09].

of both. The ITC standard lists the subtitler's priorities for SDH as follows (ITC 1999: 4):

1) Allow adequate reading time. [...]
2) Reduce viewers' frustration by:
    a) attempting to match what is actually said, reflecting the spoken word with the same meaning and complexity; without censoring
    b) constructing subtitles which contain all obvious speech and relevant sound effects; and
    c) placing subtitles sensibly in time and space.
3) Without making unnecessary changes to the spoken word, construct subtitles which contain easily-read and commonly-used English sentences in a tidy and sensible format. In the case of subtitles for children, particular regard should be given to the reading age of the intended audience.

In order to define the gap integrated titles could fill, challenges and traditional solutions of subtitling are discussed in the following. This will provide a basis for the criticism of traditional subtitling guidelines and suggestions for improvement or alternatives. As both solutions for visual and content-related challenges might offer a basis for new guidelines, content-related strategies are presented as well. The focus is on general guidelines for traditional subtitles and SDH – semi-live and live subtitles are not taken into account due to their highly specific nature.

## 1.2.1 Time & space

Time and space limitations are likely the most obvious and restricting constraints in audiovisual translation, but also one of the more frequently discussed and researched features. The various guidelines are based on an average reading speed, for example based on viewers "aged between 14–65, from an upper-middle socio-educational class" and "for a text of average complexity" (Karamitroglou 1998).[7] While Karamitroglou sets the average reading speed at 150–180 words per minute (wpm), corresponding to 2.5–3 words per second (wps), other guidelines state

---

[7]This excludes, for example, children with an average reading speed of around 90–120 words per minute (aged 6–14, Karamitroglou 1998). Karamitroglou therefore advises to adjust the subtitles for children's programmes accordingly (Karamitroglou 1998). For prelingually deaf children, the ITC guidelines state a presentation rate of 70–80 words per minute as suitable (1999: 19).

that the display speed "should not exceed 140 words per minute", with 180 wpm for "exceptional circumstances" (ITC 1999: 11; cf. Ford Williams 2009: 7). There should also be extra time allocated for unfamiliar words, several speakers, labels, flashing subtitles, visuals and graphics, placed subtitles, long figures, shot changes, and slow speech (Ford Williams 2009: 8). If subtitles are targeted at a hearing-impaired audience or are supposed to cover both audiences, the significantly lower reading speed and reading literacy for the deaf has to be taken into account (Jüngst 2010: 125).

Concerning synchronicity and rhythm, subtitles should "adhere to a regular viewer reading rhythm" and the leading-in and -out times should "reflect the rhythm of the film" (Ivarsson & Carroll 1998: 157–159; cf. Ford Williams 2009: 17). Good subtitles are in synchronicity with the film (Ivarsson & Carroll 1998: 72, Díaz Cintas et al. 2007: 88), even though Ivarsson/Carroll noted it as a challenge for viewers to follow a fast-paced dialogue and image at the same time (1998: 72). Readability, however, should not suffer in order to gain synchronicity, and content should not be subtitled before it has actually been said (Ivarsson & Carroll 1998: 75, Díaz Cintas et al. 2007: 91). While it has become customary with many professionals to display fast-paced dialogue between two speakers in one subtitle (Díaz Cintas et al. 2007: 89), the BBC guidelines state the opposite: "Do not simultaneously caption different speakers if they are not speaking at the same time" (Ford Williams 2009: 12).

All guidelines that discussed the number of lines set a maximum of two lines per subtitle. This would ensure that "no more than 2/12 of the screen image would be covered by subtitles at all time" (Karamitroglou 1998), with single-line subtitles occupying the lower of the two possible lines. Leißner (2009: 31) also sees reason for four-line subtitles in case of bilingual subtitles but mentions herself that this practice is rather rare due to the significant impact on the image. Ivarsson and Carroll give a maximum of 40 characters for cinema and 35 characters for television (cf. Karamitroglou 1998) and Karamitroglou reasons that fitting more than 40 characters per line "reduces the legibility of the subtitles" (Karamitroglou 1998). More recent articles , however, propose a maximum of 38–40 characters per line (Díaz Cintas et al. 2007: 82). Ford Williams sees the maximum at "roughly 32 or 34 characters per line" (2009: 13) – however, as BBC's subtitles are generally targeted at hearing-impaired audiences, this might be connected to the lower reading literacy and speed of these viewers.

Considering these limits, subtitle professionals regularly have to make decisions about where to insert a line break or whether to keep a long one-liner instead of splitting the sentence into two lines. Ivarsson and Carroll mention studies showing a higher reading speed for two-liners (1998: 64) while these also cover more of the image than long one-liners – therefore it's easily possible to argue for both strategies, and consistency might be the most relevant factor for a good viewing experience. If, however, a line break is necessary, the subtitle should be split into logical units (Leißner 2009: 36) that also create preferably short eye movements, and, for aesthetic reasons, with the first line shorter than the second one (Ivarsson & Carroll 1998: 77; Díaz Cintas et al. 2007: 87). Additionally, three-line subtitles are seen as acceptable in case of SDH (Díaz Cintas et al. 2007: 82) – while some might argue that the additional coverage of the image should result in further shortening, this might feel like censorship to SDH audiences and should be avoided (Jüngst 2010: 131; Neves 2009: 160). Overall, three-line subtitles are not used in many countries anymore, and it is almost impossible to find examples of four-line subtitles, even though they are mentioned now and then.

Based on the average reading speed, Gottlieb sees 2–6 seconds as the maximum durations for subtitles (2012: 162; cf. Ivarsson & Carroll 1998: 157–159), and also Díaz Cintas et al. speak of a 'six seconds rule' as the maximum duration for subtitles (2007: 96; also "six-second rule",[8] Díaz Cintas & Remael 2007: 23). This is supposed to allow the viewer enough time to read two full lines and explore the image at the same time. The maximum of 6 seconds should prevent the audience from re-reading and longer speech acts should be split into multiple subtitles (Karamitroglou 1998: 89; Ivarsson & Carroll 1998: 64). A minimum of 1–1.5 seconds is sufficient for the eye not to miss a title and 1 second is considered the minimum for even a one-word subtitle (Karamitroglou 1998; Ivarsson & Carroll 1998: 65; Díaz Cintas et al. 2007: 92).

The BBC guidelines are very precise concerning timing as they generally do not focus on language but the form. Therefore, the display times for full two- and one-liners are defined in detail: A full two-liner of about 14–16 words should be displayed for 6 seconds. Of that, 5.5 seconds are calculated by the average reading speed per word, plus ¼ to ½ second the brain needs to "start processing the subtitle" (Karamitroglou 1998). The one-liner (or single-liner) of about 7–8 words should be displayed for about 3.5 seconds, including the reaction time and the slower processing compared to a full two-liner that "signals an acceleration of the reading speed" (Karamitroglou 1998). As Karamitroglou states, this is not triggered "with the single-line subtitle" (1998). In all cases, subtitles should not stand significantly longer to prevent re-reading. The duration of $\frac{1}{3}$ second per word can be see as average time for easily processable text.[9]

---

[8]The six-seconds rule is based on television subtitle lines containing 35 to 37 characters on average, resulting in 70 to 74 characters in six seconds and therefore around 12 characters per second (Díaz Cintas & Remael 2007: 23).

[9]See the BBC guidelines for standard timing for up to three lines (Ford Williams 2009: 9).

Pauses between consecutive subtitles should be at least ¼ second to prevent "overlay" effects (Karamitroglou 1998), as "this break is necessary to signal to the brain the disappearance of one subtitle as a piece of linguistic information, and the appearance of another" (Karamitroglou 1998). This is also defined as a "minimum of four frames [that] should be left between subtitles to allow the viewer's eye to register the appearance of a new subtitle" (Ivarsson & Carroll 1998: 157–159).

Concerning cuts or camera takes, the definition is crucial: Not every change from long shot to close-up is a relevant cut, but rather "camera takes/cuts that signify a thematic change in the film product" (Karamitroglou 1998; cf. Ivarsson & Carroll 1998: 157–159). Subtitles "should disappear before the cuts" (Karamitroglou 1998) as "subtitles that are allowed to over-run shot changes can cause considerable perceptual confusion and should be avoided" (ITC 1999: 12; cf. Ford Williams 2009: 14). However, increasing use of quick shot changes and cuts in modern film making has let to some kind of acceptance of ignoring this rule now and then:

> In practice, it is recognised that the frequency and speed of shot changes in many programmes present serious problems for the subtitler. A subtitle should, therefore, be 'anchored' over a shot change by at least one second to allow the reader time to adjust to the new picture. Shot changes normally reflect the beginning or end of speech. The subtitler should, therefore, attempt to insert a subtitle on a shot change when this is in synchrony with the speaker. (ITC 1999: 12)

Concerning the leading-in time, the analysed guidelines give different instructions. While Karamitroglou states that a delay of ¼ seconds should be between speech and subtitle onset (1998), the ITC and BCC guidelines suggest an immediate appearance of the subtitles. Karamitroglou references unnamed tests of eye and brain reactions for his instructions:

> Subtitles should not be inserted simultaneously with the initiation of the utterance but ¼ of a second later, since tests have indicated that the brain needs ¼ of a second to process the advent of spoken linguistic material and guide the eye towards the bottom of the screen anticipating the subtitle. A simultaneously presented subtitle is premature, surprises the eye with its flash and confuses the brain for about ½ a second, while its attention oscillates between the inserted subtitled text and the spoken linguistic material, not realising where it should focus. (Karamitroglou 1998)

The ITC and BBC guidelines, on the other hand, insist on synchronicity, refer-
encing unnamed eye tracking research: "Research in eye movement has shown
that hearing impaired viewers make use of visual cues from the faces of television speakers. Therefore subtitle appearance should coincide with speech onset" (Ford Williams 2009: 12; cf. ITC 1999: 11). While this reasoning might be
completely justified for a hearing-impaired audience, a combination of either
both strategies or the exclusive adherence to Karamitroglou's instructions might
be better suited for a hearing audience. Titles might stand longer if scenes or
cuts allow for it, but the subtitle disappearance or "lagging-out time" (ITC 1999)
should not exceed 1.5–2 seconds or 12 frames, otherwise viewers might distrust
the translation (ITC 1999; Ford Williams 2009: 12). If possible, however, "subtitle disappearance should coincide roughly with the end of the corresponding
speech segment, since subtitles remaining too long on the screen are likely to
be re-read by the viewer" (ITC 1999: 11) and the distribution between subtitles
"must consider cuts and sound bridges" (Ivarsson & Carroll 1998: 157–159) in order to "underline surprise or suspense" (Ivarsson & Carroll 1998: 157–159). Ford
Williams emphasises that these rules of synchronicity also apply for off-screen
speakers and narrators in the case of a hearing-impaired audience "since viewers with a certain amount of residual hearing make use of auditory cues to direct
their attention to the subtitle area" (2009: 12).

Various possible strategic solutions are given by the analysed guidelines and
other authors. In order to deal with time and space constraints, interlingual subtitles are usually shortened. This can be achieved by several basic strategies that
can also occur in combination: paraphrasing, summarising, simplification, and
omission (Díaz Cintas et al. 2007: 206) as well as smaller modifications such
as altering syntactic structures (Karamitroglou 1998). Paraphrasing is usually
combined with omissions (Leißner 2009: 45), just as summaries and simplifi-
cations. Elements that can be left out include redundancies such as intrasemi-
otic repetitions or intersemiotic visible elements (Gottlieb 1998: 247; Ivarsson &
Carroll 1998: 157–159), "common comprehensible phrases" (Ivarsson & Carroll
1998: 157–159), "padding expressions" (such as "you know" or "well", Karamitroglou 1998), "tautological cumulative adjectives/adverbs" (Karamitroglou 1998)
and "responsive expressions" (Karamitroglou 1998). These decisions will always
be case-dependent:

> A decision as to which pieces of information to omit or to include should
> depend on the relative contribution of these pieces of information to the
> comprehension and appreciation of the target film as a whole. [...] The sub-
> titler should attempt to keep a fine balance between retaining a maximum

of the original text (essential for the comprehension of the linguistic part of the target film), and allowing ample time for the eye to process the rest of the non-linguistic aural and visual elements (essential for the appreciation of the aesthetic part of the target film). (Karamitroglou 1998)

## 1.2.2 Content

The number of challenges that arise with the content of spoken language and its inter- and intralingual translation in the form of subtitles is high and the following list everything but exhaustive. One of the main and most basic challenges is the textualisation of spoken language that leads to the loss of various typical characteristics such as dialects, sociolects, idiolects, colloquial language, and swear and taboo words (Jüngst 2010: 51f.; Ford Williams 2009: 5), but also intonation, emotions, accents, difficult and inaudible speech, or hesitation and interruption (Ford Williams 2009: 21ff.). Even the impact and perception of silence changes (Ford Williams 2009: 21ff.). These characteristics are not only lost due to the textualisation and time and space constraints, but also intentionally ignored in order to achieve a better readability and less distraction from the image. It can be assumed, however, that – in case of a hearing or only slightly hearing-impaired audience – some of these characteristics are still perceived auditorily, e.g. pauses, false starts, corrections, interruptions, slips, dialects, and colloquial language (Leißner 2009: 41). The transfer of sociolects, dialects, and idiolects should be handled with care and always follow an analysis of the intended effect as a literal translation or transcription might have the opposite effect (Díaz Cintas et al. 2007: 191f.) – the same goes for taboo and swear words. While these are characteristics of spoken language, other challenges occur during interlingual translation due to speech containing e.g. cultural specifics or humour.

While it is tempting to leave out as much "superfluous" (Ivarsson & Carroll 1998: 157) and repetitive information as possible, this should not be done considering hearing-impaired viewers (Ivarsson & Carroll 1998: 157–159; Ford Williams 2009: 4). Dialects and accents should not be transcribed or translated phonetically or using "syntactic transcription of the spoken form" (Karamitroglou 1998), but rather presented by using characteristic vocabulary or brackets (De Linde & Kay 1999: 13). The exception are dialects or forms that "already appeared in a written form in printed materials" (e.g. "biblical forms", Karamitroglou 1998). Swear and taboo words "should not be censored unless their frequent repetition dictates their reductions for reasons of text economy" (Karamitroglou 1998). Additionally, Karamitroglou sees no harm in using well-known acronyms, apostrophes, and symbols, as long as they are "immediately recognisable and comprehensible" (Karamitroglou 1998).

The rendering of music has been discussed widely, e.g. by Neves (2009: 164f.), Jüngst (2010: 137), and Krammer (2001). Most guidelines emphasise that "songs must be subtitled where relevant" (Ivarsson & Carroll 1998: 157–159; cf. Ford Williams 2009: 4, 31–33). The ITC guidelines (1999: 16) provide further details:

> At the very minimum, the title of the music playing should be given. Where possible the words of a song should be included. This is especially important where the programme is to be viewed by younger people. Pop programmes, opera and songs connected to the story line are particularly important areas. Song lyrics should be subtitled verbatim; but, if the pace of the song is very rapid, whole couplets or verses may be omitted.

Concerning noise transcription and indication, the challenge is not only to decide what noises should be represented in the subtitles, but also how. While hard-of-hearing and postlingually deaf audiences will understand *wuff* as indication of a barking dog, viewers born deaf will most likely not, or only with a considerably delay, make the connection. But as people that were born deaf still have a concept of noises (Neves 2009: 155), the main goal must be to only subtitle noises that are not obvious from the image and also relevant for the plot in the clearest non-ambiguous way possible (Jüngst 2010: 134; Ford Williams 2009: 34–35; ITC 1999: 15). While "context and genre [...] must be taken into consideration" (ITC 1999: 15), "descriptive statements are normally preferable to onomatopoeic spellings" (ITC 1999: 15) that is usually only targeted at children and not used for adults.

Paralanguage poses an additional challenge as meaning cannot always be accessed through a speaker's facial expressions – common solutions so far have been descriptions in brackets (Jüngst 2010: 134) while possibly more intuitive solutions such as smileys and emoticons are being researched (Neves 2009: 161; Secară 2016).

Interlingual translation additionally includes challenges such as the transfer of cultural specifics and humour. Cultural specifics are "extralinguistic references to items that are tied-up with a country's culture, history, or geography and tend therefore to pose serious translation challenges" (Díaz Cintas et al. 2007: 200). In contrast to other modes of translation, translators cannot add footnotes or any extensive explanation to subtitles and have to solve both intralinguistic features such as language-specific grammatical forms, metaphors, and idioms as well as extralinguistic features such as references to society, culture, geography, and history (Nedergaard-Larsen 1993: 211).

Karamitroglou emphasises that "there is no standard guideline for the transfer of culture-specific linguistic elements" (1998) but rather a range of strategies (based on Pedersen 2005: 9; cf. Nedergaard-Larsen 1993; Díaz Cintas & Remael 2007):

- *Omission* (Nedergaard-Larsen 1993: 219, 231; Pedersen 2005: 9; Díaz Cintas & Remael 2007: 206): In the case that a culturally specific element cannot be sustained due to the characteristics of subtitles or the lack of an appropriate equivalent in the target culture, it can be omitted. Some translators might compensate by adding another cultural specific elsewhere.

- *Transposition* (Karamitroglou 1998), *loan* (Leißner 2009: 49ff.), or *retention* (Pedersen 2005: 9): Cultural specifics such as names of streets or places can be kept, along with those that are indispensible for the plot.

- *Transposition/Loan with explanation* (Karamitroglou 1998; Leißner 2009: 49ff.): Subtitles rarely offer sufficient space for additional explanations. If, however, the space and time constraints allow for an additional element, an explanatory adjective can be used.

- *Direct translation* (Pedersen 2005: 9): If an institution or concept exists in the target culture as well and carries the same name, it can be directly translated (cf. Nedergaard-Larsen 1993: 227).

- *Imitation* (Pedersen 2005: 9) or *literal translation* (Leißner 2009: 49ff.): Literal translation of all the elements of a cultural specific – therefore "imitating" the semantic structure – that can be used for institutions or ranks. As there might already be an official equivalent in the target language, this can lead to irritation in the audience and should therefore only be used to a limited extent.

- *Official Equivalent* (Pedersen 2005), *cultural transfer*, or *adaptation* (Leißner 2009: 49ff.): Culture-specific elements can be translated with equivalents in the target culture.

- *Neutralisation* or *Specification* (Pedersen 2005: 4ff.; Leißner 2009: 49ff.): A plain explanation for a cultural specific can be given, e.g. replacing a metaphor that is well-known in the source language with the actual term or concept. Pedersen further differentiates between *explicitation* (i.e. writing out an abbreviation or acronym) and *addition* (adding information on the connotation) (Pedersen 2005: 4ff.).

- *Chunking*: Leißner (2009: 49ff.) defines chunking as the translation of a culture-specific element with a term of the same register (also comparable to *Substitution* [Pedersen 2005: 9]):
    - *Chunking up* (more general term),
    - *Chunking down* (more specific term),
    - *Lateral chunking* (more familiar term from same register).

While culture-specific elements are easily defined and recognised, humour, on the other hand, is subjective, not universal, and therefore hard to define. As it is often culturally specific, it might be seen as either an independent challenge in audiovisual translation or a subcategory of culture-specific elements as it is likely for people from the same cultural background to laugh about similar things (Leißner 2009: 54). As knowledge of the source language does not guarantee understanding of a joke, it is sometimes necessary to adjust it to the target culture. Zabalbeascoa (1996: 251) and Díaz Cintas and colleagues (2007: 221) give several categories of jokes: bi- and international jokes, national-culture-and-institutions jokes, national-sense-of-humour jokes, language-dependant jokes, visual jokes, and complex jokes. In order to deliver "humorous sequences" (2009: 29), Ford Williams underlines the importance of retaining "as much of the humour as possible" (2009: 29):

1. Try wherever possible to keep punchlines separate from the preceding text.

2. Where possible, allow viewers to see actions and facial expressions which are part of the humour by leaving the screen clear or by editing. Try not to use reaction shots containing no speech in order to gain time.

3. Never edit characters' catchphrases.

4. Puns should be clearly indicated in your subtitle. [...] (Ford Williams 2009: 29)

While these guidelines offer advice, they are not specific strategies. Díaz Cintas et al. (Díaz Cintas et al. 2007: 215f.) and Zabalbeascoa (1996: 332) emphasise that humour should not be transferred at all costs, especially not at the expense of coherence and idiomatic phrases. The subtitle's humorous effect should be as close as possible to that of the statement in the source language, but also as readable and comprehensible as possible. The purpose of a joke should be defined first (Reiß & Vermeer 1984; Stolze 1997: 180f.), as it is not always the creation of humour, and paraphrasing or the use of a similar rhetoric tool might be the better solution (Díaz Cintas et al. 2007: 215). While most mentioned strategies are similar to those listed for culture-specific elements (i.e. "adaption" [Veiga 2009: 163], "substitution" [Veiga 2009: 163], "omission" [Díaz Cintas & Remael 2007: 216], and "compensation" [Seifferth 2009: 37]), the particular challenge of translating puns is highlighted then and again, especially by Delabastita (1996: 134). He lists the following strategies in dealing with source language puns:

> *Pun → Pun*: the source-text pun is translated by a target-language pun, which may be more or less different from the original wordplay in terms of formal structure, semantic structure, or textual function
>
> *Pun → Non-pun*: the pun is rendered by a non-punning phrase which may salvage both senses of the wordplay but in a non-punning conjunction, or select one of the senses at the cost of suppressing the other; of course, it may also occur that both components of the pun are translated 'beyond recognition'
>
> *Pun → Related rhetorical device*: the pun is replaced by some wordplay-related rhetorical device (repetition, alliteration, rhyme, referential vagueness, irony, paradox, etc.) which aims to recapture the effect of the source-text pun
>
> *Pun → Zero*: the potion of text containing the pun is simply omitted
>
> *Pun ST = Pun TT*: the translator reproduces the source-text pun and possibly its immediate environment in its original formulation, i.e. without actually 'translating' it
>
> *Non-pun → Pun*: the translator introduces a pun in textual positions where the original text has no wordplay, by way of compensation to make up for source-text puns elsewhere, or for any other reason
>
> *Zero → Pun*: totally new textual material is added, which contains wordplay and which has no apparent precedent or justification in the source text except as a compensatory device
>
> *Editorial techniques*: explanatory footnotes or endnotes, comments provided in translators' forewords, the 'anthological' presentation of different, supposedly complementary solutions to one and the same source-text problem, and so forth. (Delabastita 1996: 134)

While the presented strategies enable subtitlers to transfer challenging contents into the target language and culture, yet another constraint limits the range of possible solutions: As viewers continuously have access to both the source and the target version of the dialogue, they inevitably compare these and thereby become a constant "critical lay person" (Jüngst 2010: 53, author's translation). The so-called (acoustic) "feedback effect" (Díaz Cintas & Remael 2007: 55; also "gossiping effect" [Törnqvist 1995 1995: 49]) describes this dilemma: When the audience recognises "linguistic items of the original" (Karamitroglou 1998), it expects "the exact, literal, translationally equivalent items [...] to appear in the subtitles as well" (Karamitroglou 1998). When viewers get the impression that something was not actually said that way or at all (Nagel 2009: 65), it raises "suspicions that the translation of the original text is not 'properly' or 'correctly' rendered in the subtitles" (Karamitroglou 1998).

The goal in any case should be a minimal irritation of the audience while maintaining the intended meaning and effect of the source item. Karamitroglou suggests that, in general terms and depending on context, "linguistic items of the original that can be easily recognised and comprehended by the viewers should not only be retained if they appear in a context of unrecognisable items [...] but they should also be translated word-for-word" (Karamitroglou 1998).

In addition to acoustic feedback effects, there can also be visual feedback effects – e.g. when a viewer does not understand the content but perceives the duration of the speech act. If the subtitle is obviously shorter it might be perceived as censorship (Jüngst 2010: 127). The same goes for words that might be lip-read and are not subtitled accordingly (Jüngst 2010: 127). This is also reflected in the "Code for Good Subtitling Practice": "There must be a close correlation between film dialogue and the presence of subtitles" (Ivarsson & Carroll 1998: 157–159).

### 1.2.3 Layout

The layout of subtitles is a broad field with on the one hand widely discussed aspects such as the use of specific characters, the number of lines and the right position for a line break, but also less explored features such as aesthetics, placement, and user experience.

While punctuation depends on the language  and can differ immensely between source and target language, the use of specific characters – in this case in English and German – should always be used for clarity and in a coherent way.[10] Punctuation should be used in a limited way and all used elements should have a clearly defined function to prevent irritation and therefore a possible loss of information. Following elements can be found in the guidelines:

---

[10] As there is great national variation, especially concerning e.g. the use of italics, subtitle professionals should keep it simple and avoid variation.

- *Single Dot*: Signals the end of the sentence and motivates the audience to direct its gaze back to the image (Karamitroglou 1998). Along with *question marks* and *exclamation marks*, they are used the same way as in any written text (Karamitroglou 1998).

- *Comma*: The comma is used as usual within a subtitle but should be omitted at the end of a subtitle. This allows for better clarity and the change to the next subtitle creates a break anyway (Karamitroglou 1998).

- *Dash*: Dashes are reserved as a distinguishing element for different speakers combined in one subtitle. Being a linguistic element strongly associated with written language, the dash should be avoided in other contexts (Karamitroglou 1998).

- *Three Dots*: The ITC guideline states that "sequences of dots (three at the end of a to-be-continued subtitle, and two at the beginning of a continuation) are used to mark the fact that a segmentation is taking place" (1999: 8) and that "many viewers have found this technique helpful" (1999: 8). Karamitroglou states a similar fact on "sequence dots" or "ending triple dots" (1998) and that the brain "takes more time to process" (Karamitroglou 1998) continuous subtitles without any punctuation at the end of the preceding subtitle. They should therefore not be used to "indicate ongoing thoughts or an unfinished utterance" (Karamitroglou 1998). He calls their counterpart at the beginning of the next sentence "linking dots" or "starting triple dots" (Karamitroglou 1998) and emphasises that they should always be used in combination. While this has been common practice for quite some time, more and more subtitle producers omit these dots as they seem to trust their hearing viewers to recognise connected subtitles, or prefer to rather use the space for actual content. For hearing-impaired audiences, however, this might still be an appropriate practice.

- *Italics*: Italics represent so-called "distant voices" (Leißner 2009: 34), e.g. narrators, inner monologues, speakers on the telephone, etc. Karamitroglou defines this as the indication of an "off-screen source of the spoken text" (1998). He also states that they can be used for "retaining foreign-language words in their original foreign-language version" (Karamitroglou 1998).

- *Single and double quotation marks*: They embrace alleged information and quoted information and should be used cautiously (Karamitroglou 1998).

The following linguistic elements have been deemed unsuited for subtitles due to their strong association with written language:

- *Uppercase letters*: While some argue that uppercase letters can be used to indicate screaming or increased volume (ITC 1999: 13; Leißner 2009: 35), it should generally be avoided due to the associated slower reading speed. The ITC guidelines suggest to instead use colour for "emphasis of an individual word" (1999: 13).

- *Boldface and underlining*: These design options are rarely useful for complete sentences or subtitles. Karamitroglou even sees them as "not permitted in subtitling" (1998).

- *Colons and semicolons*: While Leißner states that these should be avoided due to their strong association with written language and their similarity to each other (2009: 35), Karamitroglou only permits their use at the end of subtitles to avoid creating longer pauses than intended (1998).

- *Parentheses and brackets*: Both Leißner and Karamitroglou see parentheses and brackets as a means of explaining jokes or culture-specific elements but recommend a cautious use due to the strong association with written language (Karamitroglou 1998; Leißner 2009: 35).

- *Special characters*: Special characters can stand out too much on the screen and might have a negative impact on the reading speed. So if recognition of a rarely used special character might take too long, their meaning should be written out. Well-known characters such as the € symbol in Europe might be used cautiously.

The use of numerals and the decision whether to write them out or not depends highly on context, available time and space, and the respective situation. Ford Williams (2009: 36) offers a detailed overview of possible situations and solutions.

When subtitle layout is mentioned, it usually refers to the preference of one or two lines and the location of the line break as well as the balance between the two lines. In 2012, Gottlieb called subtitle layout "one of the relatively few aspects of subtitling tested empirically" (2012: 66) and names studies by d'Ydewalle and De (2007) and Perego (2010). While Ivarsson and Carroll (1998: 157–159) state a maximum subtitle length of two lines, the ITC guidelines and Ford Williams promote up to three lines "if the subtitler is confident that no important picture information will be obscured" (ITC 1999: 7). Concerning segmentation, the guidelines could not be more contradictory. The question is whether to distribute a long one-line subtitle evenly on two lines or not. Karamitroglou prefers two lines and states that "the eye and the brain of the viewers render a two-line subtitle as more bulky and, as a result, accelerate the reading process" (1998). Opposing this view, Ford Williams claims that "one line takes less time to read [...] and it causes less disruption to the picture" (2009: 13; cf. ITC 1999: 10). Ivarsson and Carroll also prefer the long one-line subtitle as this would avoid the break during switching to the second line.

While subtitles should "ideally [...] be self-contained" (Ivarsson & Carroll 1998: 157–159) and "start and end at logical points in a sentence" (Ford Williams 2009: 10), splitting a sentence into two subtitles often cannot be avoided. The distribution within two-line subtitles should be based on logical, grammatical, and semantic constituents. For example, determiners should not be separated from their nouns (Ivarsson & Carroll 1998: 157–159; ITC 1999: 9; Díaz Cintas & Remael 2007; Ford Williams 2009: 10). Karamitroglou demands a segmentation "at the highest syntactic nodes possible" (1998). Concerning the balance between the two lines of "unequal length" (Ivarsson & Carroll 1998: 157–159), "the upper line should preferably be shorter to keep as much of the image as free as possible" (Ivarsson & Carroll 1998: 157–159). Karamitroglou emphasises the aim of the two lines being "proportionally as equal in length as possible, since the viewers' eye is more accustomed to reading text in a rectangular than a triangular format" (1998). Ivarsson and Carroll demand left-justification as this is supposed to "reduce unnecessary eye movement" (Ivarsson & Carroll 1998: 157–159). Both the ITC guidelines and Karamitroglou see a need for "compromise between linguistic and geometric considerations" (ITC 1999: 9; Karamitroglou 1998), with both giving priority to "linguistic considerations" (ITC 1999: 9).

Regarding the typographic design of subtitles, Karamitroglou demands a "pale white" (1998) as a bright white would "render them [the subtitles] tiring to the viewers' eye" (Karamitroglou 1998; cf. Ford Williams 2009: 18). Another regularly used colour in television and DVD subtitles is yellow. To guarantee a maximum contrast, "text should normally be presented in a black box" (ITC 1999: 5; cf. Ford Williams 2009: 18; Leißner 2009: 32), even though this covers the image additionally. As it is nevertheless often used in SDH on television, the ITC guidelines define an appropriate set of suitable colours: "The most legible text colours on a black background are white, yellow, cyan and green. Use of magenta, red and blue should be avoided" (ITC 1999: 5; cf. Ford Williams 2009: 18). An alternative to black or grey boxes are shadows behind the letters or outlines (cf. Díaz Cintas et al. 2007: 84). Karamitroglou, however, demands a "grey, see-through 'ghost box' [...] since it has been proven that it is easier for the eye to read against a fixed rather than a varying/moving background" (1998) and it does not block the view on the image completely. Typefaces used should be sans-serif (Karamitroglou 1998; Díaz Cintas et al. 2007: 84; Ford Williams 2009: 20) and proportionally distributed (Karamitroglou 1998).

The position of subtitles is established in the lower part of the screen (Karamitroglou 1998; ITC 1999; Díaz Cintas et al. 2007; Díaz Cintas & Remael 2007: 8; Ford Williams 2009). They are usually placed around 10 % from the borders to compensate for various playback devices that might cut a part of the image. Karamitroglou suggests a placement of "at least 1/12 of the total screen height above the bottom of the screen, so that the eye of the viewer does not have to travel a long distance" (1998). The same amount of space should be left free to the left and right of the first and last character of each subtitle line (Karamitroglou 1998). The reason for placing the subtitles in the lower area is that it is often free of elements relevant for the plot (Leißner 2009: 30) respectively "occupied by image action which is of lesser importance to the general aesthetic appreciation of the target film" (Karamitroglou 1998). According to Díaz Cintas et al., subtitles should only be moved if necessary, e.g. if they would cover something or to avoid a weak contrast and reduced legibility (2007: 81f.). The ITC guidelines also underline the importance of not covering plot-relevant areas in the image:

> The normally accepted position for subtitles is towards the bottom of the screen, but in obeying this convention it is most important to avoid obscuring 'on-screen' captions, any part of a speaker's mouth or any other important activity. (ITC 1999: 10)

So far, the only alternative position used in traditional subtitling is at the top of the screen (Karamitroglou 1998) and should only be used in "extreme cases" (Karamitroglou 1998).

While traditional subtitles are normally centred, semi-live and live subtitles are sometimes left-oriented (Díaz Cintas et al. 2007: 88). For centred subtitles, the "distance the eyes should move is the same, no matter where the line break is inserted" (Gottlieb 2012: 23; cf. Ivarsson & Carroll 1998: 157–159). The ITC guide, however, demands that the subtitles be "displayed horizontally in the direction of the appropriate speaker, or source of sound effect" (1999: 10) by placing text "justified left, centre or right depending on speaker position" (ITC 1999: 5; cf. Díaz Cintas & Remael 2007: 14; Ford Williams 2009: 18–19).

In addition to these guidelines, which are suitable for both inter- and intralingual subtitles, some guidelines are only intended for SDH – for example those on speaker identification. Ford Williams suggests the use of colours to "distinguish speakers from each other" (2009: 15, 18–19; cf. Jüngst 2010: 129), suitable colours being yellow, cyan, and green (ITC 1999: 15; Ford Williams 2009: 18). Colours can be assigned to film characters either "throughout the programme" (ITC 1999: 13) or "in terms of scenes" (ITC 1999: 13). Other possibilities are the already mentioned placements below speakers and adding character names (ITC 1999: 13; Remael 2007: 31; Jüngst 2010: 129). The horizontal placement below speakers, however, poses an additional challenge:

> The main problem here is when characters move about while speaking. In such cases, the caption should be positioned at the discretion of the subtitler to identify the position of the speaker as clearly as possible. (ITC 1999: 13)

As the strategy of horizontal placement below speakers is being used again on recent Blu-ray releases (see Section 4.1), there seem to be strategies to handle these challenges as well. Chapter 4 gives an overview over those strategies in recent commercial films.

## 1.3 Subtitle quality and shortcomings

While the discussion of time and space constraints and content-related challenges such as humour and culture-specific elements revealed several strategic solutions, challenges originating from the placement and layout of subtitles did not quite have the same effect. Problems with contrast, collisions, and interference seem to be widely accepted as unpleasant, but unavoidable features of subtitles. Strategies so far only cover bold black boxes (rarely used in interlingual translation), shadows, and thick borders to counter weak contrasts. The only regularly used alternative to the bottom-centre position seems to be the suboptimal position at the top, and speaker identification is only done for SDH, using colours and sometimes horizontal placement.

Rarely addressed are issues such as the distance between subtitle and focus point in the image, viewers not used to subtitles (especially in dubbing and English-speaking countries), collisions of subtitles with other text elements, typographic challenges (and possibilities), and the overall visual impact of additional text elements in film. The wide range of content-related strategies should be balanced by presentation and layout-related strategies. And as many strategies, i.e. concerning timing, are already based on eye tracking studies (i.e. reading behaviour, image processing and exploration etc.) this appears to be the appropriate tool to study text elements in film further (see Chapter 6).

More recent challenges arise from further automation such as machine translation (cf. Armstrong et al. 2006; Melero et al. 2006; Volk 2008; Flanagan 2009; Volk et al. 2010; Fishel et al. 2012; Müller & Volk 2013) combined with post-editing (cf. De Sousa et al. 2011), subtitle placement (see §3.4), and crowd sourcing as well as user-generated subtitling (cf. Orrego Carmona 2015).

# 2 Overview of text elements in film – Translation and graphical impact

According to multiple award-winning film editor Walter Murch, emotion "is the thing that you should try to preserve at all costs" (Murch 2001: 18) when editing film.[1] Similar to film editors, translators should always understand a scene's emotion and atmosphere and try their best to recreate them. They should be aware that even the decision whether or not to translate a text element, and in which way, can be considered as much an act of interpretation as the content translation itself. Ideally, the audience should never wonder about a missing or unnecessary translation – or why that subtitle just moved to the top and now covers the speaker. While being historically a dubbing country, more and more German viewers prefer the original version of English film productions, and DVDs and Blu-rays released in Germany usually include subtitles nowadays. However, subtitling does not only create timing, space and content challenges but also graphical challenges related to the collision of additional text elements (subtitles) with pre-existing text elements (e.g. captions); it changes the information flow and reception of the image (cf. Rayner et al. 2001; Caffrey 2009; Romero-Fresco 2013) and possibly influences the audience's overall aesthetic experience. So far, little thought has been given to the influence that translations of text elements in film have on image composition and reception and they are rarely considered an interwoven unity.

Therefore, this chapter provides an overview of text elements in general, strategies used in their graphical translation from English into German, and the concept of typographic identity as a basis for the discussion of creative alternatives and developments.

---

[1] Parts of this chapter have been published previously in the article "Should she really be covered by her own subtitle? – Text elements in film and their graphical translation", Translation Spaces 5: 2 (2016), 244–270.

## 2.1 Representative film corpus

The examples discussed in this chapter were taken from a film corpus that was created solely for this purpose (see Appendix A). The corpus is based on the following four top 100 lists of the most popular films published between and including 2000 and 2009:

- Top-grossing feature films in the USA[2]

- Top-grossing feature films in Germany[3]

- Top-rated feature films on METAcritic (both critics and users)[4]

- Most popular feature films on IMDb[5]

Each of the films in these top 100 lists was assigned a score between 1 and 100 depending on its rank in the list (the highest-ranked film receiving a score of 100 and so on). Based on these scores, a mean score was calculated for each film mentioned in the lists. The 100 English language films with the overall highest scores were included in the final corpus. Therefore, it can be assumed that these are the 100 English language films with the strongest impact in Germany in these ten years. The corpus constitutes a representative sample of the English film industry in the 2000s and, as such, enables a detailed analysis of recent strategies in regard to design and translation of text elements, as well as the film-specific identity that can be created through the well thought-out use of typography. So far, 52 of the 100 films in the corpus have been thoroughly analysed and annotated (see Appendix A for details). These films constitute the basis for the statistics used throughout this chapter. The selection of films is a convenience sample based on availability. Other films from the corpus are used in order to illustrate specific and rare occurrences that did not occur in the analysed films. Films that are not part of the corpus but are required to illustrate cases that did not occur in the sample are marked accordingly.

The text elements were analysed using the English audio and image track as well as the German subtitles. As DVD or Blu-ray Disc (BD) descriptions do not

---

[2]Cf. http://www.imdb.com/search/title/?release_date=2000,2009&sort=boxoffice_gross_us& title_type=feature [2016–07–27].

[3]Cf. http://www.insidekino.de/DJahr/D2000--2009.htm [2016–07–27].

[4]Cf. http://www.metacritic.com/feature/the-best-movies-of-the-decade [2016–07–27].

[5]Cf. http://www.imdb.com/search/title/?release_date=2000,2009&title_type=feature [2016–07–27].

specifically state which image tracks are included, and the contents of the data carriers can vary a lot, this feature was not analysed for all films in the corpus. This point is, however, explained in more detail in the section on technical considerations and some examples are provided. Further variations can occur between cinematic versions, TV versions, and commercial versions and were not recorded in this corpus. The analysis includes films from DVD, BD, and the two online streaming services *Amazon Prime* and *Netflix*.[6] The format and version (regular, special edition, extended edition) of the respective films were based on convenience and not marked in the corpus.

## 2.2 Technical considerations

Several technical constraints should be taken into consideration due to not only the wide range of formats films can be watched in but also the variations within these formats. As mentioned before, the database includes films analysed on DVD, BD, *Amazon Prime*, and *Netflix*. These data carriers and providers mostly vary in terms of average file size, image resolution, and applied strategies concerning the use of image tracks. DVDs can either be single or double layer and can store 4.7 GB or 8.7 GB, corresponding to approximately 2 or 4 hours of standard definition information (SD, 480–540p). BD offers 25 GB and 50 GB of capacity, equating approximately 2 or 3 hours respectively of high-quality information (720/1080p) "with additional room for 2 hours [or 9 hours, resp.] of bonus material in SD quality" (Blu-ray Disc Association 2015). The online streaming services provide image resolutions of up to 4k/UHD (2160p) with corresponding file sizes. The difference in storage size between DVD and BD can be traced to the two different lasers that are used to read the information: While DVD is read by red lasers (650nm), BD uses blue lasers (405nm) that, due to their shorter wave length and therefore smaller size of focused laser spot, allow for almost five times the number of grooves and therefore a much higher storage capacity.

The data stored on these devices and platforms that are relevant for this article are the image tracks, audio tracks, and subtitle tracks. Depending on the publisher, English films in Germany can be available with the original English (unaltered) image track, the German image track that features substitutions of text elements, or both. Image tracks in one language version but with various different cuts (such as the official cinema cut versus the director's cut or an extended

---

[6]Currently, these are the only major streaming providers in Germany that offer subtitles (cf. http://www.netzwelt.de/video-streaming/kaufberatung-video-streaming-dienste-test-netflix-amazon-prime-maxdome-co-vergleich.html [in German; 2016–06–03]).

cut) are also possible. Furthermore, the option to have one major image track that only offers versions in which there are actually (translated) text elements in a scene also exists. This, as well as the various cut versions, is achieved by "seamless branching" (TFDVD Research Labs 2005) or the 'misuse' of the multi-angles option. The multi-angle option was originally intended to offer several perspectives of specific scenes. Today, while it is still used in some genres such as recorded live concerts, it is mostly used for internationalisation purposes – this version will, depending on the audio track and whether a scene has a translated version in that language, replace the source language version. Similar to this use of multi-angle videos,

> the technique of seamless branching uses a special type of interleaving [...], where multiple versions of the video are woven together into "angle blocks", and then the bits which "aren't playing" are skipped over during decoding/playback. (TFDVD Research Labs 2005)

While the information on use or existence of these multiple language versions of the image track are not included in the technical (or any) DVD and BD description, German *Netflix* client support states that they only offer the original image track provided by the studios.[7] *Amazon Prime*, on the other hand, states that they offer one or both image tracks depending on the provider and link it to the corresponding audio track.[8] Judging from personal experience, this feature is mostly used if the main target group is children – see for example *The Incredibles* (USA 2004) – or if the use of specific text elements is crucial to the film's atmosphere or plot, e.g. all films in the *Star Wars* (USA 1977-) franchise or *Avatar* (USA/UK 2009).

The number and quality of audio tracks on both DVD and BD depend on the remaining space with a limit of eight audio tracks on DVD and no limit on BD.[9] These audio tracks are used for different audio formats and different languages. Audio tracks that provide an alternative language are usually linked to the corresponding image track, if available. Even though there is no audio track limit for the streaming providers, *Amazon Prime* usually only provides the source language (if at all) and the German dubbed version, while *Netflix* seems to usually offer the English source version, the German dubbed version if available, and

---

[7] As stated during the communication with the German *Netflix* client support [2016–06–01].

[8] As stated during the communication with the German *Amazon Prime* client support [2016–06–03].

[9] Limits of data rates and balance of features on BD are discussed in detail in various BD forums, e.g. http://www.bluray-disc.de/forum/dokus-und-musik-auf-blu-ray/76647-musik-bd-welche-audioformate-und-was-geht.html [in German; 2016–06–03].

sometimes dubbed versions in other languages, such as French. This also seems to depend on the issuing studios as well as licensing costs.

Finally, there are usually multiple subtitle tracks included in DVD and BD publications. *Amazon Prime* offers a growing number of films with English and German subtitles and *Netflix* usually offers at least English and German subtitles as well as a wide range of other languages. Subtitle tracks in the corpus included English subtitles, English subtitles for the deaf and hard-of-hearing (SDH), German subtitles, German SDH, commentaries, other language subtitles, and subtitles for an additional language in the film.[10] The layout of the subtitles depends largely on the production company. *Amazon Prime* and *Netflix* offer a wide range of individual subtitle appearance settings (see Figure 2.1). While *Amazon Prime* allows users to set the size and choose one of four overall layout pre-sets, *Netflix* offers seven fonts, five different shadow settings, and various colours for either a background or box behind the subtitle, including semi-transparency.

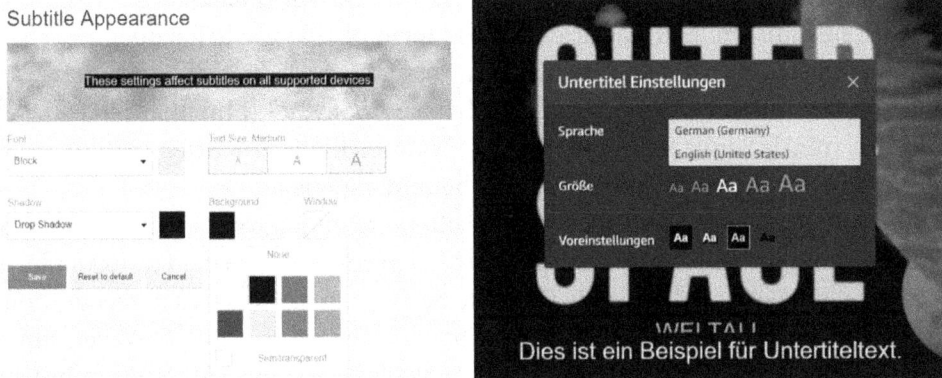

Figure 2.1: Configuration of subtitle appearance on *Netflix* (left) and *Amazon Prime* (right).

On DVD and BD, this is very different. Subtitles are saved as image files on both DVD and BD[11] and their overall layout cannot be adjusted by the viewer

---

[10]For example, the BD of *The Lord of the Rings – The Two Towers* (USA/NZ 2002) includes an English subtitle track that only translates the Elvish dialogues as well as a German subtitle track that provides the corresponding German translations. Ideally, these are linked to the corresponding audio tracks and displayed by default. If not, they are easily missed as one of many subtitle tracks, and the information of these dialogues is lost. On BD, individual subtitles can be marked as 'forced' subtitles and will be shown regardless of player settings.

[11]Cf. http://en.flossmanuals.net/avidemux/ch019_extract-dvd-subtitles/ [2017–06–06] for DVD and http://forum.videohelp.com/threads/313620-How-to-extract-subtitles-from-a-Blu-ray-and-convert-to-srt-or-sub-idx for BD [2016–06–06].

or playback device. While most studios stick to the traditional white subtitles with black border or shadow in the bottom-centre area, some recent BDs offer individually placed English SDH, e.g. *Gone Girl* (USA 2014) and *Ex Machina* (UK 2015; see §4.1). This was not observed on any other medium.

Due to this wide range of formats, layouts and combinations thereof, the decision was made to limit this first analysis to the provided image track – either the original English image track or the German image track – and German subtitles. As subtitle layout differs significantly depending on individual settings (streaming) or playback devices (DVD and BD), only the layout of the original text elements and their translations will be taken into account. It often creates its own, individual character, or even, identity.

## 2.3 Typographic film identity

Even before spoken language, written text was part of filmmaking – from the first silent films on, text appeared "in the form of title cards for opening, closing and intertitles, as subtitles, abstract character code or single character, as independent theme, image or calligraphy or ornament" (Ehrenhauser 2007: 3, author's translation). Genre-independent, various kinds of written text are used in illustrative and explanatory ways in the moving image.

These text elements and their design often create a strong identity that can make a film more distinctive and add further recognition value. For example, a well thought-out and distinctive film title design can allow for easy recognition, even without the original text. During the translation process, however, films are edited both in additive and substituting ways – be it the addition of subtitles or the substitution of the audio channel. Both forms of audiovisual translation include, depending on target group and applied guidelines, the translation and recreation of relevant text elements. This translation of both spoken and written language can result in a noticeable interference with the typographic film identity as written translations are added or replace existing text elements.

But how is this typographic film identity created and what makes viewers remember certain aspects of a film such as the title design or an opening sequence? It is the design. And it is not only the more obvious aspects such as the main colours of the images (think of the distinctive blue-green of *Avatar*) or especially aesthetic shots. The film's design also includes all the typographic elements, their typefaces, placement, effects, and colours. The overall use of text elements can support or establish a specific tone or atmosphere – just as it was intended and implemented in *John Wick* (USA 2014): When asked why they chose integrated titles, the two filmmakers Chad Stahelski and David Leitch replied that it had to do with tone: "Most people use subtitles to get across information or do what they are there for, translation. We needed hints with tone" (Graham 2014). Many typefaces evoke specific associations or emotions due to their established use. The same holds true for effects and placement strategies. Atmosphere and emotions can create continuity and strengthen the recognition value – similar to branding strategies and corporate design. This, however, should not be confused with marketing, even though they are strongly related: "Branding is not actively selling but representing: 'This is what I am.'" (Heaton 2011). Corporate design, as a part of the complexity that is corporate identity, is the design of "all visual forms of expression of a company" (Weinberger 2010: 55) that provides the "most significant distinction" (2010: 55) and "strongest recognition value" (2010: 55). Weinberger defines a number of essential elements of corporate design (2010: 55): Logo, colour, shapes, typography, communication design (all printed and digital material), industrial design (packaging), images (moving and still images), architecture, clothing, and CD manual. Apart from architecture, most of these elements can be found in film production. In regard to typographic film identity, the film title is often used as a logo (see the *Harry Potter* [UK/USA 2001–2011] or *The Lord of the Rings* [NZ/USA 2001–2003] franchises), and colour, shapes, and typography can be found in the text elements of a film. This kind of branding or corporate design often even affects the studio logos in recent films, adjusting to the film's overall design[12] – as seen for example in the *The Matrix* films (USA 1999–2003), where the Warner Brothers logo is tinted green and looks more "computerish"[13] (Quitsch 2010: 48ff.).

While an overall film design includes most of the aspects that can be found in a corporate design, the text elements form a distinctive group – creating a typographic film identity. Led by the film title, the 'logo', text elements in the film usually follow a specific design, captions are presented in one typeface and colour throughout the film, and even displays might look similar or are filmed in a similar way. The same is true for inserts, opening and closing credits, and narrative text elements (for an example, see Figure 2.2).

---

[12] Other aspects of this overall design are a film's motion design, e.g. opening titles and elements added in the post-production, props (cf. Annie Atkins, designer for the *Grand Budapest Hotel* (USA/DE/FR 2014), http://create.adobe.com/2015/12/2/the_secret_world_of_annie_atkins_graphic_designer_for_films.html [2016–06–03]), and elements created by video designers in the post-production, e.g. visualised text messages.

[13] Cf. http://www.closinglogos.com/page/Logo+Variations+-+Warner+Bros.+Pictures [2016–06–03] for examples on Warner Bros. and http://www.closinglogos.com/page/Logo+Variations+-+20th+Century+Fox+Film+Corporation for Twentieth Century Fox [2016–06–03].

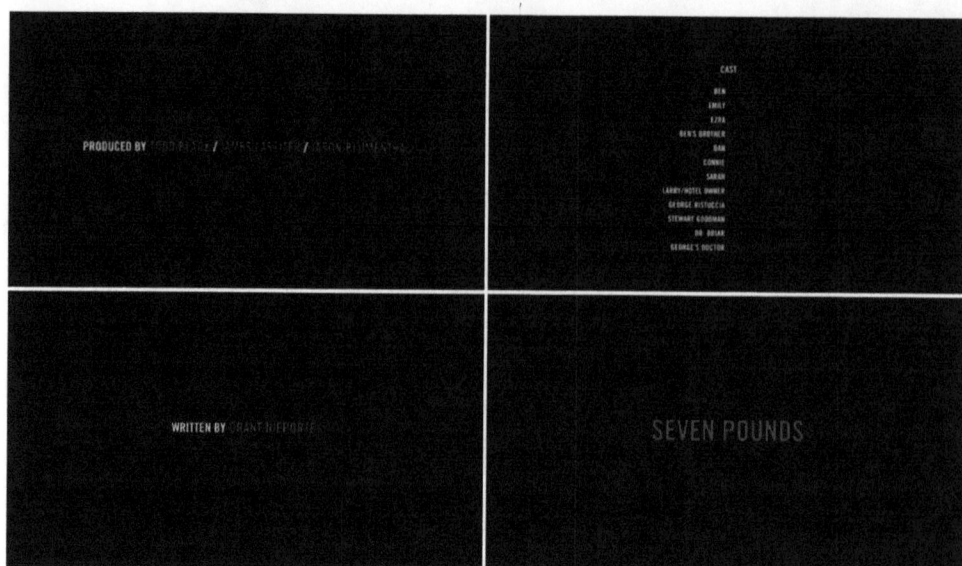

Figure 2.2: Overall typographic identity in *Seven Pounds* (USA 2008)

In the course of translation, however, text elements are often subtitled or re-placed. As explained in the technical considerations section, the design of sub-titles usually depends on either the studio or the streaming platform. On the one hand, subtitles, as a major typographic influence on the film, should ideally become a part of its typographic identity or create as little interference as pos-sible – but this is usually not the case. If taken into account, however, subtitles could probably reinforce the typographic identity which supports the film's at-mosphere. This was done, to some extent, in *Avatar*.

As can be seen in Figure 2.3, the burnt-in subtitles for the additional alien lan-guage were not the only aspect that was adapted to the film's dominant colours – creating the best possible visibility by contrasting the blue and green image with yellow subtitles – but the optional subtitles also follow the basic typographic identity of the film. Similar approaches were used in the *The Lord of the Rings* franchise, creating film-specific fonts and applying elaborate serif typefaces for the forced Elvish language subtitles.[14]

On the other hand, typefaces that are too specific and associated with other genres might not be adequate for the atmosphere of some film and irritate the audience – see for example the futuristic subtitles in the WWII historical comedy

[14]For an overview of the typefaces created for the franchise, see for example http://www.theonering.net/torwp/2014/06/26/90498-the-lord-of-the-fonts-a-guide-to-fonts-in-the-hobbit-and-the-lord-of-the-rings/2/ [2016–06–06].

Figure 2.3: Forced subtitles (left) and optional subtitles (right) in *Avatar* (00:42:07, 00:12:25)

Figure 2.4: Typographic and thematic interference in *Train of Life* (00:12:23) and in *In Bruges* (UK/USA 2008, 00:01:31)

*Train of Life* (FR/BE/NL/ISR/ROU 1998) in Figure 2.4 (on the left). Additionally, interference might occur due to the dominance of a subtitle in a scene with otherwise muted colours and text elements (see Figure 2.4 on the right).

Figure 2.5 shows the BBC television series *Sherlock* (UK/USA 2010-) and its translation into German. While *Sherlock* is a great example of the intelligent use and design of text inserts, the German version is an example of how to sometimes overlook typographic details. While it might be understandable that not the exact same typeface was used, the change from sans-serif to a serif typeface was unnecessary – and can possibly lead to a minor change of atmosphere in the corresponding scenes. While the sans-serif typeface in the original suggests a modern context in the age of smartphones and texting, the serif typeface in the German translation is associated with a rather different area of application: Serif typefaces require a higher resolution to be presented clearly and are therefore hardly used on phone screens. They are traditionally associated with printed type faces and books – not the digital world (see Figure 2.5).

Messages - Sent

if brother has green ladder
arrest brother.

SH

**Messages - Sent**

if brother has green ladder
arrest brother.

SH

**Mitteilungen - Gesendet**

Falls Bruder grüne Leiter hat,
Bruder verhaften.

SH

Figure 2.5: Original *Sherlock* scene, close-up of the English text insert, and its translation (S01E01, 00:12:14)

Examples such as *Sherlock* show that new expertise is required to deal with the various aspects of typographic film identity. Only if existing layout strategies and designs are understood and text elements and their value recognised, can they be recreated in a way that does not disturb the film's atmosphere, tone, and overall identity.

## 2.4 Text elements in film

As previously explained, translation in film does not only involve spoken language but also written text elements in the source language. In the 52 analysed films, a total of 1170 text elements with the frequencies in Table 2.1 were observed.

The following sections provide definitions and indicate the relevance of the individual text elements as well as challenges that arise due to their content and graphical translation.

Table 2.1: Frequency of text elements in the 52 analysed films

| Element | Count | Percentage (%) |
|---|---|---|
| Film title | 65 | 5.56 |
| Opening credits | 29 | 2.48 |
| Closing credits | 57 | 4.87 |
| Displays | 560 | 47.86 |
| Captions | 107 | 9.15 |
| Narrative texts | 10 | 0.85 |
| Inserts | - | - |
| Subtitles | 342 | 29.23 |
| | 1170 | 100.00 |

## 2.4.1 Film title

The film title can be seen as one of the most relevant links between the original version and translated versions of a film – at least concerning marketing and presence. Ideally, it should be possible for the audience to make the connection between the original film and the German version. However, many German film titles such as "Welcome to the Jungle" (*The Rundown*, USA 2003) or "Vergiss mein nicht!" ("Forget Me Not", *Eternal Sunshine of the Spotless Mind*, USA 2004)[15] indicate that marketing decisions are not always based on what would be an obvious translation. As Bouchehri states, it is often agencies that create the original titles in the United States (Bouchehri 2008: 30) and the distributors in Germany that choose a translation or new title (Bouchehri 2008: 20). Therefore, the linguistic translation process of film titles remains quite elusive.

The title, however, is not only relevant for marketing purposes but also for the overall image composition and identity of a film. Of the 52 films analysed, all films included at least one scene with the film title in it and 11 films showed the film title more than once. If it is presented at the beginning of a film, it can create a specific atmosphere and shape the typographic identity of the film – or subsequently strengthen it when presented after the film and before the closing credits (as in e.g. *Avatar* and *Hot Fuzz* [UK/FR/USA 2007]). Especially multi-part films and film series such as *The Lord of the Rings* or *Harry Potter* feature a clear and dif-

---

[15]See http://www.filmpilot.de/news/top-7-deutsche-filmtitel-die-uns-fuer-bloed-halten-109320 for a list of various criticised or even faulty film title translations from English into German [in German; 2016–05–11].

ferentiated typographic identity related to the film title which creates recognition value and strengthens the franchise. While the influence of the title translation on marketing is difficult to determine (Schreitmüller 1994: 72ff.), inconsistencies concerning the design or translation of the film title[16] might lead to irritation. As film titles function as names (cf. Nord 1993: 87ff.) and can be assigned a communicative function (Bouchehri 2008: 24ff.), a strongly deviating translation in the subtitles can lead to a negative feedback effect as well as irritation. In regard to the graphical translation, a dominant subtitle can interfere with a muted image composition (see the example of *In Bruges* in Figure 2.4). Thus, the question of relevance arises: What is more important at this moment – the tone and atmosphere of the scene, or reading a film title translation the audience most likely already knows (with the exception of sneak previews)? The subtitle might also collide with other subtitles if there is already some spoken content.

## 2.4.2 Opening and closing credits

Opening credits[17] and closing credits were originally 'imprints' of films (Hausberger 2006: 21; cf. McCort 2002). Thomas Edison seems to be one of the first filmmakers to include the film title and copyright in his film for economic reasons (Hausberger 2006: 3; Quitsch 2010: 12). Credits were soon regularly included due to legal requirements.[18] They received simple, but aesthetic designs: "The economy promotes, forces aesthetics" (Böhnke/Hülser 2002, author's translation). The rise of the sound film then strengthened the bridging character of the opening titles from the real to the fictional world and the titles became more complex and expensive – the studios wanted to offer a cinematic experience that television productions could not (Quitsch 2010: 21). Filmmaker Martin Scorsese described Saul Bass' work on opening credits, one of the most influential and famous designers of his time,[19] as "integral to the film" and marking the actual beginning of

---

[16] An example of inconsistency in translation would be the series of films *Pirates of the Caribbean*. The first film, *Pirates of the Caribbean* (USA 2003), was translated and marketed as "Fluch der Karibik" (Curse of the Caribbean). The second part *Pirates of the Caribbean: Dead Man's Chest* (USA 2006), obviously in an attempt to create at least some kind of continuity, was translated as "Pirates of the Caribbean – Fluch der Karibik 2" and only the third part follows the original title *Pirates of the Caribbean: At World's End* (USA 2007) with the translation "Pirates of the Caribbean – Am Ende der Welt". The fourth part then followed the same strategy.

[17] Also referred to as main titles, opening titles or title sequence (Hausberger 2006: 3).

[18] Cf. http://promaxbda.org/brief/content/the-conference-2014-title-design-from-modern-times-and-dr.-no-to-today [2016–06–05].

[19] For an overview of his work and life, see http://www.imdb.com/name/nm0000866/ [2016–06–10].

the film, opposed to "simply unimaginative identification tags, as in many films" (Meggs 1997: 17). He is said to have been the first title designer to create whole brands for films and laid the foundations for corporate design in cinema (Althen 2006). Therefore, opening credits are a strong part of the overall typographic identity of a film. Nowadays, the informative function of the opening credits often takes a back seat in favour of the overall graphical design concept (Hausberger 2006: 17; cf. Hausberger 2006: 23ff. for an overview of the various categories of opening credits). Based on the example *Psycho* (USA 1960), McClarty illustrates how "opening titles can become representative of a film text" (2012: 114):

> These credits are used, therefore, not just as an aesthetic tool, but as a means of preparing the audience for the themes and plotlines they are about to witness (in the case of Psycho, themes of split personalities and slashing)" (McClarty 2012: 144; cf. Dick 2005: 23).

However, many films do not even feature opening credits anymore (e.g. *Batman Begins* [USA/UK 2005] and *Avatar*), as due to extensive marketing and trailers such a strong transition might no longer be required (Quitsch 2010: 45–46). Films without opening credits often feature extensive and complex closing credits instead (e.g. *Iron Man* [USA 2008], *Slumdog Millionaire*). Other films feature opening and closing credits that follow a similar design (e.g. *Se7en* [USA 1995]). However, complex and aesthetic opening credits seem to be here for good, attracting a growing audience and recognition in the industry.[20]

In terms of content, opening and closing credits mostly feature names, professions, and prepositions such as "with", "from" or "produced by" etc. Of the 52 films analysed, all films included closing credits and 29 films included opening credits. None of the analysed films featured any kind of translation of their opening or closing credits, emphasizing their mainly aesthetic, atmospheric, but also legal function – they have to exist, so filmmakers and designers often seem to work hard to make the most of it.

## 2.4.3 Displays

Displays are defined as "writing that has been recorded by the camera and has significance for the plot" (Ivarsson & Carroll 1998: 97). They are already part

---

[20]Evidenced on websites such as "Forget the film, watch the titles" (http://www.watchthetitles.com/ [2016–06–10]) and "The Art of the Title Sequence" (http://www.artofthetitle.com/ [2016–06–10]) or the "Excellence in Title Design Award" by the SXSW Film Festival Austin, Texas (cf. Hausberger 2006: 18).

of the image, be they street signs, newspapers, headlines, or handwritten notes. Therefore, with the exception of animated or drawn films, they cannot (or only with immense cost and effort) be edited.

The analysed films included 560 displays,[21] corresponding to an average of 10.77 displays per film. It is the most frequent text element in the corpus subset, with only nine out of 52 films not featuring any displays. The most displays were found in *District 9* (ZA/USA/NZ/CAN 2009), including 62 displays over 112 minutes of runtime, and *The Departed* (USA/HK 2006) containing 46 displays (151 minutes).

Displays pose quite a challenge for subtitle professionals as they are the text element that requires the most interpretation by the translator – the relevance has to be determined (which can be quite subjective and differs from translator to translator) and even if categorised as important, deciding whether a display requires translation is also challenging. For example, an EXIT sign might be very relevant in a scene, but usually does not require translation for a German audience, especially if accompanied by the corresponding symbol.

### 2.4.4 Captions

Captions[22] are defined as "texts that have been added to the film or tape after shooting, texts that tell the audience when and/or where a scene is taking place or, in programmes of a more documentary nature, the name of a speaker and perhaps his position and title" (Ivarsson & Carroll 1998: 97; cf. Díaz Cintas & Remael 2007: 60). Captions are therefore additional superimposed text elements that are relevant to the plot and are added in post-production. There were 107 captions in the 52 films, which equals to 2.06 captions per film on average. As they only appeared in 17 of these films, however, this works out as an average of 6.29 captions for films with captions.

While the content translation of locations, professions and short phrases such as "Three months later" (*The Incredibles*, 01:45:41) does not usually seem to require exceptional skill, mistakes can happen, especially if the translator did not

---

[21]The interpretation of a display as plot-relevant can slightly vary depending on the translator. In the analysis, reoccurring displays were only counted once or whenever they received translation.

[22]While the term 'captions' is often used to describe additional text elements such as name and place indicators, in the United States they refer to the subtitles for the deaf and hard-of-hearing (SDH) – either simply as "captions" or "closed captions" (CC, Díaz Cintas & Remael 2007: 14), discussed in depth by Remael (2007).

have access to the image or did not understand the context.[23] Captions are usually placed in the lower or upper third of the screen and, with more recent films, often edited and therefore substituted in the German image track. If caption editing is not possible, similar challenges as for display translation arise and the translational subtitle might collide with subtitles for spoken content. In contrast to displays, however, the accompanying image is often static. Captions, from a graphical perspective, often form part of the overall typographic film identity and are part of the atmosphere and 'illusion' of the film (see *Bad Company* [USA/CZE 2002] with its caption formatting similar to intelligence files, and *District 9* including captions in a documentary style).

## 2.4.5 Narrative text

Narrative text elements can easily be considered as a subcategory of captions as they are superimposed text elements that are added in post-production. However, they are usually more dominant and feature full-length sentences, are more relevant to the plot and often function as an introduction to the film or as the beginning of a new chapter in the film. They can appear as prologues, epilogues, and title card-like between major chapters of a film. Only six of the 52 films featured narrative texts, accounting for ten of the overall 1170 observed text elements. A translation with subtitles might pose a challenge due to the length of the text and limited space and time. A replacement, as seen in the dominant prologue in the *Star Wars* films (see §2.5.3) seems to be an appropriate solution, especially when the content is highly relevant and little or no space for subtitles remains.

## 2.4.6 Inserts

'Insert' is a term used for text elements that are designed and animated in a way to fit the image composition (Molerov 2012: 3). They are superimposed text elements added in the post-production process and the most modern of the various groups of text elements, mentioned in Díaz Cintas/Remael (2007: Glossary) and Hickethier (2007: 98). Molerov further references the terms of "iconogram" and "Iconokineticgram" used by Ehrenhauser (2007: 32). They could also be seen as a subgroup of captions as they are created in post-production. An overview of the origin and forms of inserts can be found in Molerov (2012: 9ff.) who sees the

---

[23]Such as the caption translation of "Hasaad Instruments" and "Hasaad Instrument Repair" (00:40:10 and 00:40:19 in *Eagle Eye*, USA 2008) as "Hasaad Werkzeuge" and "Hasaad Werkzeugreparatur" ("tools" and "tools repair") while the image clearly shows a shop for musical instruments.

aesthetic function of inserts in their visualisation of thoughts (2012: 15). This can be observed in *Stranger Than Fiction* (USA 2006), *Sherlock* (see Figure 2.5), and *Limitless* (USA 2011). As inserts are obviously such a relevant part of the plot, substitution seems like the most viable option. The films included in the corpus, however, do not feature any inserts.

### 2.4.7 Subtitles

The final group of text elements to be discussed is burnt-in subtitles that are created during the post-production of a film, usually for one or more additional language(s) in the film. They are a fixed element of the image that usually cannot be switched off and are featured in films such as *Avatar* (for the alien language Nav'i), *Star Trek Into Darkness* (Klingon; USA 2013), and the *The Lord of the Rings* franchise (Elvish), and usually receive a design that fits the overall typographic identity and atmosphere of the corresponding film (see also §2.3). In those cases when the original film already features a set of interlingual subtitles, another set of subtitles in the new target language is often added. Graphically, these subtitles can easily collide with each other due to their frequent placement in the traditional bottom-centre area. While one solution is the use of forced subtitles or a subtitle track that only includes these additional subtitles, subtitles that are part of the image track have to be subtitled – resulting in additional crowding of the image – or replaced with the translation. As McClarty states, "if opening titles can become representative of a film text, it then stands to reason that subtitles, when designed creatively, can also become representative of the narrative and the mise en scene in each specific film, and even in each specific scene" (2012: 144). They can therefore become part of the film's typographic identity and overall design, conveying tone and atmosphere.

## 2.5 Strategies

While the "Code of Good Subtitling Practice" (Ivarsson & Carroll 1998: 157ff.) states that "all important written information in the images [...] should be translated and incorporated wherever possible" (Ivarsson & Carroll 1998: 157), no specific definitions of 'important' or the corresponding strategies are mentioned. The following strategies for graphical translations were found in the corpus and will be discussed:

- No translation

- Translation through subtitles

- Translation through substitution

- Translation through (subtitled) verbalisation

- Translation through additional scenes[24]

Regarding the list, the first choice that has to be made seems to be whether to translate a text element at all. Several criteria should be taken into account: Is the text element plot-relevant? Is the translation necessary? Is it worth including despite the danger of 'distracting' from the image? In addition to this interpretation of the relevance of the text element, graphical challenges also arise: Can the text element be edited? Can it be recreated in the same way? Molerov also mentions the lack of rights, technical tools, and financial resources (2012: 13) as possible hindrances. Concerning technical requirements, most text elements are created during post-production of a film and added digitally into a film. Therefore, this data can theoretically be made accessible to the film distributor of the target language and text elements be replaced with their translations. Displays, however, are part of the film image and would require a more complex and therefore most likely more expensive and time-consuming process, i.e. replacing them with CGI (computer-generated images). While costs and time requirements might differ, both groups of text elements mainly require that someone decides for these elements and the overall design to be important enough to not just subtitle them. However, the interference with the original film image might be criticised as corruption. The following Table 2.2 provides an overview of the derived frequencies of the strategies in the 52 films.

As can be seen in Table 2.3, the most frequent strategy was translation using subtitles, followed by no translation and substitution. Translation through subtitled verbalisation was the least frequent strategy. In the following, the observed strategies and their frequencies will be discussed.

---

[24]This strategy has only been observed in German image tracks that were not analysed (*The Incredibles, Brother Bear* [USA 2003]). It therefore does not appear in the statistics.

Table 2.2: Overview of the derived graphical translation strategies of text elements in film

|  | Strategy | Frequency | % | Films |
|---|---|---|---|---|
| Film titles | No translation | 37 | 56.92 | 34 |
|  | Subtitle | 22 | 33.85 | 18 |
|  | Substitution | 6 | 9.23 | 4 |
|  | Verbalisation | - | - | - |
|  |  | 65[a] | 100 | 52 |
| Opening credits | No translation | 29 | 100 | 29 |
|  | Subtitle | - | - | - |
|  | Substitution | - | - | - |
|  | Verbalisation | - | - | - |
|  |  | 29 | 100 | 29 |
| Closing credits | No translation | 57 | 100 | 52 |
|  | Subtitle | - | - | - |
|  | Substitution | - | - | - |
|  | Verbalisation | - | - | - |
|  |  | 57 | 100 | 52 |
| Displays | No translation | 254 | 45.36 | 36 |
|  | Subtitle | 256 | 45.71 | 36 |
|  | Substitution | - | - | - |
|  | Verbalisation | 50 | 8.93 | 16 |
|  |  | 560 | 100 | 43 |
| Captions | No translation | 26 | 24.30 | 10 |
|  | Subtitle | 75 | 70.09 | 12 |
|  | Substitution | 6 | 5.61 | 3 |
|  | Verbalisation | - | - | - |
|  |  | 107 | 100 | 17 |
| Subtitles | No translation | 3 | 0.88 | 1 |
|  | Subtitle | 246 | 71.93 | 6 |
|  | Substitution | 93 | 27.19 | 5 |
|  | Verbalisation | - | - | - |
|  |  | 342 | 100 | 12 |
| Narrative text | No translation | - | - | - |
|  | Subtitle | 8 | 80 | 5 |
|  | Substitution | 2 | 20 | 1 |
|  | Verbalisation | - | - | - |
|  |  | 10 | 100 | 6 |
|  |  | 1170 |  | 52 |

[a]The number of film titles is higher than the total amount of films as it is sometimes displayed more than once, e.g. three times in *The Departed*. The same applies to closing credits, as some films include a combination of static and scrolling closing titles that are disrupted by a final film scene.

Table 2.3: Overview of the strategies in the corpus

| Strategy | Frequency | % |
|---|---|---|
| No translation | 406 | 34.70 |
| Subtitle | 607 | 51.88 |
| Substitution | 107 | 9.15 |
| Verbalisation | 50 | 4.27 |
| | 1170 | 100 |

## 2.5.1 No translation

The existence of a text element does not equal the need to act. A loan from the originally ethical considerations of translation by Michael J. McCann might provide a basis for the corresponding decision-making process:

> However, apart from the 'doing' of a translation, the translator can at times be faced with a dilemma – be mindful please of its original etymology of the Greek *dí lemma* 'two assumptions' – to translate or not to translate at all. The first ethical consideration of the translator is almost Hippocratic as with the medical profession – 'primum non nocere' – first do no harm. If the translation is going to do harm, the translator should try to avoid it [...]. (2005: 1)

Graphically speaking, this is obviously an ideal case as no additional interference with the image composition is created and no thought has to go into creating a translation that fits the typographic film identity. In the analysis, 56.92 % of film titles, 45.36 % of displays, 24.30 % of captions, and 0.88 % of subtitles were not translated and neither were any opening or closing credits. For narrative text elements, this strategy was not used at all. The high frequencies for film titles most likely results from proper names, simple words that do not seem to require translation into German (e.g. *Ice Age* [USA 2002]), and marketing considerations. The equally high frequency of untranslated displays might, on the one hand, be based on the strongly subjective decision-making process here, but on the other hand also on the high number of displays that could be plot-relevant, but are easy to understand for a German audience (see the address in Figure 2.6) or clearly inferable from the overall image or scene. The untranslated captions mostly consist of names and places that do not require translation into German – they might, however, be translated through replacement in German image tracks, if available.

Figure 2.6: No translation of a display in *Finding Nemo* (USA 2003, 00:31:56)

## 2.5.2 Translation through subtitles

With a share of about 52 %, translation using subtitles was the most frequent strategy in the translation of text elements. It is additive and isosemiotic as it stays in the same channel while adding an additional typographical element. Translation through subtitles is used for film titles, displays, captions, pre-existing subtitles, and narrative text. While the high frequency of the subtitle strategy for displays is not surprising – 45.71 % of all observed displays (256 of 560) – this strategy was also used for about 33.85 % of film titles (22 of 65), 70.09 % of captions (75 of 107, see Figure 2.7), 71.93 % of subtitles (246 of 342), and 80 % of narrative text elements (8 of 10). All groups besides the displays could technically be substituted graphically and this might be the case in German image tracks, if available.

## 2.5.3 Translation through substitution

Translation through substitution is isosemiotic as well and includes a wide range of cases. Simply put, it is a translation that replaces the source element – be it through editing of the source text element, deletion of the source element and creation of a new element trying to imitate the source element, or substitution of an optional element. This includes substitutions that still contain the English source term, e.g. "The Departed – Unter Feinden" ("The Departed – Among Ene-

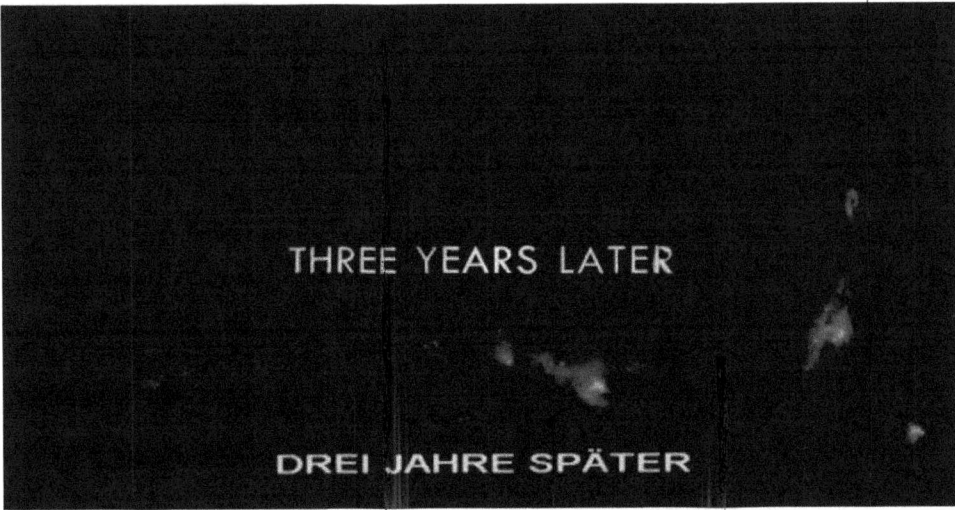

Figure 2.7: Caption translation through subtitle (*Star Trek*, USA 2009, 00:27:05)

mies", *The Departed*). The choice between replacing a text element and subtitling seems similar to the choice between dubbing and subtitling. Replacing a text element prevents additional distraction from the image, a negative feedback effect by displaying the original and the translation, as well as the additional subtitle which covers the original or anything else relevant to the plot or image composition.

In the 52 films, the strategy of substitution was used for 9.23 % of the film titles (22 of 65), 5.61 % of the captions (6 of 107), 27.19 % of the subtitles (93 of 342), and 20 % of the narrative text elements (2 of 10). It was not observed for any of the opening or closing credits when the English audio track was selected. Concerning displays, the strategy is most likely so very rare because of effort and costs. So far, it was only observed in very few films targeted at children, e.g. *Lilo & Stich* (USA 2002; not part of the corpus). While the intention behind the substitution in *Lilo & Stitch* surely was good, the appropriateness of the used typeface, retention of the exclamation mark for the question in the German version, and the overall translation quality can easily be challenged (see Figure 2.8).

While there are no films that feature inserts in the corpus, the German versions of *Sherlock* (see Figure 2.5) and *Non-Stop* (UK/F/USA/CAN 2014) include a wide range of translated inserts that replaced the English original text elements. The substitution of the narrative text in the *Star Wars* franchise, however, might be one of the most noted and remembered – and also a good example of a strong typographic film identity (see Figure 2.9).

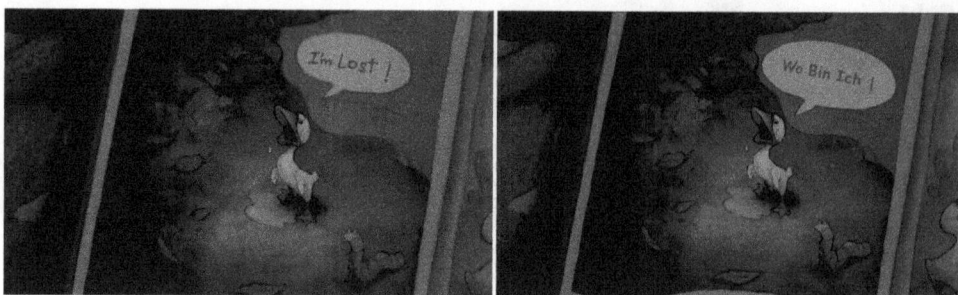

Figure 2.8: Substitution of a display (*Lilo & Stitch*, 00:40:33)

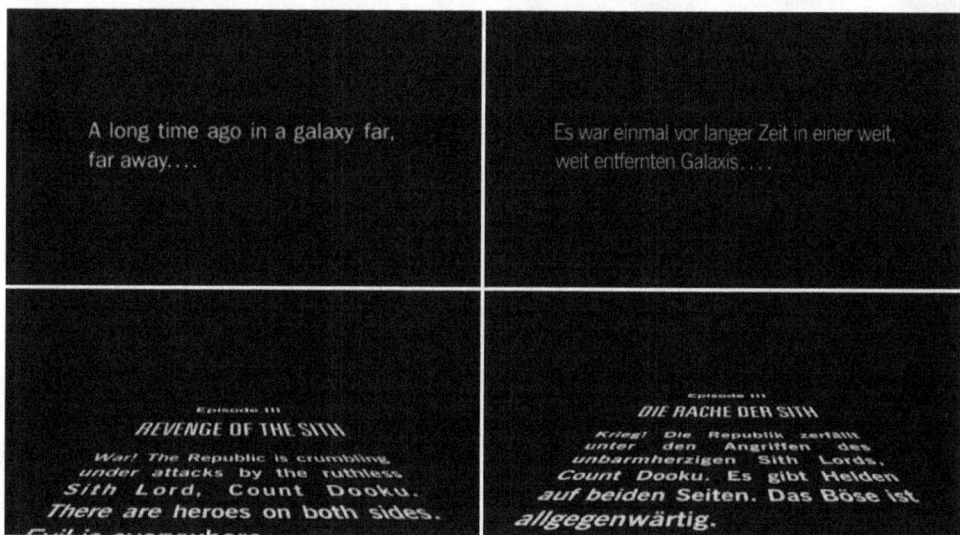

Figure 2.9: Substitution of narrative text elements (*Star Wars: Episode III – Revenge of the Sith* [USA 2005], 00:00:16 and 00:01:10)

## 2.5.4 Translation through subtitled verbalisation

While this strategy includes both the reading (through a speaker or off-voice) performed in the original version of a film and that in a dubbed version, this article only takes into account the first case. The second case is nevertheless interesting due to the possibility of adding verbalisation when the corresponding actor (or at least his or her mouth) is not visible in a shot. So far, this strategy has only been observed for displays, as superimposed text elements are usually not visible to possible 'readers'.[25] Due to the reading, the translation of the corresponding text

---

[25]With some exceptions of characters breaking through the fourth wall and noticing superimposed text elements as happened in the segment "Desperanto" in *Montreal Stories* (CAN 1991).

element appears in the subtitles of the spoken content of the film (see Figure 2.10). While this could also be rated as being translated using a subtitle, the source of the subtitle is a different one. In the analysis, 8.93 % of the overall displays were translated this way, equating to 50 of 560 displays.

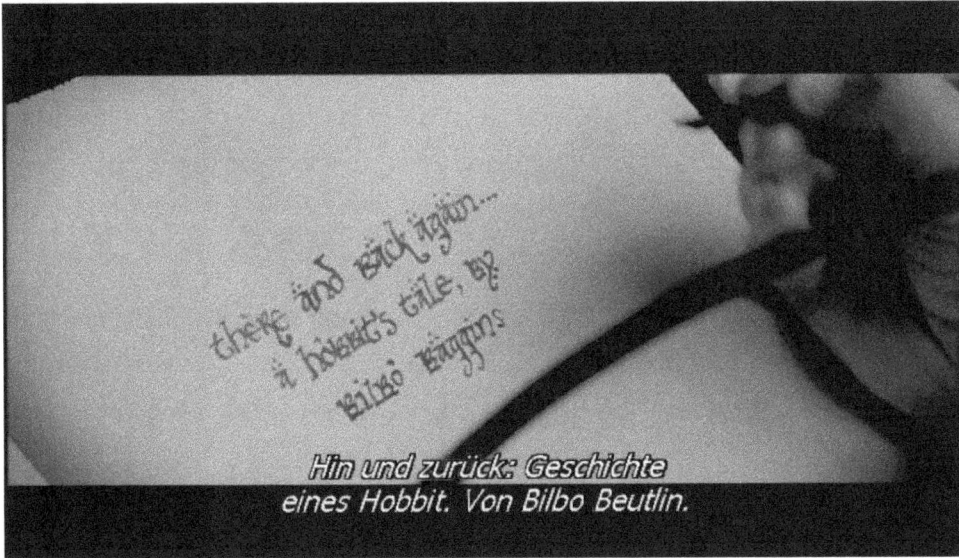

Figure 2.10: Display read aloud by a character (*The Lord of the Rings – The Fellowship of the Ring*, NZ/USA 2001, 00:08:07)

### 2.5.5 Translation through additional scenes

Translation through additional scenes has so far only been observed within German image tracks of Disney productions such as *Brother Bear* and *The Incredibles*. This strategy is not only isosemiotic towards the translated element but also additive towards the whole film. As seen in Figure 2.11, the same typefaces and positions were used and the overall layout was imitated as closely as possible, recreating the typographic identity of the film.

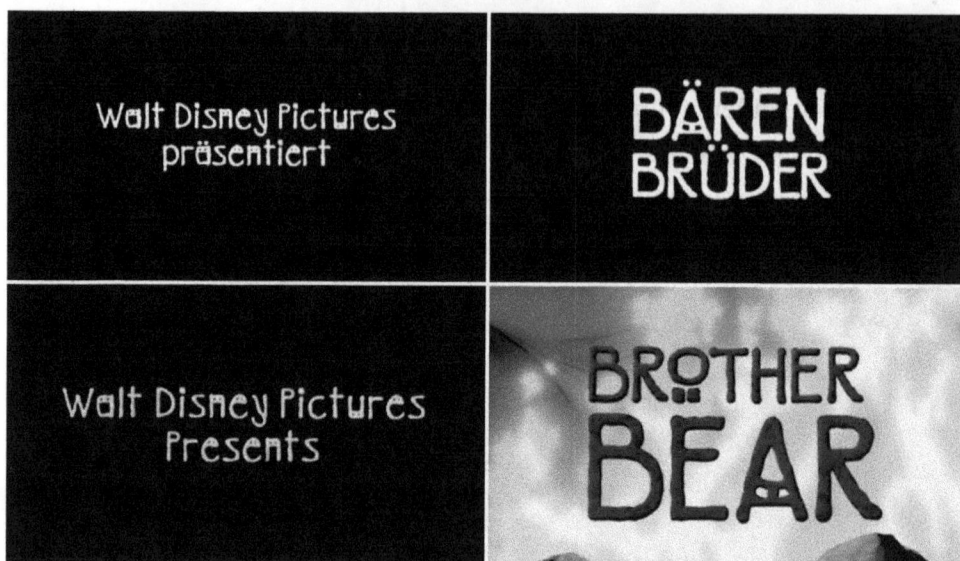

Figure 2.11: Additional scene translating the following film title scene (*Brother Bear*, 00:00:15)

## 2.6 Shortcomings and challenges

Various shortcomings and challenges are linked to the different text elements and translation strategies. As mentioned before, the first challenge seems to be the decision whether to translate or not. Translation when none is needed or no translation when a translation might be needed can easily lead to irritation, frustration or even amusement. As illustrated in Figure 2.12, some translations might raise the question of necessity.

Other text elements might include a culture-specific element, phrase or name that is not included or different in the target text. When the only option is a subtitle, the decision will have to be made to either translate that text element and possibly create a negative feedback effect due to the deviating term in the subtitle – while "Happy Birthday" does not pose a problem, "Bilbo Baggins" is known as "Bilbo Beutlin" in Germany – or to leave it out and possibly cause confusion for viewers that do not know the term or name from the source text (see Figure 2.13).

A major shortcoming of translation using subtitles, the most frequent strategy (52.02 %), however, is the possibility of collisions. Collisions can occur due to the conventional subtitle's static position in the bottom-centre area while occasionally being moved to the top-centre area. The subtitle can collide with plot-

Figure 2.12: Possibly unnecessary caption translation (*Star Trek*, 00:13:48)

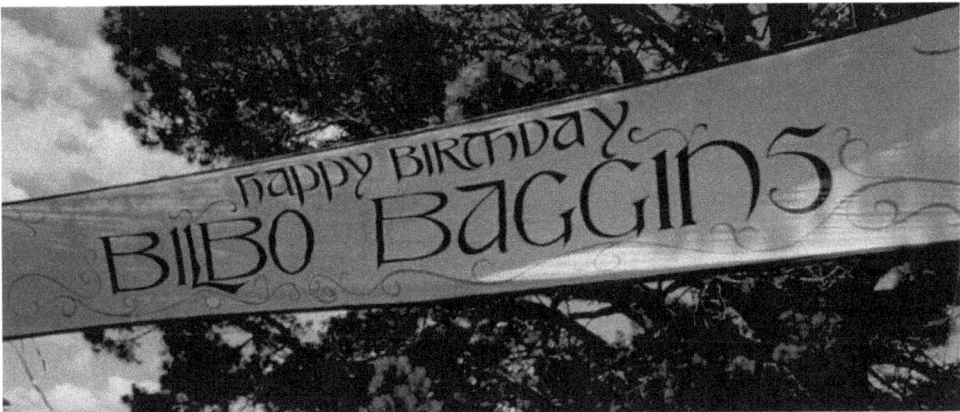

Figure 2.13: No translation of a display in *The Lord of the Rings – The Fellowship of the Ring* (00:10:06)

relevant image areas, other text elements, or even subtitles that translate the spoken content.

Two types of collisions occurred in the analysed corpus, spatial and temporal collisions. Spatial collisions describe the actual act of covering another text element (see Figure 2.14 on the left) and so far are mainly prevented by moving the subtitle to the top-centre area. Temporal collisions can occur when there is both spoken content and a text element that require translation. If this is achieved through subtitles, the only observed solution is to display one of the otherwise simultaneous subtitles slightly earlier or later.

Collisions were present in at least 26 of the 52 films. In *District 9*, so many collision-prone situations exist in the first 40 minutes of the film that almost half of the subtitles were moved to the top-centre area. However, the top-centre area does not always constitute an ideal solution, as visible from the right example in Figure 2.14, where the subtitle covers the main focus area – the speaker.

Figure 2.14: Spatial collisions in *Avatar* (00:14:49) and *District 9* (00:03:32).

Figure 2.15 is an example of both a spatial and temporal collision. The caption is translated first even though the speaker has already started talking. As a result, not only the speaker is covered partially by the subtitle but also the display time of both elements (translation of the caption and translation of the spoken content) is shortened.

These collisions are, of course, quite dependent on genre and specific films – the pseudo-documentary style of the science-fiction film *District 9* is more prone to collisions than e.g. a romance such as *Pride & Prejudice* (FR/UK/USA 2005) that does not feature any text elements besides film title and closing captions.

Even though subtitles are added as images to DVD and BD, *Avatar* is the only film analysed so far which features optional subtitles adjusted to the film's typographic identity and overall design. The other films either featured unremarkable subtitles with standard readability or minor problems concerning readability and

Figure 2.15: Caption translation (left) with the shifted subtitle (right) while the speaker has already started to talk. (*District 9*, 00:01:56).

design (e.g. low resolution, pixelated or lacking a border or shadow). The films on *Amazon Prime* and *Netflix* included clear and readable subtitles which – due to the personalised settings and options – never reflect the overall design of the film. However, it raises the question whether it is more important to provide viewers with these options or to allow professionals to be more creative.

One of the main shortcomings observed during this analysis is the lack of information on the provided image tracks. Neither DVD and BD nor the streaming providers offer clear information on the availability of multiple image tracks. In addition, even if there are multiple image tracks available, they cannot be selected by the viewer and are usually linked to a specific audio track (e.g. it is not possible to watch the German image track with English audio and German subtitles). Based on this shortcoming, the analysis could only be performed on a mix of English and German image tracks. The following Table 2.4 illustrates the differences that can arise from the different image versions using the example of *The Incredibles*:

As illustrated in Table 2.4, there are quite a number of differences between the two image versions. The opening credits and film title were replaced with their German translations, as well as nine of the displays. An additional scene was added to replace a written display with a symbol. Furthermore, five displays were removed from the film. The two captions were both replaced with their German translations. While the significant differences between the two image tracks might to a large extent be explained by the intended target group, replacements of captions and film titles were observed in at least five other films.

For a future study, a feature that could be added to the corpus annotation is an overview of the available image tracks and the applied translation strategies to clarify this topic further.

Table 2.4: Differences between the graphical translation strategies of the English and German image tracks of *The Incredibles*

|  | Strategy | English | German |
|---|---|---|---|
| Film Titles | No translation | 2 | - |
|  | Substitution | - | 2 |
| Opening Credits | No translation | 1 | - |
|  | Substitution | - | 1 |
| Closing Credits | No translation | 1 | 1 |
| Displays | No translation | 20 | 9 |
|  | Subtitle | 1 | - |
|  | Verbalisation | 4 | 1 |
|  | Substitution | - | 9 |
|  | Removed | - | 5 |
|  | New Scene | - | 1 |
| Captions | No translation | 2 | - |
|  | Substitution | - | 2 |
| Subtitles | Substitution | 4 | 4 |

## 2.7 Summary

Based on a film corpus of 100 films, 52 of which were thoroughly analysed, text elements and the observed graphical translation strategies were presented and discussed. The concept of corporate design was applied to films and the newly created term of typographic film identity was explained. Also, technical considerations and constraints were discussed. While the image-based subtitles on DVD and BD would allow for a more individual design and placement following the typographic identity of films, this has only been observed in one of the analysed films. Streaming providers offer personalisation of subtitles that cater to readability issues but prevent any inclusion of the subtitles in overall branding or typographic identity.

The analysis showed that film titles and closing credits were found in all analysed films but only 29 films included opening credits, 43 films included plot-relevant displays, 17 films featured captions, 12 films featured subtitles, and six films had narrative text elements. Plot-relevant displays were the most frequent text element with 560 cases, equating to 47.86 % of the 1170 observed text elements. Additionally, 342 subtitles, 107 captions, and 10 narrative text elements were observed. With 52.05 %, subtitling was the most frequent strategy to translate these text elements, followed by non-translation with 34.44 %, substitution (9.32 %), and a character reading a text element aloud, adding its translation to the subtitles of the spoken content (4.19 %).

With subtitling as the main strategy, the interference with shot compositions and typographic identity, the focus on the lower image area, and the possible collisions with other relevant image and text elements need to be mentioned. Due to the developments of increasingly creative and complex text elements and effects, the translation of inserts (as well as many captions) are a good example of how films can profit from substitution rather than subtitling. On the other side, integrated titles (Fox 2012, see Chapter 3) are an example of how the typographic design and image composition can effectively be incorporated into and respected by the translation while at the same time increasing the time spent exploring the image (see Chapter 7). Due to their individual positions, collisions with relevant image and text elements can be prevented and additional information such as the identification of the current speaker and the speaking direction might be attractive for SDH audiences. However, the possibility to choose between both English and German audio and image tracks as well as subtitle tracks creates unique possibilities for the German audience.

# 3 Integrated titles

So why look for an alternative or improvement? What do subtitle concepts such as 'integrated titles' have to offer? The previous chapters illustrated that, while there has been much research and focus on content-related challenges, there is still much to learn concerning the reception and aesthetics of subtitles, and text elements in film overall. Therefore, this chapter introduces integrated titles and insights from associated fields of study.

Technically speaking, the creation of individually placed titles has been possible for quite a while now. While the changeover from analogue to digital processing and the rise of non-linear video editing in the 90s made it possible not only for professionals but also for amateurs at home to edit film material, there were already ways of adding text into film before that (see §1.1). Nowadays, video editing software that allows to place text elements in videos (e.g. *Adobe Premiere Pro* as example for a professional tool) or subtitle programmes such as *Aegisub* that can create subtitle files with individual positions are sufficient to create integrated titles. For more elaborate purposes such as 3D titles that are placed in the depths of the image, software programmes such as *Adobe After Effects* are more suitable.

While guidelines focused on SDH seem quite thoughtful – at least in terms of speaker identification and horizontal placement – traditional or "conventional" (Foerster 2010: 81) subtitles are sometimes still seen as "a blemish on the film screen" (Díaz Cintas & Remael 2007: 82) and "intrusion into the visual space of film" (Thompson 2000: 1) that have the "potential to 'drown' the images [and] instead of watching images, the audience starts literally to see only texts" (Sinha 2004: 174). This perception shows that, even though the content is at least as often under criticism – the authentic and aesthetic experience of the audience is a relevant part of subtitling. The created split visual attention, the distraction of inexperienced viewers particularly, and the traditionally thoughtless design (and often layout) of subtitles call on the paradox of the demanded invisibility of translation, and therefore subtitles. In addition to well discussed challenges such as the afore-mentioned time and space constraints and the transfer of humour and cultural-specific elements, the position and design of traditional subtitles can be seen as one of the major drawbacks. Especially viewers from countries that do not make major use of subtitling – mainly English speaking countries and those that have a long tradition of dubbing films – might find it hard to focus on both reading the subtitles and perceiving the visual aspects of the plot. British director Danny Boyle, appreciated for films such as *Trainspotting* (UK 1996) and *Slumdog Millionaire*, described the problem by stating that "you don't watch the film – you read the film and you scan occasionally to the actors" (Beckman 2008). And he does not stand alone with this opinion. Rawsthorn describes conventional subtitles as "limply at the bottom of the screen" (2007) and only legible "if you're lucky" (Rawsthorn 2007). But "mostly, they're not" (Rawsthorn 2007). She goes even further in saying that

> subtitles are almost always badly designed. Illegible typefaces drift on- and off-screen at the wrong moments, lurking so low that the bottoms of the letters are chopped off, and obstructing the audience's view of gripping twists in the plot, or especially beautiful scenes. It doesn't seem to matter how good – or bad – the film is, the size of its budget, the quality of the cinematography, sets, costumes or titles, because the subtitles are still dire. Every other area of movie aesthetics has a proud design history, except subtitling. (Rawsthorn 2007)

Stuart Comer, the curator of film at the Tate museum in London, gives one of the main reasons for these shortcomings: "Subtitling often takes place after the film is completed. It is not necessarily done by the director, and there is less quality control. That's why it can seem thoughtless" (Rawsthorn 2007). While it is understandable that before digital technology took over, the complex and time-consuming process of adding subtitles to film did not spark much interest in adding additional effort and costs to the design process, today's processes are much more flexible. However, few filmmakers and producers have adjusted to this not so new reality. "Purely utilitarian" (Vit 2005) subtitles are predominant and keep "interfering with the beautifully framed and considered shot of the director" (2005). The demand for the cheapest possible solution might seem to be an understandable explanation – but how much might a slightly higher investment into subtitling actually weigh, especially compared to the horrendous costs of dubbing? Combined with Romero-Fresco's observation that "half of the revenue of [...] both top-grossing and award-winning Hollywood films comes from foreign territories" (Romero-Fresco 2013: 202) while "translation and accessibility services only account for 0.1% – 1% of the budget of an average film production (Lambourne 2012)" (2013: 202), it can only be in the interest of film producers to take a critical look at the perception of the translated version of their film.

SDH guidelines already propose a more logical placement of titles and incorporate colour and layout into the relevant aspects that affect viewer's perception. Various researchers, however, defined less traditional concepts of subtitling based on a quite contrary form of subtitling – fansubs. Of these, Nornes appears to be one of the first to discuss subtitles not only based on content but also layout (1999). He recognises the criticism concerning the graphical intrusion of subtitles into the film image:

> Spectators often find cinema's powerful sense of mimesis muddied by subtitles, even by skillful ones. The original, foreign, object – its sights and its sounds – is available to all, but it is easily obscured by the graphic text through which we necessarily approach it. Thus, the opacity or awkwardness of subtitles easily inspires rage. (1999: 17)

As Nornes considers it "likely that no one ever has come away from a foreign film admiring the translation" (1999: 17), he emphasises the need for exploring new methods such as what he calls "abusive" subtitles (1999: 17). Abusive subtitles include not only "textual abuse" (Nornes 1999: 18) but also "graphical abuse" (1999: 18) that means "experimentation with [...] visual qualities" (1999: 18). Nornes sees the roots of these experiments within Japanese cinema: Japanese subtitles can be placed "both horizontally and vertically" (1999: 21) and are therefore prone to abusive application. Not only can subtitles therefore be modified in a way to provide a "graphic representation of the materiality of the speech" (Nornes 1999: 25, concerning the Japanese subtitles for the film *M* [USA 1951]) but also following the image composition of the film:

> Furthermore, Japanese subtitlers routinely placed their titles in different areas of the scene depending on the cinematographer's position. It was thought that the position of the words should complement mise-en-scène and movement. At the same time, there are indications that subtitle positioning depended upon narrative as well. One story from critic Yodogawa Nagaharu describes a dreamy Hollywood love scene where the subtitles appeared *between* the two lovers. Of course! (Nornes 1999: 25)

Even back then, Nornes realised that the possibilities for modifications concerning e.g. placement, size, and colour of subtitles were not a problem of technical constraints and "nothing was preventing them [students in an exemplary class] from indulging in the most outrageous innovations" (1999: 31) but rather professionals and students being held back "by the inertia of convention and the ideology of corruption" (1999: 31). The advantage of early Japanese anime fandom was the subtitler's position "outside of the mainstream translation industry"

(1999: 31) and following their "instinct" (1999: 31): They used "different colored subtitles", additional definitions, footnotes, cultural explanations, and "different fonts, sizes, and colors to correspond to material aspects of language, from voice to dialect to written text within the frame" and they "freely insert their 'subtitles' all over the screen" (1999: 32). Nornes therefore defines this "abuse" as "directed at convention, even at spectators and their expectations" (1999: 32).

Díaz Cintas and Muñoz Sánchez seem to follow this definition when they discuss what they call "hybrid" subtitles (2006: 51). While subtitles are supposed to "pass unnoticed to the viewer" (2006: 47) and "be as invisible as possible" (2006: 47), "some of these new conventions are nowadays making an appearance in the commercial versions of some programmes (Díaz Cintas 2005)" (2006: 47). Ferrer Simó (2005) provides the following "comprehensive list of key features that define fansubs" (2006: 47):

Use of different fonts throughout the same programme.

Use of colours to identify different actors.

Use of subtitles of more than two lines (up to four lines).

Use of notes at the top of the screen.

Use of glosses in the body of the subtitles.

The position of subtitles varies on the screen (scenetiming).

Karaoke subtitling for opening and ending songs.

Adding of information regarding fansubbers.

Translation of opening and closing credits.

While the use of colours for speaker identification, subtitles longer than two lines, additional information, and varying positions are similar to the SDH guidelines presented earlier, fansubs distinguish themselves through several additional features such as varying fonts, glosses, and karaoke subtitles. They are "a hybrid resorting to conventions used both in subtitling for the hearing as well as in subtitling for the deaf and the hard-of-hearing" (2006: 51). Thus, this more thoughtful approach has its roots in Japanese subtitling that influenced fansubs for Japanese anime films and seems to combine features of both traditional subtitles and SDH.

While the terms 'abusive' and 'hybrid' focus on subtitles in the context of Japanese productions and Nornes' 'abusive subtitles' are often seen as mainly "making translations linguistically visible" (Foerster 2010: 86), researchers such as Foerster (2010) and McClarty (2012) approach the topic from a more aesthetics- and creativity-based perspective. Foerster criticises the conventional guidelines' aim of invisibility and the resulting "register and [...] design for subtitles that never call attention to themselves" (Foerster 2010: 82), defining subtitles "solely as a means of understanding what is being said on screen" (2010: 82). Mentioning examples such as *Monty Python and the Holy Grail* (UK 1975), *Annie Hall* (USA 1977), and "Desperanto" (segment in *Montreal Stories*, CAN 1991) and discussing the subtitles of *Nochnoy Dozor*[1] ("Night Watch", RUS 2004; see §4.2.1), she defines "aesthetic subtitling" (2010: 85) as a practice that "draws attention to the subtitles via aesthetic means exploring semiotic possibilities, which include the semantic dimension without being restricted by it" (2010: 85) and is "predominantly designed graphically to support or match the aesthetics of the audiovisual text and consequently develop an aesthetic of their own" (2010: 85).

McClarty follows a more film studies-based approach when she speaks of "creative subtitles" (2012: 138). Like Foerster, she sees "subtitling practitioners [as] mere norm-obeying machines" (2010: 135) that "continue to have their hands tied by the constraints of the field and the norms of the profession" (2010: 135) while failing to "acknowledge the insights that could be gained by referring to audiovisual translation's parallel discipline: film studies" (2010: 135). While McClarty sees the roots of creative film titles in the "artistry involved in the design of intertitles during cinema's silent era" (2012: 136) that "completed the scene" (2012: 136), she also acknowledges the failure of Japanese anime distributors to fulfil the "specific demands of that fan community" (2012: 137) and thereby providing the motivation for fans to create their own subtitles – or, fansubs. By using their own concept of typefaces, colours and placements they "forced the hand of anime distributors, leading them to adapt their subtitling styles" (2012: 137). McClarty sees the solution in a multidisciplinary approach similar to the recent turn to more practical approaches in theatre translation:

> Regardless of how timely, beneficial or aesthetically pleasing a creative subtitling strategy may be, referring only to ideas from within translation studies and audiovisual translation will fail to produce a new form of subtitling that is truly innovative. (McClarty 2012: 138)

Instead of 'abuse', she sees the need of a 'creative' approach that does not simply "describe a subtitling practice that differs from the norm but [that denotes] an approach that looks outward from its own discipline as well as its own culture" (McClarty 2012: 138) and aims for "difference rather than sameness" (McClarty 2012: 140). McClarty emphasises that not the creativity of a translator or subtitle

---

[1]Released in the USA by Twentieth Century Fox and Fox Searchlight Pictures in 2006 with English titles.

practitioner leads to innovative titles such as those visible in *Slumdog Million-aire, La Antena* (AR 2007) or *Austin Powers in Goldmember* (USA 2002), but the "imagination of film directors and editors" (2012: 140) that did not only want to provide a translation but also create additional effects of comedic or artistic na-ture (2012: 140–142). Thus, subtitles can not only convey content but also sound (McClarty 2012: 146) or speaker location (McClarty 2012: 148). The goal should not be a new set of norms but a "creative response to individual qualities within and between films" (2012: 148.), created by a "translator-title designer" (McClarty 2012: 149) that aims for both linguistically and aesthetically pleasing titles. These should be produced within the postproduction phase of a film's making and in cooperation with the film maker, editors, and title designers.

Another term that can be found in recent studies that is more strongly focused on usability and automation is that of "dynamic subtitles" (Armstrong & Brooks 2014, Brown et al. 2015). The concept is based on placing the titles close to the speaker and allowing for an easier speaker identification and more time for the image exploration. The two eye tracking studies dealing with this concept are presented in §6.3.

In similar fashion to these approaches, the studies by Park et al. (2008), Hong et al. (2010) and Hu et al. (2013) focus not only on the improved perception but also on the automation of the process. They use terms such as "speaker-following subtitles" (Hong et al. 2010; Hu et al. 2013) that relate to the automatic speaker recognition systems of their software. These studies are presented in §3.4.

While the presented terms are still based on the concept of subtitles that are placed below or at the bottom of the image, even Nornes back in 1999 put the "sub" in parentheses "because they were not always at the bottom of the frame" (Nornes 1999: 23). As Bayram and Bayraktar speak of "text information" pre-sented in "integrated formats" (2012: 82) when combining text and image, the term of "integrated titles" was chosen for the pilot study in 2012 and kept for the following studies as even Armstrong and Brooks mention the enhancement of subtitles through "integrating them with the moving image" (2014). Even though this approach could also be deemed 'creative' or 'aesthetic' and the title place-ment 'dynamic' and 'speaker-following', using the term 'integrated' seems to include both these concepts while emphasising the relationship between image and title. The various terms, however, show the wide bandwidth of possible ap-proaches that cannot be defined by tight norms or strict guidelines.

As Foerster (2010), McClarty (2012), and others stated, not only the analysis (cf. Chaume 2004) but also the creation of subtitles should not purely be based on translation studies. Film studies can offer insight into image composition and storytelling, communication and graphic design can offer definitions of aesthetics and creativity, usability studies provide basics of user experience design as well as interface design, and computer sciences provide insight into potential automation processes and software design. Therefore, the following sections discuss these fields of study in regard to integrated titles.

## 3.1 Communication design: Aesthetics and layout

In the previous §1.2.3, various challenges regarding the layout of traditional subtitles were presented and discussed. While the main criticism was that subtitles with a conventional layout can cover interesting or plot-relevant image regions and objects, further points of criticism should be considered as well, such as the loss of aesthetic value and the disruption of the intended image composition. Aspects such as aesthetics, creativity, and layout were mentioned – but how are these similar sounding concepts defined and how are they relevant for title reception? First of all, they can be put into an order following relevance: Graphical aspects such as readability, legibility, and contrast are highly relevant to the overall experience and information transfer while characteristics of good design and aesthetic concepts are not always that specific to be easily and directly applied. Readability is affected by the "way in which words and blocks of type are arranged" (Loyd 2013) while legibility "refers to how a typeface is designed and how well one individual character can be distinguished from another" (Loyd 2013). Therefore, readability is tightly connected to rule-based decisions such as the position of the line break (see §1.2.3), the position of the subtitle in general (see §1.2.3 and Chapter 4), and the decision between one- and two-liners. Legibility, on the other side, refers to the choice of typeface, the character spacing and kerning as well as the line spacing, and the size and style of the typeface. Based on these characteristics, subtitles can be easy to read – or not. While there are detailed discussions and analyses of readability and legibility of printed typefaces, there is not that much material on subtitles yet. Projects such as "Screenfont"[2], however, provide insight into the challenges and shortcomings of typefaces used for subtitles:

> Because of careful hinting and special adaptation for computer displays, these screenfonts are generally more pleasant and easier to read than many other fonts. But their purpose is to display static pages of text. [...] They don't appear and disappear like pop-on captions or subtitles, nor do they

---

[2]See http://www.screenfont.ca [2016–03–25].

scroll or paint on like certain other captions. You don't have a single nominal chance to read the text that uses those fonts before that text disappears. (Screenfont 2016)

While these problems might become less relevant with higher resolutions and the rise of the BD, it should be taken into account that a bad choice of typeface, style, and size can render any subtitle unreadable. Organisations such as the Irish National Disability Authority (NDA) list several more criteria of readable subtitles (NDA 2016):

- Rationale
- Standard readable language
- Start and end at natural, logical points
- Carefully chosen linebreaks
- Adequate reading time
- Clear visual presentation
- Position of subtitles that avoids obscuring important content

In the section on 'clear visual presentation', the Centre for Excellence in Universal Design (CEUD) of the NDA puts emphasis on the importance of subtitles staying within the so-called 'safe area' that is never cut regardless of the video size or playback device. Furthermore, suitable typefaces and a strong contrast as well as legible colour combinations are demanded. While the most legible colour combinations are seldom suitable for most image concepts (blue/white, red/white, cyan/blue and blue/cyan), the recommendation of using "colours with a saturation index of less than 85 % to avoid distortion and flicker" (NDA 2016) can easily be followed when working with colours (and also black and white typefaces). Interestingly, the CEUD also demands to not obscure the speaker's mouth, burnt-in subtitles or "any important activity" (NDA 2016). As the recommended colour combinations might not suit most films, calculating the contrast might be a useful tool in ensuring legibility. Due to the way the eyes work (especially the rods and cones and our sensitivity to light), luminance and contrast are most relevant in distinguishing colours and therefore objects. While "contrast in light and dark is the most effective" (Bradley 2016), there's also complementary colours, temperature, and saturation. These can be retrieved from tables or through calculation.[3] Even though readability and legibility are discussed concerning design and aesthetics, they are tightly connected to usability and accessibility as well.[4] While there is no perfect set of required characteristics of subtitle text, some aspects are clear: A bold, sans-serif typeface that provides a strong contrast due to its colour and possibly an outline and offers good legibility due to a spacing that allows a clear distinction of each letter is likely to be a good fit for most films.[5]

Aesthetics, on the other hand and by itself, is difficult to define. Most aspects that would be used to define it are normally entirely subjective and can vary between different viewers. This is why in his book on the "aesthetic experience and literary hermeneutics" Hans Jobert Jauß demands that "aesthetic judgment" should be based on "both instances of effect and of reception"[6] (1991: 9). Thus, aesthetics is not only about the superficial effect of a piece of art, or a film in this case, but also about how it is interpreted. And if it can be interpreted, then there is usually also an intention behind it, an intended effect of the film. If we regard any film, including translated film, as an artistic synthesis, then we can therefore critically examine the intention behind the target language adaptation. The current appearance of subtitles basically suggests that the intention behind the adaptation normally includes little more than the goal of providing access through translation, combined with considerations of time and cost efficiency. In the worst case, the audiovisual translation of (older) films is subject to censorship.[7] Furthermore, there are only few examples based on more advanced aesthetic considerations. A problem in this regard could be, of course, the recipients' "expectation and experience" mentioned by Jauß (1991: 13). Since users of subtitled films are usually not accustomed to or do not know any other way of subtitling, they do not make demands regarding the aesthetics of the adaptation.

---

[3]See i.e. calculation of luminance and contrast ratio (http://vanseodesign.com/web-design/luminance-contrast-ratio-accessibility/ [2016–08–01]) and tools for colour contrast check (http://www.snook.ca/technical/colour_contrast/colour.html#fg=33FF33,bg=333333 [2016–08–01] and http://openweb.eu.org/articles/text-contrasts) [2016–08–01].

[4]Cf. https://www.nngroup.com/articles/low-contrast/ [2016–08–01] on low contrast and accessibility issues.

[5]Further and more detailed discussions can be found here: http://webdesign.tutsplus.com/articles/typographic-readability-and-legibility--webdesign-12211 [2016–04–18].

[6]In German, the passage from *Ästhetische Erfahrung und literarische Hermeneutik* reads "[das] ästhetische Urteil [aus den] beiden Instanzen von Wirkung und Rezeption [zu] bilden".

[7]See, for example, the German dubbed version of the American film *Die Hard* (USA 1988), where the nationality of the originally German alleged terrorists was altered (see http://www.schnittberichte.com/schnittbericht.php?ID=1105 [2016–07–29]). *Casablanca* (USA 1942), as well, was subject to denazification (see http://www.dradio.de/dkultur/sendungen/zeitreisen/918145/ [2016–07–29].

And if the target group makes no demands, the industry apparently rarely feels compelled to act.

So if we accept film as a work of art, even if it is such an 'ephemeral' one as a television series, and apply these basic design rules, then what are the probable consequences for subtitling?

- Film should not be subject to any negative influences due to translation and should not be altered to its detriment as a consequence of translation.

- Concerning layout, audiovisual translation should either follow the original as closely as possible or should compensate losses caused by the transfer in another way.

- The value of the translated film should not be reduced by an aesthetically unambitious presentation.

- Film and translation should not be created and judged separately from each other.

Based on these assumptions, translators can only deliver a quality translation if they have full access to the source film as well as the inserted texts (e.g. captions) and the texts to be inserted, so that they can connect the non-verbal visual channel with the other channels. To show that this mode of translation is indeed possible, and that film can be translated graphically in an appealing and respectful manner, this study also analyses the aesthetics of the newly created integrated titles. As the aesthetic experience cannot be measured via eye movements recorded with an eye tracker, a questionnaire was designed according to the recommendations of the WPGS (*Wirtschaftsspsychologische Gesellschaft*, Society for Behavioural Economics and Economic Psychology). It included a number of questions on information processing and the aesthetic experience. The study is presented in Chapter 7, the results and the discussion in §8.2.

Gottlieb, however, judges the aesthetics of subtitles based on subtitle design – referring to line breaks etc. – and comfortable reading speed as well as subtitle duration (2012: 53). He therefore defines subtitle aesthetics through their usability, and criticises the low standards that can sometimes be observed:

> Although in most countries subtitling companies that produce bona fide subtitles allow subtitlers enough time to cue subtitles in advance, not all countries focus on oral synchrony — or visual, for that matter. Worse still, in news programs and other direct transmissions in any country, live and

semi–live subtitles are, inevitably, often grossly out of sync with the speaker on screen. (Gottlieb 2012: 41)

As discussed earlier, interlingual and intralingual subtitles created for deaf and hard-of-hearing audiences provide several additional features that allow an easier speaker identification, e.g. through colour, and "although color identification may indeed be less relevant to a hearing audience, certain dramatic film sequences with overlapping speech may benefit from a (modest) use of colors, so that two or three main characters may be distinguished throughout fast verbal exchanges" (Gottlieb 2012: 68). In addition, "letter size [...] and alignment are suited for the purpose" (Neves 2007: 94–95) and varying screen sizes and target groups should be taken into account (Gottlieb 2012: 68). However, "viewers are not as aware of 'quality' in subtitle content and design as researchers and practicing subtitlers would like them to be" (Gottlieb 2012: 69) and the common minimum should be the "synchronous cueing and harmonious subtitle design" (2012: 69). Gottlieb reasons that subtitling "has not yet proven to be reader-*un*friendly" (2012: 69):

1. Sentence-level synchrony between dialogue and subtitles is secured, helping viewers identify speakers and comprehend the original dialogue.

2. Subtitles will appear as an integral part of the polysemiotic totality of the production, thus creating semiotic cohesion (Díaz Cintas & Remael 2007: 49–52) and the illusion in readers that they can follow the original dialogue.

3. Each subtitle is a self-contained entity, making sense even in isolation from the previous and following subtitles. This, however, should not lead to staccato-like sequences of isolated subtitles: grammatical and logical cohesion is indispensable.

4. Subtitles do not cover important pictorial information.

5. Subtitles do not give away important information to the tar-get audience that the original audience has not yet obtained through the dialogue.

6. Well-designed subtitles pave the way for a 'fuller' translation of the spoken lines. Reader-friendly segmentation, including effective line breaks, allows for more positive intersemiotic feedback and may result in higher reading speeds. In other words, well-designed subtitles mean less condensation – and minimal loss of information. (Gottlieb 2012: 69)

In combination, the definition of aesthetic subtitling seems to be based on being pleasing and useful to the audience. Similarly, creativity can be defined as an "achievement [that] emerges from the awareness of a problem and presents something new that in a certain time within one culture is accepted as sensible by experts" (Preiser 1976: 5) and a creative product as "a new product that is regarded usable or satisfactory at a certain time by a certain group" (Stein 1953). Foerster summarises these needs in a similar fashion:

> The evaluation of a creative solution is thus based on two pillars: the awareness of a problem, as innovations have to meet certain parameters and norms to eliminate the discontent and to be regarded as satisfactory by experts (Kußmaul 2000: 17). (2010: 95)

This combination of creative and aesthetic elements with features of the common subtitling guidelines might then "form the essence of an approach that is professional and yet of artistic value" (2010: 95) that transports the plot to the audience in the best possible way. As the demanded usefulness of these new approaches is emphasised as much as the possible improvements in aesthetics and creativity, a look at usability studies and user experience design might provide further insight into what would be a good future approach for innovative subtitling strategies.

## 3.2 Usability studies: Interface and user experience design

Although there is no specific set of usability guidelines for subtitles, Mosconi and Porta argue that those concerning web accessibility and usability "can be applied generally to them" (2012: 106). They define usability in the context of subtitles as pursuing a concept that works as "intuitively and efficiently as possible" (2012: 106), based on the definition of usability being a "quality attribute that assesses how easy user interfaces are to use" (Nielsen 2003). Nielsen himself defines five quality components of usability — learnability, efficiency, memorability, errors resp. error management, and satisfaction:

> According to this idea, it will be easy for users to accomplish basic tasks the first time they come across a new usable interface (*learnability*). Once the way the usable interface functions has been digested and learnt by new users, new tasks will be performed quickly (*efficiency*). When users return to a given usable interface after a period of not using it, it will be easy for them to re-establish proficiency (*memorability*). As far as errors are concerned, within usable interfaces their frequency and seriousness are generally acceptable and it is easy to recover from them. Lastly, also satisfaction is important: using a usable interface should be a pleasant task. (2012: 114)

Part II of the "Ergonomics of Human System Interaction" (ISO 9241–11, 1988), for example, defines usability as "the extent to which a product can be used by specified users to achieve specific goals with effectiveness, efficiency and satisfaction in a specific context of use" (Mosconi & Porta 2012: 115). The importance of not only usefulness but also satisfaction can be related to the goals of the demanded aesthetic approach in the previous chapter and are also reflected in basic design guidelines. As highlighted by Foerster (2010), not only the aesthetics and usefulness are relevant, but also consistency – additional effects and individual placement within a film must follow comprehensible rules or make it a rule to break those. So, while web usability typically deals with command wording, layout, position of page elements, site 'intuitiveness', and other user-oriented criteria (cf. Cherim 2007), it can be applied to subtitling, e.g. in terms of a consistent layout and readability (Mosconi & Porta 2012: 107). In combination with the rules of good design by Shneiderman (1998), demands for good subtitling – or good integrated titles – can be split into four major aspects:

- Consistency

- Readability/Legibility

- Usefulness

- Satisfaction

These aspects should be obeyed when making decisions concerning subtitle layout, timing, length etc. Consistency can refer to the position of line breaks, the length of titles, the timing, rhythm, and contents, but also layout decisions such as typefaces, contrast-increasing features, and individual title placement, e.g. below speakers in order to provide speaker identification. Readability and legibility were already explained in the context of graphic design earlier in this chapter and the need for these aspects is obvious. The usefulness is a combination of a suitable translation, consistency, readability and legibility. In turn combined with a layout and design concept that not only pleases the viewer's need for information but also provides an aesthetic experience, satisfaction can be reached.

Usefulness and the aesthetic experience can also be based on the closely related film studies as these can offer insight into image composition and provide an understanding of the filmmaker's goals in an overall film as well as specific scenes – overall, allowing the subtitle creator to 'read' the film the way it was intended.

## 3.3 Film studies

Obviously, film studies are very closely related to audiovisual translation. When watching a film, "viewers make sense of visual and acoustic sign systems that are complemented by an acoustic channel and presented to them on a screen (Díaz Cintas & Remael 2007: 45). Therefore, "subtitles have to become part of this semiotic system" (2007: 45) and "must interact with and rely on all the film's different channels" (2007: 45). But in order to being able to "follow the movement of the camera" (Díaz Cintas & Remael 2007: 53) or "ignore the different camera positions" (2007: 53), a subtitle creator has to understand the use of cameras, shots and cuts to begin with. As Foerster phrases it: A "more creative space means more responsibility and the obligation to fully understand traditional practice in order to be able to divert from it successfully" (2010: 96). Thus, an understanding of both the underlying film and the traditional subtitling strategies is needed. Only then a decision can be made whether to adhere to these strategies and guidelines or to break the rules.

Walter Murch, a well-known (sound) editor who worked on films such as *The Godfarther: Part II* (USA 1974) and *Apocalypse Now* (USA 1979), gives an overview over film composition in his book "In the Blink of an Eye: A Perspective on Film Editing" (2001). He mentions the "rule of six" (2001: 18) that rates the six most important aspects of filmmaking:

- Emotion (51%)

- Story (23%)

- Rhythm (10%)

- Eye-trace (7%)

- Planarity (5%)

- Three-dimensional space of action (4%)

While the mediation of 'emotion' and 'story' make up the biggest part in this distribution, the point of 'eye-trace' with after all 7% is striking and a significant argument for integrated titles. 'Planarity' and the 'three-dimensional space of action' describe the creation of a three-dimension space with a two-dimensional product and the position and relation of people in a room to one another (2001: 18). McClarty sees the importance of conveying emotion as a reason for titles to "respond to the emotion of the moment" (2012: 145) in "both linguistic and graphic forms" (2012: 145), including "colours, styles or special effects" (2012: 145). She also understands "Murch's criterion of 'eye-trace' [as] significant when considering a creative subtitling practice, as it seems to pose an argument for subtitles being raised into the heart of the on-screen action" (2012: 146). A subtitle professional should therefore understand from the film the importance of these aspects for the respective filmmaker – one might focus on emotion, another one on story or eye-trace. Creative decisions should be made accordingly.

Similar to subtitling guidelines, "the rules of cinematic composition are not written in stone" (Mercado 2010: XIV) and an "integrated approach [is needed] to understanding and applying the rules of cinematic composition [...] that takes into account the technical and narrative aspects that make shots [...] so powerful" (2010: XIV). However, a decision-making model or workflow based on more commonly found shots and knowledge on the technical and visual conventions could provide the foundation to create integrated titles that suite the respective film and its image system. Image systems refer "to the use of recurrent images and compositions in a film to add layers of meaning to narrative" (Mercado 2010: 21). As this can be a "powerful tool to introduce themes, motifs, and symbolic imagery" (2010: 21), it allows the audience to make "connections not only within, but also between shots" (2010: 21). Similarly, integrated titles should follow a continuative system that provides recognition value to the audience and, much like image systems, "work best when they support and add meaning to, and not become, the point of [your] film" (2010: 21). Some principles of composition and technical concepts of filmmaking can support decision-making, for example when placing titles individually:

- Rule of thirds

- Hitchcock's rule

- Balanced/Unbalanced compositions

- High/Low angles

- Open/Closed frames

- Focal points

The "rule of thirds" (Mercado 2010: 7) indicates the frequent "looking room" (2010: 7) that prevents a static feel and creates a "dynamic composition" (2010: 7) and sometimes even "walking room" (2010: 7), thereby offering space for title placement – or, in the case of 'waking room', preventing a placement. Another rule from filmmaking that can be applied to title layout is "Hitchcock's rule" (Mercado 2010: 7ff.) that says that "the size of an object in the frame should be directly related to its importance in the story at that moment" (2010: 7ff.). Balanced and unbalanced compositions can both define suitable areas for titles and lend their definition to creative titles:

> Every object included in a frame carries with it a visual weight. The size, color, brightness, and placement of an object can affect the audience's perception of its relative visual weight, making it possible to create compositions that feel balanced when the visual weight of the objects in the frame is evenly distributed, or unbalanced when the visual weight is concentrated in only one area of the frame. (Mercado 2010: 8)

So if a balanced composition provides an "evenly" or "symmetrically distribution" and "convey[s] order, uniformity, and predetermination" (2010: 8), titles integrated into this scene should do the same. The same goes for an unbalanced composition that is often "associated with chaos, uneasiness, and tension" (2010: 8). Similarly, high and low angles can – always depending on the situation – communicate either confidence and control or weakness and passiveness. The use of closed or open frames can directly be connected to the decision whether or not – and in what way – to indicate a speaker's position and the direction of someone's speech: Closed frames can be created in a way that they "do not acknowledge or require the existence of off-screen space to convey their narrative meaning" (Mercado 2010: 10) and open frames "do not contain all the necessary information to understand their narrative meaning" (2010: 10). Focal points help defining the "center of interest in a composition, the area where the viewer's gaze will gravitate to because of the arrangement of all the visual elements in the frame" (Mercado 2010: 11) – thus, any title placement in a scene with one or more focal points should take place accordingly. These focal points can be created with the afore-mentioned rules and additional technical aspects such as the used lenses and the use of depth. Mercado (2010) and Kenworthy (2011) mention various common shots that can be distinguished in film. These can in turn be split into two basic groups – one being rather content-related and one illustrating the 'size' of the frame. The following sizes of shots are commonly distinguished:

- Extreme close up

- Close up

- Medium close up

- Medium shot

- Medium long shot

- Long shot

- Extreme long shot

While the extreme close up and close up isolate "single, visual details from the rest of the scene" (Mercado 2010: 29), medium and long shots create relationships between characters and the space around them. Close ups should be kept free of "any visual elements that might distract the audience from the main subject" (Mercado 2010: 31) while medium shots "can contain a lot of visual detail" (Mercado 2010: 47) and usually need to stay longer on the screen to allow processing. These shots can make use of Hitchcock's rule, create several layers of depth or a narrative between characters through their respective placement in the frame (Mercado 2010: 60). A content-based categorisation of shots would at least include the following groups:

- Establishing shot

- Over the shoulder shot

- Subjective shot

- Two shot

- Group shot[8]

Understanding the usually three layers of an 'over the should shot', the technical features of a 'canted shot' that makes vertical lines "run diagonally across the frame" (Mercado 2010: 101) or the relationships created through placement, scale or depth can allow for a considerate placement of text elements. As they become part of the image, they will "be interpreted by an audience as being there for a specific purpose that is directly related and necessary to understand the story they are watching" (Mercado 2010: 2) and have to respect the "direct connection between what takes place in the story and the use of a particular composition" (Mercado 2010: 3).

---

[8]Many more shots such as macro and zoom shots, canted and tilt shots, emblematic shots, abstract shots, dolly shots, crane shots etc. can be found in recent films (see Mercado 2010).

From a translation studies perspective, Chaume (2004) proposed a "film studies-based approach for the analysis of audiovisual texts" (McClarty 2012: 138), based on ten "signifying codes of cinematic language" (Chaume 2004: 16). This multidisciplinary approach aims at translators knowing the "functioning of these codes" (McClarty 2012: 138):

1. The LINGUISTIC CODE as translators are faced with a text "written to be spoken as if not written" and that "has to appear oral and spontaneous" (Chaume 2004: 19).

2. The PARALINGUISTIC CODE concerning the representation of paralinguistic signs such as silence or a pause.

3. The MUSICAL CODE and the SPECIAL EFFECTS CODE, e.g. highlighting music lyrics by using italics.

4. The SOUND ARRANGEMENT CODE that allows a differentiation of diegetic and non-diegetic sound, e.g. italics for narrative text.

5. Various ICONOGRAPHIC CODES that, for example, acknowledge the challenge of the visual feedback effect.

6. Various PHOTOGRAPHIC CODES that relate to scenes that might make it necessary to use different orthography in the subtitles, e.g. italics in dark scenes where the speaker is unclear.

7. The PLANNING CODE that refers to types of shots, e.g. the application of Hitchcock's rule with the close up of a plot-relevant poster.

8. Various MOBILITY CODES such as "proxemics signs", "kinetic signs", and "phonetic articulation" (Chaume 2004: 21) that relate to distances between characters and characters and the camera, movement and relating a subtitle to a visibly speaking character.

9. Various GRAPHIC CODES.

10. Various SYNTACTIC CODES of editing, as the "process of shot associations chosen by the director can have repercussions on the translation" (Chaume 2004: 22), as well as "audiovisual punctuation marks" (2004: 22), e.g. a fade to black resulting in a subtitle change.

Thus, Chaume bases his analysis not only on translation theory and discourse analysis but also film studies and communication studies, and demands that an audiovisual translator is "capable of transmitting not only the information contained in each narrative [visual and verbal] and each code [...] but the meaning that erupts as a result of this interaction" (Chaume 2004: 23) and adds value (Chion 1993) or additional meaning (Fowler 1986: 69).

Desiderata that can be derived from this design- and aesthetics-based perspective are discussed in §3.5. However, as one of the main arguments against new approaches based on communication design and film studies seems to be the additional workload for a subtitle creator, possible automation of the placement processes will be discussed in the following section.

## 3.4 Computer science: Automatic subtitle placement

In recent years, various automation solutions for individual title placement were developed and tested. One of the first studies that can be found was done by Park et al. (2008), describing a "framework for displaying synchronized text around the speaker" (Mosconi & Porta 2012: 129) with the aim to develop a "new media player, namely MoNaPlayer, which displays subtitles near by speakers" (Park et al. 2008: 166) that reuses existing subtitle formats (2008: 166). Their concept includes a module that automatically transforms existing information from the subtitle file and an "automatic subtitles localization through speaker identification" (2008: 168) and fulfils three tasks:

(a) Extracting descriptive context (e.g., text, styling, timing model, and etc.) and contents from existing timed text formats,

(b) Analyzing video source for subtitles region detection and speaker identification, and

(c) Transforming the timed text to a new spatio-temporal text and generating SMIL[9] document in order to integrate the video and the subtitles (2008: 168).

Additionally, Park et al. defined three cases of speaker identification: a speaker visible in the screen, a speaker that "may not appear" or "can not [sic!] be identified exactly due to particular reasons" (2008: 169), and "open captions, recorded in video itself, for explaining the scene or situation even though there are no

---

[9]SMIL stands for "Synchronized Multimedia Integration Language", cf. https://www.w3.org/TR/1998/REC-smil-19980615/ [2016–07–30].

sound and speakers" (2008: 169). After evaluating their system, Park et al. found several limitations in their first version of the system: the system could only detect speakers facing the camera, had problems "detecting subtitle regions as a consequence of multiple moving objects" (Park et al. 2008: 171), produced subtitles overlapping with the speaker's face, and did not offer a method for "detecting reusable regions" (2008: 171). Overall, their system represents a first encouraging approach that they propose as a future solution targeted at "foreign-language and visual learners, for beginning readers, and for a videoconferencing" (2008: 171).

Similar to the approach by Park et al., Hong and colleagues wanted to illustrate that "existing captioning techniques are far from satisfactory in assisting the hearing impaired audience to enjoy videos" (Hong et al. 2010). Opposed to the traditional "static captioning" (2010), they propose the concept of "dynamic captioning" (2010) as an "assistive approach" (2010) for hearing-impaired audiences. They identified the following problems with traditional subtitles: Confusion of the speaking characters and the tracking of captioning (meaning the speaking pace), and the lost of volume information (2010). Hong et al. refer to a study by Gulliver and Ghinea (2003) that concluded that "the conventional captioning approach can hardly add significant information" and that "information from other sources such as visual content and video text will be significantly reduced" (2003). They therefore developed a script-based "automatic approach to intelligently present captions" (2003) that puts the titles in "suitable regions, aligns them with speech and also illustrates the variation of voice volume" (2003). The system includes face detection, tracking and grouping, script-face mapping (including lip motion analysis with a recognition accuracy above 80 %), non-intrusive detection, and voice volume analysis. To test their system, Hong et al. conducted a user study with 60 mostly prelingually deaf participants with sign language as first or preferred language that watched video material in three modes – no caption, static captions, and dynamic captions. In their user study, they asked the participants questions concerning the content, enjoyment and naturalness, and their preference. They could not find a difference between static and dynamic mode concerning the content but "remarkably higher [scores] for the questions that are related to video text or visual content" (2003). However, the dynamic captions "remarkably outperform" (2003) the other two modes concerning enjoyment and preference – 53 out of 60 participants choose dynamic captioning over static captions. They mainly focused on the "technical part of dynamic captioning and [cared] less about user interface, such as the visualization of volume variation [...] and the style of script highlight" (2003). However, they stated user interface design to be "crucial for real-world application" (2003) and that it should be considered in future approaches to automation.

Based on the system by Hong et al. (2010), Hu and colleagues (2013) attempted to improve the automatic placement. They reason that humans can "only read text clearly in a narrow vision span" (2013) of "approximately 6 degrees of arc, which yields a region with a diameter of 5.23 cm when viewed from 50 cm away" (2013; cf. Rayner 1975, Just & Carpenter 1987, McConkie et al. 1989). Therefore, viewers have to "constantly move their eye gaze between the main viewing area and the bottom of the screen, leading to a high level of eyestrain" (Hu et al. 2013). To improve the existing system by Hong et al. (2010), they present a "new speaker detection algorithm to accurately detect the speakers based on visual and audio information" and an "efficient optimization algorithm [...] to place the subtitle based on a number of factors" (Hu et al. 2013). While it might seem obvious to consult strategies of text placement in comics (see, for example, Kurlander et al. 1996, Chun et al. 2006, Groensteen 2007), Hu et al. argue that placement strategies for single, static frames "cannot easily be extended to video subtitles because they cannot ensure cross-frame coherence" (2013). Therefore, their placement is based on speaker detection that works through face tracking combined with lip motion and center contribution, as "a speaker is more likely than non-speakers to be located towards the center of the screen" (2013), as well as audiovisual synchronicity. The subtitle placement was based on the following rules:

1. In each frame, the subtitle should be close enough to its speaker so not to cause any confusion that it is spoken by another person;

2. Across consecutive frames, the overall distance between all subtitle placements should be small to reduce eyestrain;

3. Subtitles should not be placed near screen boundaries so not to detract the viewer from the central viewing area;

4. Subtitles should not occlude any important visual contents (e.g. faces) (2013)

Based on these rules, Hu et al. only considered eight positions around the speaker – above left, above, above right, below left, below, below right, left, and right. The ultimate position was then "computed based on the speaker's location and size of the speaker's face and the length and font size of the subtitle" (2013). In order to alleviate eye-strain, "subtitles of subsequent speaking video segments [were] to follow the positions of the preceding subtitles" (2013) and "not be placed at the screen boundaries in order to allow the viewer to focus more on the central viewing part of the screen" (2013). Additionally, subtitles should follow moving speakers – splitting subtitles into shorter segments that would follow the speaker's path "rather than letting the subtitles float with the speaker" (2013). If a cut would render a subtitle in an unfavourable position or the speaker disappears, it should be placed "at a default position (such as the bottom of the screen)" (Hu et al. 2013). Compared to Hong et al. (2010), Hu et al. found an improvement by 7.5–17 % which they reasoned to be based on a better placement algorithm that was not solely based on a saliency map but also placed subtitles far away from non-speakers. In their final evaluation, they showed 11 videos of about 2.3 minutes length in one static and three slightly differing dynamic versions. The 219 participants scored the videos on a scale 1–10 on overall viewing experience and eyestrain level. Hu et al. found the speaker detection of their system to be "more accurate than the method by Hong et al. (2010)" (Hu et al. 2013) and achieved an accuracy of over 90 % for speaker detection for their so-called "speaker-following subtitles" (2013) they also see suitable for 2D and 3D games – with the limitation of identifying off-screen speakers.

   While this can only be a basic overview of some of the recent studies concerning automatic speaker detection and text placement in audiovisual material, it is visible that automation is indeed possible and audience feedback is already quite positive. However, these systems have only been tested with questionnaires and it is unclear whether traditional subtitling guidelines were adhered and how far. Furthermore, not much thought went into layout, interface design, and usability of the created subtitles. No analysis of existing integrated titles has taken place so far, the reception of 'speaker-following subtitles' has not yet been analysed with eye tracking or EEG, and the studies apparently were not combined with film studies, translation studies or any other connected field of study.

## 3.5 Summary

This chapter has provided a basic overview of integrated titles and associated fields of study. In addition to the objective shortcomings determined in §1.3, emotional reactions and the audience's view have to be taken into account as well. These are neutral at best, and as Rawsthorn puts it, even when quality, budget size, set, costumes, and cinematography are at their best, "subtitles are still dire" (2007). As the subtitling takes place after the film's post-production, there is less or even no control through the filmmakers and producers. Furthermore, development is held back "by the inertia of convention and the ideology of corruption" (Nornes 1999: 31). Technologically speaking, there have not been limitations that would prevent the creation of more creative titles since the digitalisation of film.

This has, however, not led to a paradigm change in either research or the industry and the statement by Nornes still holds true. Therefore, it seems like research has to lead the way this time and show how these recent developments can improve reception and enjoyment as well as accessibility for audiovisual products – with the aim to motivate further change and developments in the industry.

The few creative examples in commercial films come from the "imagination of film directions and editors" (McClarty 2012: 140), that, similarly to the intentions behind additional text elements discussed in Chapter 2, intend to not only translate but also add or support tone and atmosphere. Beyond traditional translation skills in the area of audiovisual translation, the following skills are therefore required for the creation of integrated titles:

- Understanding of filmmakers' intentions and basic film studies to interpret atmosphere and tone:
  - Shot compositions
  - Tools and rules
  - Emotion and story (e.g. for layout, but also timing and content translation)
  - Rhythm (e.g. for title timing)
  - Use of three-dimensional space (speaker identification, indication of speaking direction, atmosphere)
  - Image systems: titles should follow a continuative system that provides recognition value and supports the film without becoming the main focus
  - Eye-trace (title placement)
- Ability to read typographic identity of a film; understand design and layout choices

Based on the criteria from communication design studies, usability studies, film studies, and automation processes, the following characteristics are required from good integrated titles:

- Intuitiveness (learnability, efficiency, and memorability)
- Usefulness
  - Suitable translation (e.g. preventing negative acoustic feedback effects)

- Consistency (following comprehensible rules and avoid irritation, frustration or amusement when not intended)
- Readability and legibility
- Reduced eyestrain (small distance between consecutive titles)
- Close to action and close to speaker (speaker identification)

• Satisfaction, based on the combination of pleasant layout and comprehensible design concept:

- Titles are within safe area
- Suitable typeface
- Legible colour combinations
- Saturation index <85 %
- Not obscuring speaker's mouth, other text elements or important activity

Provided with full access to existing text elements and this basic set of additional skills, the creation of integrated titles should be possible. However, especially the sources on usability demand comprehensible rule sets for titles (at least within a film). As the layout and design should be an individual decision process for each film, what remains are the placement strategies. Therefore, the following chapter gives an overview of existing commercial integrated titles and the most frequent placement strategies in mainstream films.

# 4 Placement strategies in commercial integrated titles

While Chapter 2 already provided an overview over the design of text elements and their translation in film in general, this chapter will focus on the placement strategies of commercially-used integrated titles – how they came into existence, what the critics and audiences thought, and, most importantly, what placement strategies are used frequently.[1] The goal is to create a basic set of strategies for the creation of the titles used in the study as well as to draft a recommendation for rules and strategies that can be used for the creation of integrated titles in general.

The analysis is product-based and was conducted by taking screenshots (of static titles) and short clips (of animated titles) from a selection of films. The first selection of three films is a sample analysis based on several criteria: The films are in English and offer subtitles that are placed on individual horizontal positions as illustrated in the ITC guidelines and by Karamitroglou, they are state-of-the-art by being released on BD and not older than 2010. As the existence of these 'partially' integrated titles is not listed as a specific characteristic, there is no way of creating a complete list of films that offer this feature. Therefore, the chosen films can only be a convenience sample. However, as they reflect the discussed guidelines for SDH in §1.2.3, they can be seen as representative of this recent resurrection of supposedly outdated rules, and there should be little variation, irrespective of the number of films.

The sample for the second part of this analysis consists of – to the investigator's best knowledge – all examples of English films released between 2000 and 2015 that contain integrated titles that translate an additional language into English as well as the so far only known film that made use of integrated titles throughout the whole length of the film, translating Russian into English. Contrary to the partially integrated SDH, there are no pre-existing guidelines or rules these integrated titles are based on. Therefore, all known examples were

---

[1]Parts of this chapter are also published in the article „Placement strategies for integrated titles – Based on an analysis of existing strategies in commercial films" (Fox 2017) in a special issue of inTRAlinea (see http://www.intralinea.org/specials/building_bridges [2017–12–20]).

included in the sample analysis to reflect the state-of-the-art as accurately as possible while being able to exclude rare strategies due to their lower frequency.

Therefore, the following analysis takes into account two groups: Integrated titles for the hearing-impaired audience with only horizontal displacement ('partially integrated titles') and integrated titles targeted mainly at hearing audiences with the subcategories 'partial translation' and 'complete translation'. The placement strategies used in these films are analysed concerning their frequency and possible shortcomings. The most frequent strategies are then summarised in a first basic set of placement strategies that forms the basis for the placement of the titles in the present study. Their evaluation will show whether this set can later become the basis for a set of general guidelines for the creation of integrated titles.

## 4.1 Partially integrated titles for the hearing-impaired audience

Subtitles for the Deaf and Hard-of-Hearing have been around for quite some time and there have definitely been many attempts, both successful and unsuccessful, to add more information than the mere text can convey. Especially in television, SDH such as live subtitles often use colours to allow for an easier speaker identification. Additionally, there have also been a few films that make use of it – for example *The Dancer* (FR 2000), that (hardly by chance as the main protagonist is deaf) combines the use of colour with a basic attempt to indicate the speaker by additionally aligning titles to the left and right in the bottom area:

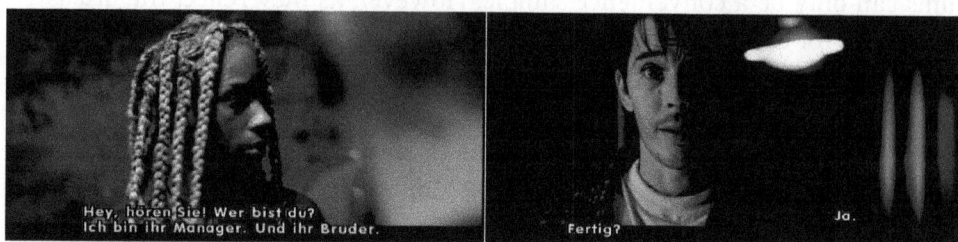

Figure 4.1: Speaker indication through colour and placement in *The Dancer* (00:48:06 and 00:54:12).

Since then, not many subtitles have gone far beyond this. Therefore, it is even more gratifying that some BD releases offer SDH that actually follow the guidelines concerning speaker identification through placement: Titles that not only use the left and right corner as alternative positions but that are also placed in between and thus allow for a clearer speaker identification. These partially integrated titles for a hearing-impaired audience can be found on some BDs, namely the following three most recent examples produced by Universal Pictures and Twentieth Century Fox (also the producers of the titles for *Nochnoy Dozor* ("Night Watch", RUS 2004), see §4.2.1):

Table 4.1: Overview of recent films with English partially integrated titles on the German BD releases

| Name | Release | Country | Director | Production studio(s) | Main distributor |
|---|---|---|---|---|---|
| *Jaws* | (1975) 2012 | USA | Steven Spielberg | Zanuck/Brown Universal Pictures | Universal Pictures |
| *Gone Girl* | 2014 | USA | David Fincher | 20th Century Fox Regency Enterprises TSG Entertainment | 20th Century Fox |
| *Ex Machina* | 2015 | UK | Alex Garland | DNA Films Film4 | Universal Pictures |

BDs offering much more space[2] might be one of the reasons of this recent development regarding SDH, but the integrated titles in films such as those discussed in the next chapter might have also played a central role in this process. Found to be representing the overall used placement strategies in the respective films well, only the first three scenes of these films were analysed, resulting in slightly differing time spans. The differing number of titles, however, is more connected to the density of spoken dialogue in the films than the analysed time span. In the following, the three films are analysed and an overview of the derived placement strategies is given.

---

[2]While DVDs offer 4.7 or 8.5 GB, BD offer up to 50 GB of space (see http://www.audiogurus.com/learn/news/blu-ray-vs-dvd-upgrade/2616 [2015–12–30] and also §2.2).

### 4.1.1 Sample analysis

Being an already well-known film classic from 1975, the American production *Jaws* tells the story of a gigantic white shark haunting the fictional island community of Amity that is finally killed by two residents and a marine scientist.[3] The release on BD in 2012 brought a new layer to this special experience: The subtitles for the hearing-impaired are not placed solely in the centre of the bottom area but move around horizontally depending on the positions of speakers and noise sources.

The titles in *Jaws* seem to follow the strategy of using the traditional position in the bottom-centre area as long as another position does not provide a better solution. Therefore, noise transcriptions and titles for off-screen speakers were placed about equally as often in the centre position as below a visible source in the image. For dialogues, however, titles were most likely placed below the speaker or below and in between multiple speakers. The combination of a speech act with a noise transcription took place three times in the analysed time frame and was either placed under the speaker that also made the noise or assigned two individual positions to the two elements in the title (see Figure 4.2).

Figure 4.2: Speech and noise in one title but with individual positions in *Jaws* (00:09:20)

Concerning the layout, the titles use a simple sans-serif typeface in regular line width, coloured in white and with a thin black outline. While the titles are legible in front of a dark background, some titles in front of brighter image areas do not create a very strong contrast and are harder to read.

---

[3]See http://www.imdb.com/title/tt0073195/?ref_=fn_al_tt_1, http://www.blu-ray.com/movies/Jaws-Blu-ray/7547/, and http://www.jawsonbluray.com/ [2016–04–21].

*Gone Girl*, based on the thriller novel of the same name by Gillian Flynn and published in 2012, was released to the cinemas in 2014 and directed by David Fincher. The American film tells the story of Nick Dunne and his wife Amy who Nick reports as missing on their fifth wedding anniversary. Under pressure from media, police and relatives, Nick does not handle the situation very well and his strange behaviour makes more and more people suspect him to be the murderer of his wife.

The titles in *Gone Girl* were most likely placed below the speaker respectively noise source (see Figure 4.3) or below and in between multiple speakers. As with *Jaws*, it seems like the titles were placed in the traditional position whenever there was no visible benefit from placing it somewhere else.

Figure 4.3: Noise transcription placed below source (*Gone Girl*, 00:02:52)

Overall, the titles in *Gone Girl* offer good legibility due to the clean, sans-serif typeface with a thin, black outline and titles close to the focus points. Even in front of a bright and diverse background the titles are comfortably readable.

The British production *Ex Machina*, written and directed by Alex Garland, was released to the cinemas in 2015 and is a fiction thriller on the topic of artificial intelligence. The young programmer Caleb Smith wins an in-house competition and is invited to spend a week at the private retreat of his eccentric employer Nathan Bateman. He is asked to test the authenticity of what Nathan claims to be the first ever real artificial intelligence, but feels like there is more to it. The two first scenes analysed in *Ex Machina* contain almost no titles placed in the traditional bottom-centre area of the screen. The sources of off-screen noises and the majority of noises with sources visible in the image were indicated through the title placement (see Figure 4.4). Titles for speakers outside the frame were placed almost exclusively below the focus point in the image; the same goes for the majority of titles for visible speakers.

Figure 4.4: Indication of noise source in *Ex Machina* (00:06:06)

Despite the thin stroke width and the pale white tone, the typeface and layout used for the partially integrated titles in *Ex Machina* offer a sufficient contrast to be legible and reader-friendly – most likely due to the black outline and the wide character spacing of the sans-serif typeface.

## 4.1.2 Shortcomings

All in all, the titles in these films show that steps are taken to convey more information for the hearing-impaired audiences by making an effort to allow for an easier identification of speakers and noise sources. However, some problems could be identified in the sample and will be discussed here.

The main problem with the partially integrated titles for the hearing-impaired audience seems to be the creation of simultaneity in dialogues that does not actually take place (see Figure 4.5). The reason is most likely that these titles are still based on the traditional formatting and therefore contain speech acts of multiple speakers in single titles. Guidelines such as those by BBC clearly state that different speakers should not be captioned simultaneously "if they are not speaking at the same time" (Ford Williams 2009: 12). All three analysed films created this alleged simultaneity by displaying two consecutive speech acts at the same time. A solution would be to separate these titles and display the respective speech act when it actually takes place. Alternatively, the text for the second speaker can be delayed as an "add-on" (ITC 1999: 14ff.) or "cumulative title" (1999: 14ff.) that co-incides "with the onset of the second utterance, while the subtitle corresponding to the first utterance remains on screen" (1999: 14ff.), preserving the "natural relationship between speech onset and subtitle presentation" (1999: 14ff.). Both these solutions would not have to be performed by hand but can be achieved through algorithms such as the automatic splitting and pre-processing of subtitles files proposed by Hu et al. (2013).

Figure 4.5: Alleged simultaneity in *Jaws* (00:09:12)

Another problem that should be addressed is the top area as a position for alternative placement. This area is being proposed again and again (e.g. Karami-troglou 1998, ITC 1999) as suitable for the placement of a title if the placement in the traditional bottom area would result in it covering other relevant text or image elements. The problem is, while the bottom area is normally quite suitable as only few important image elements are placed here, this does not apply for the top area (especially in 16:9 film material; cf. Mercado 2010). And even if there is sufficient space and a title can be placed e.g. above a speaker (see Figure 4.6), viewers might be less likely to notice a title being placed there. In *Gone Girl*, one out of the 86 analysed titles was placed in the top area, and no title in the other two analysed examples *Jaws* and *Ex Machina*. That makes it quite unlikely for viewers to expect a title in that area. Their reaction might be too slow and the result could be irritation and a reduced enjoyment. Another counter-argument might be directing the focus so far away from an obviously relevant element or area in the image (see the boardgame in Figure 4.6).

Figure 4.6: Title placed above the speaker in order not to cover the board game relevant for the dialogue (*Gone Girl*, 00:02:38)

All in all, the partially integrated titles analysed in these films offer a good middle way in between traditionally placed subtitles and integrated titles. They should not, however, create simultaneity where it does not belong and if possible avoid the top area of the screen if other areas in the image can provide sufficient contrast and a logical placement. While the layout could still be improved, this approach offers easier access to the film and therefore possibly better entertainment. Yet, the partially integrated titles are only available in English on the German BDs. The German titles included in the release are placed traditionally and do not offer any of the benefits of their English counterparts.

### 4.1.3 Derived placement strategies

The placements used in the three SDH samples basically follow the supposedly outdated guidelines on SDH placement that demand placement close to the appropriate speaker or noise source (ITC 1999: 10) or below speakers (ITC 1999: 13, Jüngst 2010: 129, Remael 2007: 31). In order to create categories for these placements, main groups according to the visible position of the speaker(s) or source of noise – based on both the human faces as almost irresistible "gaze catchers" (Lautenbacher 2012:142; cf. Birmingham et al. 2008) and the gaze direction visible from the eyes (Lautenbacher 2012: 142) – were created:

- Noise

- Off-screen noise

- Noise + Speaker

- Off-screen speaker

- 1+ Speaker(s)

Based on these categories on the number and visibility of speakers and noise sources, the following placements could be identified in the partially integrated titles for the deaf and hard-of-hearing:

- Traditional (Bottom-centred)

- Traditional (Top-centred)

- Above speaker or noise source

- Below speaker or noise source

- Above focus (other than the speaker or noise source)

- Below focus (other than the speaker or noise source)

- Indication of noise source outside the frame

- Below & In between

- Next to speaker

- Simultaneity

The listed strategies are now summarised following the distribution of visible speakers or noise sources. An example for the combination of speaker and noise can be seen in Figure 4.2, an example of the indication of an off-screen noise is illustrated in Figure 4.4. The problem of simultaneity is illustrated and discussed in the previous §4.1.2. The following additional strategies were derived from the sample: Figure 4.7 shows the identified positions for noise sources, Figure 4.8 shows the positions for off-screen speakers, and Figure 4.9 shows the identified positions for visible speakers.

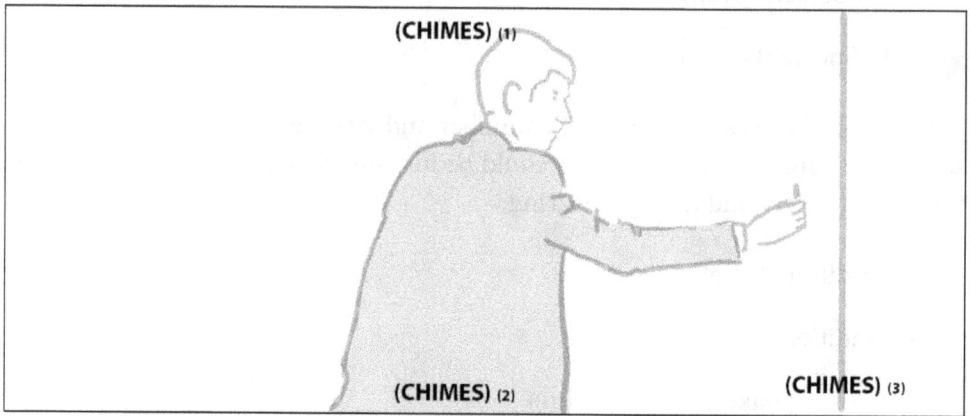

Figure 4.7: Examples for identified positions for visible noise sources: 1) Traditional (top-centre), 2) traditional (bottom-centre), and 3) below noise source (sketch after a scene from *Ex Machina*, 00:07:44).

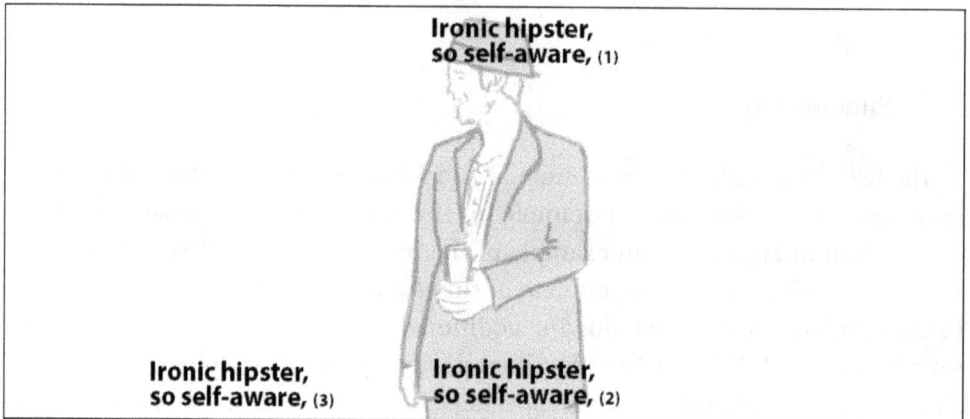

Figure 4.8: Examples for identified positions for off-screen speakers: 1) Traditional (top-centre), 2) traditional (bottom-centre), and 3) below focus (sketch after a scene from *Gone Girl*, 00:04:25).

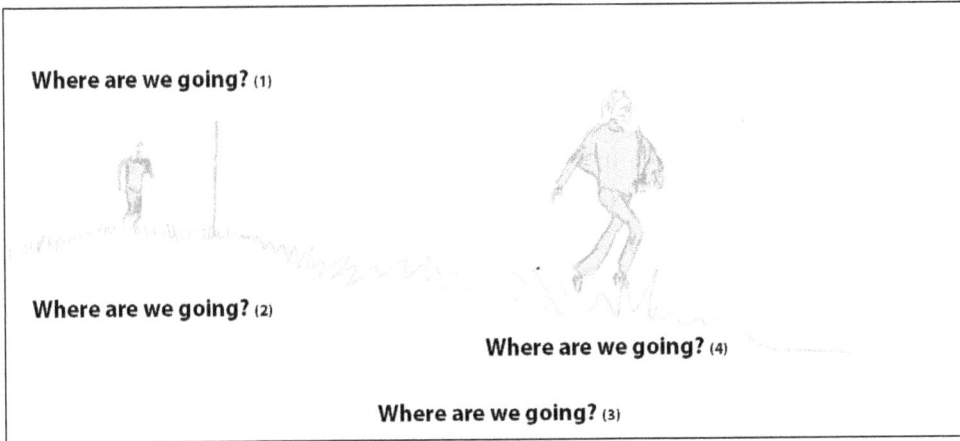

**Where are we going?** (1)

**Where are we going?** (2)

**Where are we going?** (4)

**Where are we going?** (3)

Figure 4.9: Examples for identified positions for visible speakers: 1) Above speaker, 2) below speaker, 3) below & in between/next to speaker, and 4) traditional (bottom-centre) (sketch after a scene from *Jaws*, 00:02:31).

Table 4.2: Overview of the derived placement strategies for partially integrated titles

| Visible speakers | Placement strategy | Jaws | GG | EM | All | % | Film count |
|---|---|---|---|---|---|---|---|
| Noise | Traditional (bottom) | 11 | 5 | 2 | 18 | 5.61 | 3 |
| | Traditional (top) | - | 2 | - | 2 | 0.62 | 1 |
| | Below source | 10 | 5 | 5 | 20 | 6.23 | 3 |
| Off-screen noise | Source indicated | - | - | 2 | 2 | 0.62 | 1 |
| Noise + Speaker | Below source(s) | 3 | - | 2 | 5 | 1.56 | 2 |
| Off-screen | Traditional (bottom) | 5 | 10 | 1 | 16 | 4.98 | 3 |
| speaker | Traditional (top) | - | 2 | - | 2 | 0.62 | 1 |
| | Below focus | 2 | 2 | 8 | 12 | 3.74 | 3 |
| 1+ Speaker | Above speaker | - | 1 | - | 1 | 0.31 | 1 |
| | Below speaker | 55 | 43 | 86 | 184 | 57.32 | 3 |
| | Below & In between | 12 | 7 | 6 | 25 | 7.79 | 3 |
| | Traditional (bottom) | 6 | - | - | 6 | 1.87 | 1 |
| | Next to speaker | 1 | - | 4 | 5 | 1.56 | 2 |
| | Simultaneity | 6 | 9 | 8 | 23 | 7.17 | 3 |
| | | 111 | 86 | 124 | 321 | 100.00 | |

The following placement strategies could be identified in the analysed films *Jaws*, *Gone Girl* (GG), and *Ex Machina* (EM). The following Table 4.2 includes the individual counts per film as well as the summary of all three films.

For the noise transcription, the traditional position at the bottom-centre and placement below the source were used in the majority of the analysed situations and in all three films. As mentioned before, the top area can hardly be classified as suitable and was only used in two cases, accounting for less than 1% of the overall titles. While the source indication of an off-screen noise was only used two times, it appears to be a suitable solution for a simply quite unlikely situation and can therefore be indicated by the placement of the title (see Figure 4.4). Concerning off-screen speakers, the traditional position and the position under the presumable main focus point had the highest frequency. No placements were used that would indicate a speaker's positions outside the frame, even though suitable situations were identified (see Figure 4.10 for an example).

CALEB: Yeah, this is great.

Figure 4.10: Title in the bottom-centre area even though it could have been placed closer to the right border indicating the speaker position outside the frame (*Ex Machina*, 00:08:13)

While the strategies used for one and more speakers include a variety of solutions such as the placement below a speaker and below and in between multiple speakers, there were also 23 titles (accounting for more than 7% of titles in similar situations) that indicated the mentioned simultaneity of two speech acts that actually did not take place in the audio channel (see Figure 4.5).

Of the 111 titles analysed in the first two scenes of *Jaws*, six titles were placed in the traditional position in the bottom-centre area in situations with one or more speakers. It is not comprehensible from the scenes why the titles were not placed below the speakers – Figure 4.11 for example shows sufficient place and contrast below the speaker but the titles in this scene remain in the bottom-centre area. As with the placement in the top area, these solutions were only used in one of the three films and made up less than 2 % of all analysed titles. These two solutions will therefore not be taken into consideration for the final set of placement rules.

Figure 4.11: Title in the traditional position despite the sufficient space below the speaker (*Jaws*, 00:07:34)

After the exclusion of suboptimal strategies – such as the placement in the top area of the image and those creating simultaneity – and strategies with low frequencies, a basic set of placement strategies for partially integrated titles for the hearing-impaired can be derived from this analysis. Titles are placed below sources, foci and speakers, in between multiple speakers or in indication of a noise source or speaker outside the frame (see Table 4.3). While the speaker indication was not used in the analysed scenes, it makes sense to include it in order to add further information for a hearing-impaired audience.

More importantly than with the completely integrated titles that are discussed in the following section, positions outside the traditional (and therefore expected) areas should only be used if they are likely to lead to a better processing and experience than the bottom-centre area could offer, and not at all costs.

Table 4.3: Derived basic placement strategies from the sample analysis

| Visible speakers | Placement strategy |
| --- | --- |
| Noise | Traditional (bottom) |
| | Below source |
| | Source indication |
| Noise + Speaker | Below source(s) |
| Off-screen | Traditional (bottom) |
| | Below focus |
| 1+ Speaker | Below speaker |
| | Below & In between |
| | Speaker indication |

## 4.2 Integrated titles for the hearing audience

Tony Scott's *Man on Fire* might not be the first film ever to use a more creative approach on its subtitles for additional languages,[4] but it seems to be the most frequently mentioned modern example (Kofoed 2011; McClarty 2012; Romero-Fresco 2013), followed quickly by the Russian film *Nochnoy Dozor* with its creative subtitles for the English-speaking target audience. Together with *Nochnoy Dozor*'s sequel *Dnevnoy Dozor*[5] ("Day Watch", RUS 2006) and *Slumdog Millionaire*, this "quartet of high-profile releases from Twentieth Century Fox and its specialty-film unit Fox Searchlight has initiated a radical, popular re-conception of the subtitle's status in its previous distinction between inter- and intra-lingual contexts – as graphically additive captions and as linguistic translation" (Kofoed 2011). They offer titles that are a "central aspect of the filmic mise-en-scène" (Ko-

---

[4]Early creative approaches include the "subtitles for people who don't like subtitles" (DVD description, EMI Films, UK 1975) in *Monty Python and the Holy Grail* with the text being taken from Shakespeare's *Henry IV, Part II* (cf. Foerster 2010: 84), Jean-Luc Godard's *Vivre Sa Vie* (FR 1962) that features a main protagonist with subtitles instead of a voice (2010: 84), Woody Allen subtitling unspoken thoughts in *Annie Hall*, and subtitles in "Deperanto" that illustrate the language barrier in a foreign country (cf. Rozema 2004: 65–67).

[5]This film could not be analysed as it is even harder to come by than its prequel. It was released in the USA in 2007 with English titles by Twentieth Century Fox and Fox Searchlight Pictures.

foed 2011)[6] and underline the fact that "subtitles as a graphic presence [are] in-separable from its medium as film" (Egoyan & Balfour 2004: 68). While *Man on Fire* includes 219 integrated titles that translate from Spanish into English (com-pared to 1332 subtitles if watched with English subtitles, therefore accounting for approximately 16.44 % of the film's dialogue), the English subtitled version of *Nochnoy Dozor* offers a complete translation for the foreign English-speaking audience with integrated titles accounting for around 6.46 % of the overall subti-tles. Therefore, two kinds of integrated titles can be identified here: Titles that are part of the original version of a film and translate an additional language (cf. *Man on Fire*, *Slumdog Millionaire*), and titles that translate an entire film into another language for a foreign target audience (cf. *Nochnoy Dozor*, *Dnevnoy Dozor*).

## 4.2.1 Sample analysis

While the integrated titles for the hearing-impaired audience described in the pre-vious chapter seem to be a fairly new development with recent examples only a few years old, the integrated titles as translation tool for an additional language in an English film reach, as already stated, at least back to 2004 (*Man on Fire*) and are often traced back to the very beginnings of text elements in film, namely intertitles (McClarty 2012: 136; Romero-Fresco 2013: 205). Apart from *Nochnoy Dozor*, the films discussed in this section were all produced in the USA. The fol-lowing Table 4.4 represents the analysed sample.

"Subtitles are boring" – this simple opinion stated by Tony Scott (Scott, in-terview[7]) led to a new view on subtitles after decades of lacking interest from directors and producers. Without knowing that he would establish a new trend, if not even a future paradigm shift, he wanted the subtitles to be conceived as a "kind of character in the scene" (Kofoed 2011).

Therefore, the American remake[8] *Man on Fire* provides a variety of integrated and aesthetically pleasing titles. The film takes place in Mexico and tells the story of ex-legionnaire and soldier John Creasy. While he appears to have already given into his alcohol addiction, his best friend convinces him to take on a job as bodyguard for the 9-year-old Pita, the daughter of a rich married couple. Very

---

[6]For a definition of mise-en-scéne, see http://www.elementsofcinema.com/directing/mise-en-scene-in-films/ [2015–10–01].

[7]Interview with Tony Scott, performed by Daniel Robert Epstein for UGO in 2007, as quoted in Kofoed (2011).

[8]Information on the 1987 original of the same name can be found here: http://www.imdb.com/title/tt0093489/ [2012–06–25]. Information on the remake: http://www.imdb.com/title/tt0328107/ [2012–06–25].

slowly and hesitantly, a strong friendship develops and John seems to recover – until Pita is abducted and John seriously injured. When the handover of the ransom money fails and Pita is killed, John sets out to find the kidnappers. With the setting in Mexico, several words and phrases in the film are in Spanish. However, not only this spoken content is subtitled, but also some English statements – presumably to underline and intensify the corresponding content:

Table 4.4: Overview of the analysed films with integrated titles for an additional language

| Name | Release | Director | Production studio(s) | Main distributor | Languages[a] |
|---|---|---|---|---|---|
| *Man on Fire* | 2004 | Tony Scott | Warner Bros. International | Twentieth Century Fox | English *Spanish* |
| *Nochnoy Dozor* | 2004 2006 | Timur Bekmambetov | Channel One | Twentieth Century Fox | Russian |
| *Heroes (Episode 01)* | 2006 | Tim Kring | Tailwind Productions | Universal Pictures | English *Japanese* |
| *Slumdog Millionaire* | 2008 | Danny Boyle | Celador Films Ltd. | Twentieth Century Fox | English *Hindi* |
| *Fast Five[b]* | 2011 | Justin Lin | Original Film One Race Films, Dentsu | Universal Pictures | English *Portuguese* |
| *Star Trek Into Darkness* | 2013 | J.J. Abrams | Bad Robot | Paramount Pictures | English *Klingon* |
| *John Wick* | 2014 | Chad Stahelski David Leitch | 87Eleven | Lionsgate Entertainment | English *Russian* |

[a]The main language in the film is given in the first line, the additional, subtitled language in italics in the second line. As *Nochnoy Dozor* was subtitled completely from Russian into English, only the source language is stated.

[b]There is also a small number of similar titles in the following films of the series (*Fast & Furious 6* [USA 2013], *Fast & Furious 7* [USA/JP 2015]). The same goes for further *Heroes* episodes.

The traditional, translating purpose of the subtitle is directly questioned, as characters speaking in accented English are selectively subtitled, until even Denzel Washington's mixed language dialogue is transcribed according to purely aesthetic considerations during emotionally heightened scenes. This non-translative doubling of the dialogue with its textual equivalent marks a radical reconception of a text's potential function in another otherwise typical Hollywood production, an inescapably heightened awareness and assertion of the visual nature of the subtitle. (Kofoed 2011)

Another interesting aspect is the conscious placement in the mise-en-scène or "within the shot's depth of field, such that characters and objects may move before the subtitles, obscuring them from the reader's gaze" (Kofoed 2011). In addition to several fading animations (see Figure 4.12), a wide variety of kinetic effects was used to underline the active role of the titles in *Man on Fire*. Concerning the layout, the titles are rendered mostly in Franklin Gothic[9] and well readable due to their sans-serif and bold character that provides a good contrast to film image. They are "not confined to the top layer of the film, they have depth and perception" (Vit 2005).

Figure 4.12: Additional fading effect in *Man on Fire* (01:03:18).

As mentioned before, the integrated titles in *Man on Fire* (see Table 4.6) account for approximately 16.44 % of titles needed to subtitle the complete film (219 out of 1332 titles). Titles for off-screen speakers were either placed quite traditionally in the bottom-centre area or close to focal points in the image. With one speaker

---

[9]See, for example, https://typekit.com/fonts/franklin-gothic-urw [2015–09–11]. Two other unidentified typefaces were used in a small number of titles, one of them resembling type printed in newspapers.

visible in the image, the titles were mostly placed below him or her. About 19 titles were placed next to the speaker, even if there would have been space to indicate the speaking direction, as it was done with 54 titles. Therefore, the most frequently used positions for one visible speaker were below the speaker or in speaking direction (approximately 84 %). If there were at least two speakers visible, the titles were placed in between them. Only one title is placed below the person that is spoken to.

As stated above, another interesting feature of *Man on Fire* is the use of titles not only for translation, but also emphasis of already English terms and statements (adding intralingual translation to the otherwise interlingual titles), which account for 17.35 % of the integrated titles (38 out of 219).

The reactions to *Man on Fire* were mixed. While some critics celebrated the innovative titles as "small, visual victories that add charisma and personality to commonly bland and uninspiring subtitles" (Vit 2005), others such as film critic Brian Gallagher refer to them as an example of "how NOT to do subtitles" (Gallagher 2004). While *Man on Fire* displays several aesthetic types of text integration, it is not always comprehensible on what basis the present effect was chosen. Some titles are displayed word by word, corresponding to the actual speed of speech, while others are displayed in a whole or line by line, flicker, re-appear after a scene cut or move through the image. A smaller, but more comprehensive selection of effects might have had a stronger and more thoughtful impact.

Furthermore, these integrated titles seem to only be part of the English original version of the film. For the German DVD and BD releases, the titles were removed and replaced with traditional subtitles.

"Rejoice – subtitles have been freed!" With this exclamation, the Washington Post celebrated *Slumdog Millionaire's* titles when the film came to the cinemas in 2008 (Beckman 2008). *Slumdog Millionaire* tells the story of the young orphan adult Jamal who participates in the Indian version of "Who Wants to Be a Millionaire?" to find the love of his life. While the film was initially supposed to be completely in English, the British director Danny Boyle quickly realized that the child actors would not be able to deliver their lines credibly in English (2008). He therefore decided to let them speak Hindi and promised Warner Independent[10] "that the film would be even more exciting because of the subtitles" (Beckman 2008; cf. Kofoed 2011). He "came up with the idea to have the subtitles look more like the dialogue in comic books, which float depending on where the characters are positioned" (Beckman 2008). According to McClarty, this "works to keep the audience engaged with the plight of the young boys" (2012: 143). The

---

[10]Later replaced by Fox Searchlight Pictures as main production studio.

titles were also "placed within coloured caption boxes" (Kofoed 2011)[11] and inspired not only by comic book captions but also the nontraditional subtitles of *Nochnoy Dozor* (Beckman 2008; Kofoed 2011). The coloured boxes ensure both "visibility" (McClarty 2012: 143) and legibility against the changing background and slightly resemble compositions on posters and in comic books. While traditional subtitling conventions often suggest black boxes (e.g. Karamitroglou 1998), the "colour of the transparent box changes according to the colour scheme of the mise en scène" (McClarty 2012: 143) in *Slumdog Millionaire*. The 202 integrated titles account for about 17.99 % of the film's dialogue (out of approximately 1123 subtitles if watched with closed captions).

The Washington Post's film critic Rachel Beckman described the titles in *Slumdog Millionaire* as bouncing "around the screen in a rainbow of colors" (Beckman 2008) and "stylish and splashy and original. They're liberated" (2008). McClarty underlines the importance of these titles not only fulfilling "their linguistic, translational function" (McClarty 2012: 143) but "also fulfilling an equally important aesthetic function through their colour and an affective function through their positioning in the heart of the on-screen action" (2012: 143). However, she notes that these titles rather allow for an "overall understanding of the situation and dialogue, rather than a word by word comprehension of each subtitle" (2012: 143) and also Romero-Fresco sees that "the translational role of these subtitles (and even their legibility) often takes a back seat to their affective use of colour and position to advance plot and character development" (Romero-Fresco 2013: 210). This discussion of the titles in *Slumdog Millionaire* shows that decisions concerning the significance awarded to the translational function of the titles on the one hand and the aesthetic and affective function on the other have a strong influence on the final product and translators and designers involved in the postproduction have to work hand-in-hand to achieve a good result.

In addition to ignoring the layout instructions of the traditional guidelines, the titles also lack periods at the end of the only or last sentence within a title. This might lead to irritation of the audience as it might not be clear whether the sentence was finished or will continue in a following title. The typography is modest and makes use of a single typeface with soft edges and a legible stroke width. The combination of typeface, drop shadow and coloured box, however, might lead to a decrease in legibility. From examples such as Figure 4.13, it appears as if the image composition was considered more important than indication of speaker or speech direction, but then there are also titles that disturb the image composition strongly even though better solutions would have been possible. While

---

[11]Created by London-based title designer Matthew Curtis.

Figure 4.13: Indication of speaker outside the frame in *Slumdog Million-aire* (00:34:49).

the placement of the titles could be improved by decreasing the distance to the speakers and focus points, the overall layout and especially the coloured boxes support the atmosphere and emotions in the respective scenes and most likely had a strong impact on the reception of *Slumdog Millionaire.*

The American television show Heroes was produced and broadcast by NBC between 2006 and 2010.[12] It consists of four seasons and its dubbed German version was broadcasted by the Swiss channel "SF zwei" and the German channel "RTL2".[13] *Heroes* tells the story of a group of people all over the world that developed supernatural abilities. While there seems to be no connection between the various stories, shared fate brings them together and everyone has to decide for themselves on which side of the fight for Earth's future he or she will stand.

While almost all characters in *Heroes* speak English, the Japanese friends Hiro and Ando speak their mother tongue at the beginning of the first season and only learn English bit by bit due to their continuous stay in the United States.[14] Thus, Hiro and Ando are the only characters in the first season to be subtitled. These titles were integrated into the image dynamically, seemingly on the basis of the placement of speech bubbles in comics as Hiro is a huge fan of them

---

[12] Also taking into account its sequel *Heroes Reborn* (USA 2015–2016) with a similar concept of integrated titles.

[13] For further information, see http://www.imdb.com/title/tt0813715/ [2015–10–02].

[14] There is also a South American pair of siblings in the second season that speaks Spanish. However, the corresponding English subtitles were placed traditionally – the only noticeable difference is the yellow colour that might be intended to refer to their Southern origin or offers a better contrast to the often dark green image.

and draws all his knowledge of supernatural abilities and other characters from them. The integrated titles in the first episode of the first season of *Heroes* (see Table 4.6) make up about 13.56 % of the film's dialogue, accounting for 96 titles out of 708 in total. For speakers outside the frame, the titles were more frequently placed traditionally in the lower centre area of the screen or in an area providing a good contrast than as an indicator of speaking direction. In the case of one visible speaker, the titles were most likely placed below this person, also accounting for over 53 % of all placed titles in *Heroes* (Season 1, Episode 1; S01E01). For two or more speakers, the titles were often placed in the lower area, but in between the speakers, therefore allowing the viewer to read the titles while switching between the speakers of a conversation. Alternatively, if the frame offered enough space, the titles were placed in between the speakers faces (see Figure 4.14).

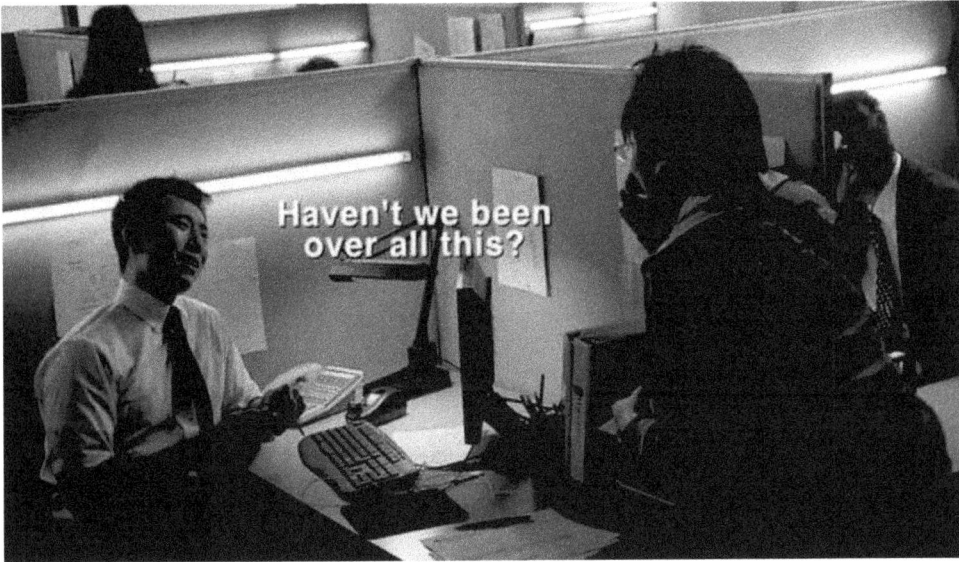

Figure 4.14: Title placed in between speakers during a dialogue in *Heroes* S01E01 (00:14:12)

Overall, the first episode of the first season of *Heroes* showcases many interesting placement strategies and might include some of the first film material that was actually shot in a way that would provide space and sufficient contrast to allow for the title placement in the postproduction.

*Fast Five* was released to cinemas in 2011 as a joint production between Original Film, One Race Films and Dentsu, distributed by Universal Pictures. Even though the screened version included 101 individually placed titles translating Portuguese conversations and statements into English, no mention of this can be found in critic's reviews of the fifth part of the *Fast & Furious* series. In the film, the former cop Brian, his girlfriend Mia and her brother Dom fled the United States to Rio de Janeiro after they helped Dom escape prison. To finally end their escape, they decide to accept one last job involving a heist and antagonising even more criminals and both the local and American authorities.

The integrated titles make up 7.49 % of the subtitles that would be required to watch *Fast Five* completely subtitled (101 out of 1348 subtitles in total, see Table 4.6). While off-screen voices were primarily placed close to a focus point (14 out of 17), the titles for visible speakers were most frequently placed below a speaker or indicating speaking direction (see Figure 4.15). Almost 12 % of the titles were placed next to a speaker even though there are several cases in which the image composition would have offered space and sufficient contrast below the speaker or in speaking direction. This does not only increase the distance between focus and title but might also lead to a misidentification of the speaker.

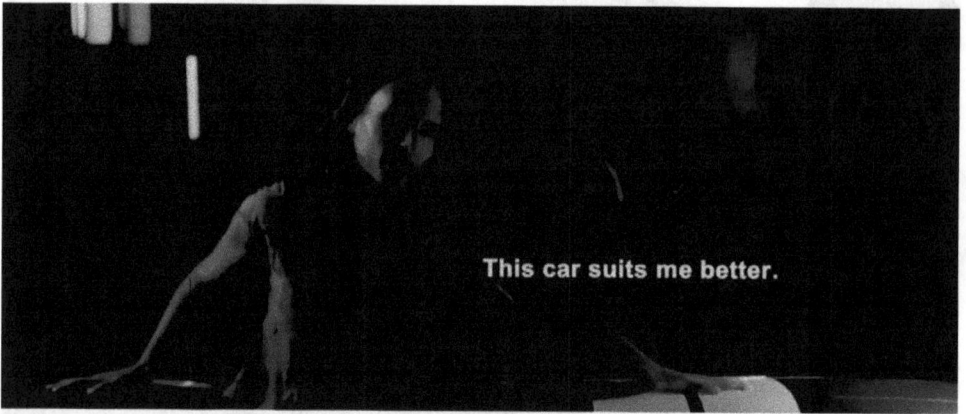

Figure 4.15: Title indicating speaking direction (*Fast Five*, 00:11:51).

The typeface is a bold white sans-serif with a slight shadow and creates a strong contrast to most backgrounds. In one case, single words are highlighted in italics, reflecting the speaker's emphasis. All in all, the titles are usually placed close to the speaker or in speaking direction and allow for a close focus for the audience. Even though the titles were not mentioned in any major film critic's review, the production studio and directors seemed content and continued the practice in the following sequels of the *Fast & Furious* franchise – *Fast & Furious 6* and *Fast & Furious 7*, both distributed by Universal Pictures and following similar layout and placement strategies.

Figure 4.16: Titles indicating speaking direction and reflecting the colours in the shot in *Stark Trek Into Darkness* (00:51:30)

After the immense success[15] of the first film in the reboot of *Star Trek* in 2009, the second part *Star Trek Into Darkness* followed quickly in 2013, directed by J. J. Abrams and produced by Bad Robot. While the use of integrated titles was discussed in-depth concerning earlier films such as *Man on Fire* and *Slumdog Millionaire*, critics did not mention the few integrated titles in this film. While this might be due to the fact that there are just eight titles in total (therefore accounting for about 0.45 % of the film's dialogue) in one scene,[16] the American (and other) audiences might also be becoming accustomed to the more frequently occurring integrated titles for the translation of an additional language in a film[17] – in this case, of the fictional language Klingon.

The placement in *Star Trek Into Darkness* is very simple and always indicates speaking direction – whether towards a person outside the frame (see Figure 4.16) or from a speaker outside the frame. Even though uppercase letters are normally rated disadvantageous concerning readability and reading speed (Liebig 2016), the negative effect should be negligible due to the very short scene and number of titles in it. The bold typeface and uppercase letters fit the rather 'brutish' and guttural Klingon language well. The text colour reflects the colours in the shot and makes it fit well into the scene, resembling the use of coloured boxes in *Slumdog Millionaire*.

---

[15]See http://www.imdb.com/title/tt0796366/business?ref_=tt_dt_bus for the box office numbers [2015–10–21].

[16]The discussed scene can be found on YouTube (00:00–00:45): https://www.youtube.com/watch?v=K0cFLb-JmaQ [2015–10–22].

[17]See http://variety.com/2014/film/columns/why-u-s-audiences-are-more-comfortable-with-subtitles-than-ever-1201160162/ [2015–10–21].

*Star Trek Into Darkness* might not offer a big variety – or even number – of integrated titles, but the designers nevertheless did a good job of integrating the Klingon to English translations into the scene. The focus was obviously set on making titles and scene match and there is definitely room for improvement concerning the distance between focus and title as well as legibility. But out of the films analysed in this chapter, it is the film with the highest gross from cinema screenings in the United States (about $228,778,546).[18] Thus it can be seen as promoting integrated titles to the so far biggest audience and – much like *Avatar* with its handling of an additional fictional language (see §2.3) – increase the probability of directors and producers putting additional thought into their handling of translation within their films and audiences to actually welcome creative and integrated titles.

In the 2014 blockbuster *John Wick*, mainly produced by 87Eleven[19] and directed by Chad Stahelski and the uncredited David Leitch, both traditional subtitles and integrated titles were used to translate Russian dialogues into English. *John Wick* is the only American film in the sample to combine traditional subtitles and integrated titles and slightly resembles *Nochnoy Dozor* in doing so. While the reason behind this decision might differ for the two films, the effect is quite similar and discussed in the following. *John Wick* tells the story of the return of an ex-hit man who quit his criminal life for love years ago. After several criminals break into his house and take his last keepsake of his recently deceased wife, he swears revenge and goes after them – even though one of them is his former employer's son.

During an interview[20] performed by the film critic Bill Graham, the two filmmakers of *John Wick* were asked for their reasons for choosing integrated titles: "I think it had to do with tone. Most people use subtitles to get across information or do what they are there for, translation. We needed hints with tone" (Stahelski; Graham 2014). They see *John Wick* as a "graphic novel" (2014) and themselves as story tellers who want their audience to enjoy the film. Using integrated titles "puts you at ease" (Stahelski; Graham 2014) and allows you to "relax and just watch it" (2014). Inspired by *Man on Fire* as well as graphic novelists such as Frank Miller (known for works such as *Sin City* [USA 2005], *300* [USA 2006] and *Ronin* [UK/FR/USA 1998]) they wanted "the subtitles to be part of the story" (2014) and use them "as if it were just story text, not just subtitles" (2014).

---

[18]Followed by *Fast Five* and *Slumdog Millionaire* with a gross from cinema screenings about $209,837,675 and $141,319,195 (cf. imdb.com [2016–07–30]).

[19]And several more credited and uncredited production companies as listed on IMDb: http://www.imdb.com/title/tt2911666/companycredits?ref_=tt_dt_co [2015–10–22].

[20]Cf. http://thefilmstage.com/features/john-wick-filmmakers-on-how-to-direct-action-dga-keanu-reeves-advice-and-more/ [2016–07–27].

Out of the roughly 561 subtitles that make up the closed captions of the film, 58 are integrated into the image (see Table 4.6) and 12 are traditional subtitles – therefore, the integrated titles account for approximately 10.34 % of the film's dialogue. Added together, the subtitles and integrated titles account for about 12.48 % of the film's dialogue. The placement strategies in *John Wick* include a variation of possible positions, but focuses on the areas below a speaker or focus point (12.86 % of the titles were placed under focus points and 17.14 % were placed under speakers, see Figure 4.17) and next to a speaker (22.86 %). The speaking direction was indicated in 14.29 % of the titles.

Figure 4.17: Title placed below the speaker and with highlighted swear word (*John Wick*, 01:02:15).

If mentioning them at all, film critics and viewers had only praise for the titles in *John Wick*. Describing them as "unique [...] by either highlighting certain words or positioning them in different areas" (Abreu 2014), "stylized" (2014) and as "throwing color and extra font impact" (Robinson 2014), it's appraised as "nice to see something being done with those subtitles just to make reading them a bit more engaging with the film" (Mistry 2015).

This apparently thoughtful approach, however, raises the questions why the first 12 subtitles follow the traditional conventions and are not even using the same typeface. A possible reason might be the same as for the use of the integrated titles: The directors wanted to convey a 'tone' with the titles – so two sets of different titles might be able to deliver different tones or at least support different atmospheres. While John is obviously on his way to become the 'hero' of the film when the integrated titles are introduced, we do not know what will happen to him at the beginning when the traditional subtitles are used. They are passive and do not tell us anything about the relationship between John and Iosef (see Figure 4.18).

Figure 4.18: Traditional subtitle in the first chapter of *John Wick* (00:12:18)

All in all, the titles in *John Wick* are a showcase of what is possible with the thoughtful use of typefaces, colours and placement. They convey tone and might make the audience more interested in the titles and the translations they offer. Additionally, the titles are comparatively dominant and have their own character, much like Tony Scott's titles in *Man on Fire*. Unlike the overwhelming number of different effects, placements and layouts in *Man on Fire*, however, *John Wicks'* titles convey a clear design and message. They add a visual component to the image that is normally reserved for comics. While the titles below speakers and focus points work well and often indicate speaker and speaking direction, a few titles might not offer a high legibility, are prone to speaker misidentification, and probably implicate simultaneity that does not take place.

The Russian production *Nochnoy Dozor* ("Night Watch"), based on the book of the same name by Sergei Lukyanenko, was released to Russian cinemas in 2004 and directed by Timur Bekmambetov. The film tells the story of the so-called "Others" that possess a variety of supernatural abilities and include creatures such as vampires and shape shifters. Divided into Light and Dark, they fight over the control over modern-day Moscow. As it "became the biggest Russian hit since the Soviet Union's collapse" (Rosen 2006), Fox Searchlight purchased the international rights and released it to US cinemas in 2006. It's not completely clear who then made the decision of imposing "digitized subtitles" (Rosen 2006) instead of traditional subtitles or dubbing the film. Rawsthorn claims that Bekmambetov "insisted on subtitling it and took charge of the design process himself" and quotes him describing the subtitles as "another character in the film, another way to tell the story" (2007). However, the way Kofoed (2011) and Rosen report it seems much more likely as Fox Searchlight would rather be the driving force and decision maker concerning the localisation of the film:

> Deeming the Russian-supplied English subtitles to be of insufficient quality, Gilula worked with Bekmambetov and American Laeta Kalogridis to develop a re-cut and re-write for the "international" version of the film, adding "digitized subtitles" that he felt "enhanced the experience" (Kofoed 2011).

Rosen quotes Stephen Gilula, the then chief operating officer for Fox Searchlight, that they "thought we'd do subtitles that enhance the visual experience" as the "original English-language subtitles provided by the filmmakers were of poor quality" (2006). In her review of *Nochnoy Dozor*, film critic Leslie Felperin stated that the reason for that decision was to "help those subtitles slip down more easily with mainstream viewers" (2005: 79). The decision to use slightly animated and sometimes integrated titles to translate the film from Russian into English seemed to have paid off as the film "finished first on the indieWIRE Box Office Tracker (iWBOT) of per-screen averages over the four-day Presidents' Day weekend" (Rosen 2006) and "also had the highest three-day per-screen average" (2006) at that point of the year.

The vast majority of the titles in *Nochnoy Dozor* are in a white sans-serif typeface while a small percentage (15 out of 1006 subtitles, amounting for 1.49 %) is coloured in red and sometimes dissolves into a blood trail in the 'air' (see Figure 4.19).

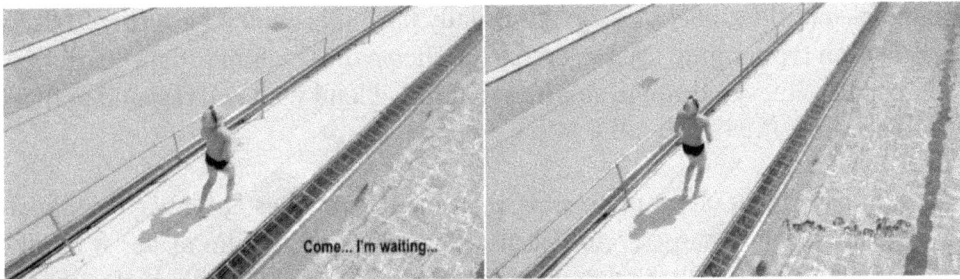

Figure 4.19: Title dissolving into a blood trail (*Nochnoy Dozor*, 00:11:12)

The 65 integrated titles in *Nochnoy Dozor* (see Table 4.6) only account for about 6.46 % of the film's dialogue, the other 941 titles (accounting for 93.54 % of the 1006 titles in total) being placed traditionally in the bottom-centre area. Many titles appear to be placed in the depth of field as they disappear behind objects or characters walk in front of them. In five scenes, a title follows a moving object (e.g. at 00:44:30) or dissolves into the scene. Kofoed sees "all the textual effects of *Man on Fire* [...] replicated in *Night Watch*" (2011). The reasoning behind the placement strategies is not always comprehensible – McClarty calls it "far from consistent" (2012: 149) – and the audience can just wonder what led to the decision of placing some titles integrated into the image and others in the traditional bottom-centre area. And similarly to the release of *Man on Fire*, this version of *Nochnoy Dozor* is hard to come by. It is not sold in Germany and only included in a special 2-DVD version sold in English speaking countries while the "subsequent release on Blu-ray and DVD of a new high-definition digital master does not feature the embedded subtitles" (Kofoed 2011; cf. McClarty 2012: 149). The German DVDs and BDs only offer traditional subtitles and the dubbed version.

McClarty also mentions the Argentinian art film *La Antena* as an example of creative subtitling throughout the whole film. It is a near-silent film "similar in design to early German expressionist films" (IMDb-1 2016), set in a city where the inhabitants have lost their voices:

> Motion typography is therefore used to represent the characters' dialogue [...]. Rather than being used for comedic effect as in the first example, these 'subtitles' perform both a narrative and an artistic function. [...] these 'subtitles' are fully integrated into the mise en scène, providing a vehicle for understanding for both the characters and the audience. Clearly the film was always intended to be read with subtitles, even by its native audience, and was therefore filmed and edited in such a way that the subtitles could be integrated into the mise en scène without very great difficulty. Interlingual subtitlers, of course, do not usually have this luxury. Nevertheless, the motion typography used in *La Antena* shows the levels of artistic merit that can be achieved through subtitles that fully blend with and respond to their backdrop. (McClarty 2012: 141)

While *La Antena* offers interesting placement strategies and image composition, its silent film character and clear affiliation with art film makes it hardly comparable with the other more mainstream productions including interlingual titles. While the titles in the other analysed films mostly exist as a tool of translation and are interlingual, the titles in *La Antena* are not only part of the story and overall concept of the film but also the only information channel – there is no translation taking place through the titles. Therefore, it was decided not to include *La Antena* in this analysis.

## 4.2.2 Shortcomings

While the titles in scenes with two or more speakers were found to be generally well-placed below the speaker or in speaking direction (in between the speakers), there are some situations in which these titles are visible at the same time even though only one person is speaking. While this is unlikely to lead to a misidentification of the speaking character as stated in the previous sample analysis (as these titles are targeted at a hearing audience), this might lead the audience in perceiving the scene as faster and more hectic than it actually is (see Figure 4.20).

Figure 4.20: Titles indicate simultaneity that does not actually take place (*Fast Five*, 00:49:21)

Most of the titles in the sample, such as the ones depicted in Figure 4.17, are well integrated into the image composition and colour schemes, but some just do not offer a good contrast and are therefore hardly legible. The title in Figure 4.21 offers neither a good contrast due to the grey-blue background nor is it very legible as the line spacing and number of lines is just too high in relation to the time the title is visible. It also blocks the view on a relevant focus point in the image – John's target, Iosef's hiding place.

Similarly, some titles in *Star Trek Into Darkness* could have been placed closer to the speakers to decrease the distance the eye has to travel in some of the shots (especially considering cinema screens). While the contrast is very strong in most of the titles, there's still room for improvement. The additional 3D and light effects make it sometimes difficult to distinguish the individual letters from each other and might have a negative impact on the legibility.

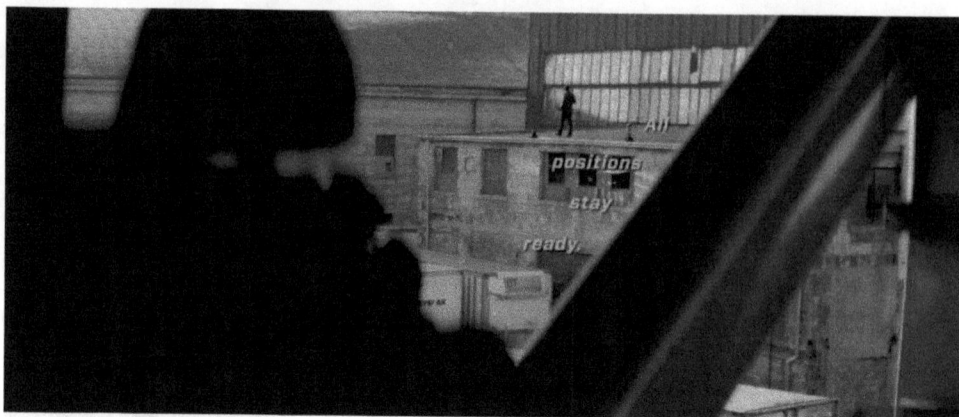

Figure 4.21: Title in *John Wick* with a too wide line spacing and weak contrast and that collides with a relevant image area (01:14:46)

Besides the small number of cases of alleged simultaneity and issues with readability, the main problem that can be identified with the analysed integrated titles is consistency. Some films offer a clear design (cf. *John Wick, Fast Five, Star Trek Into Darkness, Slumdog Millionaire*) but struggle sometimes with the placement or legibility, other titles seem to not only having been positioned all over the place but also do not follow a consistent layout (cf. *Man on Fire, Nochnoy Dozor*). Future productions should take viewer's expectations of subtitle placement more into consideration while using a consistent layout and comprehensible placement strategies.

### 4.2.3 Translation into German

For the German versions in cinema and on DVD and BD, the titles of *John Wick* were the only ones that were translated. In *Man on Fire* and *Fast Five*, the titles were removed and replaced with conventional subtitles. In *Star Trek Into Darkness*, the original English integrated titles are still visible and translated by additional subtitles, overcrowding the otherwise well-orchestrated image composition (see Figure 4.22). The titles in *John Wick,* however, follow the same graphical rules as in the original version and similar typefaces and colours (see Figure 4.23).

This hopefully marks a new trend of distributors actually spending the time and money to both linguistically and graphically translate integrated titles, as so far, *John Wick* remains the only example of integrated titles that were recreated for the German release – at least on BD.

Figure 4.22: Additional German subtitle in the German BD version of *Star Trek Into Darkness* (00:52:23)

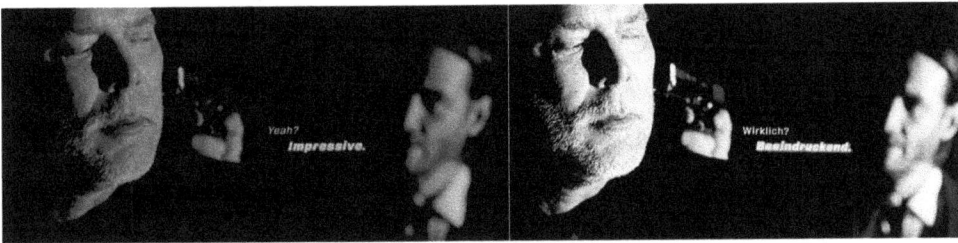

Figure 4.23: English original on the left and graphically and linguistically translated title in the German BD version of *John Wick* on the right (00:47:32)

In *Slumdog Millionaire, Nochnoy Dozor,* and *Heroes,* no trace remains of the creative translations – the titles were removed and the relevant parts dubbed in German. This does not only take away the creative aspect of the titles becoming part of the image composition, but also the multilingual character of the films is removed. While this is already a very strong graphical and linguistically intervention, it even changes the storyline in *Heroes,* as the two characters learn more and more English during the whole series and speak less and less Japanese. Situations arise from their lack of English as well as their improving English that could not take place without this aspect of their characters. In *Man on Fire,* the protagonist sometimes struggles with the Spanish language, resulting in others correcting his pronunciation or him mixing both languages within sentences. The question is whether these removals simply happened in order to save time and money by not having to recreate the integrated titles or if it was based on an interpretation of this aspect not being important or relevant enough to spend additional thought on it. However, the result remains the same: The films were altered immensely and German audiences denied access to the original experience.

## 4.2.4 Derived placement strategies

The previous chapter gave an overview of integrated titles as a means of translation of an additional language in an English film – so far the only known commercial use of integrated titles. While *Nochnoy Dozor* is often mentioned as an example for the complete translation of a film with integrated titles, these titles only make up about 6.5 % of the otherwise traditional subtitles. The often praised creative effects only account for less than 1.5 % of the titles. This makes *Star Trek Into Darkness* the only film with a lower percentage of integrated titles in proportion to the spoken dialogue (see Table 4.5). Being the earliest examples of integrated titles, *Man on Fire* and *Slumdog Millionaire* still offer the highest percentage of

Table 4.5: Overview of the proportional amount of integrated titles in the discussed examples

| Film | Year | Duration (min) | All titles | Integrated titles | Integrated titles (%) |
|---|---|---|---|---|---|
| *Man on Fire* | 2004 | 146 | 1332 | 214 | 16.07 |
| *Nochnoy Dozor* | 2006 | 114 | 1006 | 65 | 6.46 |
| *Heroes S01E01* | 2006 | 45 | 708 | 96 | 13.56 |
| *Slumdog Millionaire* | 2008 | 120 | 1123 | 202 | 17.99 |
| *Fast Five* | 2011 | 131 | 1348 | 101 | 7.49 |
| *Star Trek Into Darkness* | 2013 | 132 | 1753 | 8 | 0.45 |
| *John Wick* | 2014 | 101 | 561 | 58 | 10.34 |

integrated titles in the analysed films. Considering that only one episode (out of at least 79 episodes) of *Heroes* was analysed and one episode already included more than 96 integrated titles (accounting for 13.56 % of the spoken dialogue in the episode), it's safe to say that all seasons of *Heroes* combined most likely offer the highest number of integrated titles.

As the placement strategies of integrated titles for a hearing audience were analysed and grouped following the number of visible speakers as important criterion and relevant feature of the image composition, these strategies are now summarised following the same distribution. Even though the issue of misleading simultaneity was observed in this sample as well, it was not recorded in a separate group, as these titles are directed at a hearing audience that is most likely still able to assign the titles to the respective speaker. The strategies illustrated in Figure 4.24 were derived from the sample:

Figure 4.24: Examples for identified positions for off-screen speakers (sketch after a scene from *Fast Five*):
1) Traditional (bottom-centre), 2) below focus (e.g. person spoken to), 3) next to focus, and 4) indicating speaking direction (e.g. speaker on the right outside the frame)

Figure 4.24 illustrates the derived positions for off-screen speakers. Besides the traditional position in the bottom-centre area (1), speakers and their speaking direction can be indicated (4) or the titles placed below or next to the focus (2, 3).

Figure 4.25 shows the identified positions for visible speakers. Below (and alternatively above) the speaker (1, 5) allows for a quick identification. Indication of the speaking direction (2) can be useful in conversations to allow for a quick focus change between speakers. The position next to a speaker (4) seems to be

Figure 4.25: Examples for identified positions for one visible speaker (sketch after a scene from *John Wick*):
1) Traditional (bottom-centre) and below speaker, 2) speaking direction, 3) around speaker, 4) next to speaker, and 5) above speaker. Other positions were effect-based (e.g. following an object or person through the frame) or based on the image composition.

used in order not to cover important elements in the image, and the very specific position around the speaker in *John Wick* (3) supports the central position of the speaker, allowing to focus on his face during the reading of the title.

Finally, Figure 4.26 illustrates positions derived for two or more visible speakers. The first decisions seems to be whether the focus is supposed to be on the

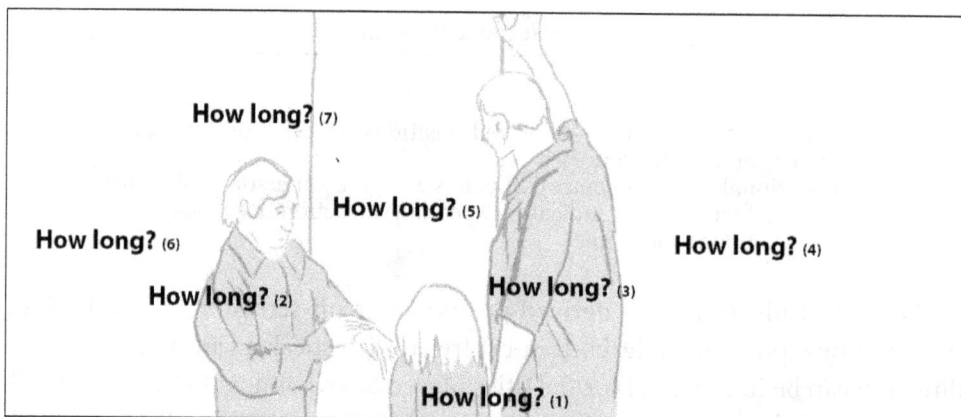

Figure 4.26: Examples for identified positions for two or more visible speakers (sketch after a scene from *Man on Fire*): 1) Traditional (bottom-centre), 2) below focus (e.g. person spoken to), 3) below speaker, 4) next to speaker, 5) in between speakers, 6) next to focus, and 7) above focus.

speaker or the person spoken to. Accordingly, titles were placed below speaker or focus (2, 3), in between them (5) or above (7). The positions next to speaker and focus (4, 6) again only seemed to be used in order not to cover important image areas or elements. The derived frequencies are listed in Table 4.6.

As visible from Table 4.6, placement below the focus or focal point in the image (e.g. a person spoken to or an object that is discussed) and next to a focus make up the biggest percentage of the derived strategies and were used in at least three of the six analysed films. The indication of speaking direction can also be seen as relevant strategy as it was used in 50 % of the films. The indication of speaking directing for one visible speaker was used in all analysed films, followed by placement below the speaker and next to the speaker. The derivation from this strategies is minimal (4.1 %) and only takes place in *Slumdog Millionaire* where the titles do not seem to follow clear placement strategies.

The only strategy for situations with two or more speakers used in more than two of the analysed films was the indication of speaking direction which accounted for about 13 %. Even though a placement close to the actual speaker seems like a favourable solution in scenes with multiple speakers and was in fact used for about 6.3 % of these titles, only one film made use of it. While a placement close to a relevant object or focal point might be a good solution, placing the title close to a person that is not the speaker might lead to confusion and misinterpretation of the scene (see Figure 4.27) – especially for hearing-impaired audiences. This leads to the importance of defining an overall concept for the placement strategies being used in the translation of a film with integrated titles and will be discussed in detail in Chapter 5 (workflow for the creation of integrated titles) and Chapter 7 (hypotheses and study).

In summary, the placement strategies used in these analysed films are not as diverse as they might appear at first glance. For all of the three defined situations, three basic strategies can be defined due to their high frequency: below and next to a focus or speaker and indicating speaking direction (as listed in Table 4.7).

The result of this analysis is a first basic set of placement strategies for integrated titles that can be extended by additional individual strategies such as the placement around the speaker in *John Wick* or those based on overall image composition in *Slumdog Millionaire*. These alternative positions for integrated titles, however, should only be used if this leads to a better processing and experience than the traditional placement could offer. The goal of integrated titles should not be the use of alternative positions at all costs.

Table 4.6: Overview of all derived strategies for one visible speaker

| Visible Speakers | Placement Strategy | MF | ND | H | SM | FF | ST | JW | ALL | % | Film count |
|---|---|---|---|---|---|---|---|---|---|---|---|
| Off-screen | Traditional (bottom) | 15 | – | 2 | – | 3 | – | – | 20 | 2.67 | 3 |
| | Below focus | 18 | 2 | – | 3 | – | – | 9 | 32 | 4.28 | 4 |
| | Next to focus | 22 | – | 3 | 12 | 14 | – | 1 | 52 | 6.95 | 5 |
| | Speaking direction | – | – | 1 | 4 | – | 1 | – | 6 | 0.80 | 3 |
| | Image composition | – | – | – | 7 | – | – | – | 7 | 0.94 | 1 |
| 1 Speaker | Traditional (bottom) | – | – | – | – | – | – | 5 | 5 | 0.67 | 1 |
| | Around speaker | – | – | – | – | – | – | 3 | 3 | 0.40 | 1 |
| | Below speaker | 54 | 8 | 51 | 33 | 16 | – | 12 | 174 | 23.26 | 6 |
| | Next to speaker | 19 | – | 7 | 39 | 12 | – | 16 | 93 | 12.43 | 5 |
| | Speaking direction | 54 | 14 | 16 | 23 | 13 | 7 | 3 | 130 | 17.38 | 7 |
| | Effect-based | – | 15 | – | – | – | – | – | 15 | 2.01 | 1 |
| | Image composition | – | – | – | 25 | – | – | – | 25 | 3.34 | 1 |
| | Below focus | 1 | 17 | – | – | – | – | – | 18 | 2.41 | 2 |
| 2+ Speakers | Traditional (bottom) | – | – | – | – | – | – | 2 | 2 | 0.27 | 1 |
| | Above focus | – | – | – | 1 | – | – | – | 1 | 0.13 | 1 |
| | Below speaker | – | – | – | – | 27 | – | – | 27 | 3.61 | 1 |
| | Below focus | 1 | – | – | 13 | – | – | – | 14 | 1.87 | 2 |
| | Next to speaker | – | – | – | 16 | – | – | – | 16 | 2.14 | 1 |
| | Next to focus | – | – | – | 12 | – | – | – | 12 | 1.60 | 1 |
| | In between speakers[a] | 35 | – | 16 | 14 | 16 | – | 7 | 88 | 11.77 | 5 |
| Television | Placed in television | – | 8 | – | – | – | – | – | 8 | 1.07 | 1 |
| Integrated | | 219 | 65 | 95 | 202 | 101 | 8 | 58 | 748 | 100.00 | 7 |
| Traditional | | 941 | | | | | | 12 | 953 | | 2 |

[a]Includes "speaking direction".

Figure 4.27: Title placed below the person spoken to despite the scene offering enough space for it to be placed under the actual speaker or in between speakers (*Slumdog Millionaire*, 00:31:26)

Table 4.7: Overview of all derived strategies with a high percentage and film count

| Visible speakers | Placement strategy |
| --- | --- |
| Off-screen | Below focus |
| | Next to focus |
| | Speaking direction |
| 1 Speaker | Below speaker |
| | Next to speaker |
| | Speaking direction |
| 2+ Speakers | Below focus / speaker |
| | Next to focus / speaker |
| | In between speakers |

## 4.3 Summary

The "interference" of professionals from the film business without any background in translation and subtitling might have brought this industry on the long overdue new course towards a more integrated approach towards film translation and hopefully leads to better cooperation in the future. All in all, the derived strategies of the partially and completely integrated titles differ much less than might have been suspected. Noise transcriptions are placed below their source or indicate a source's position outside the frame. The same goes for a combined title of noise transcription and dialogue. Titles for off-screen speakers can be placed below a focus or focal point, next to it or in indication of speaking direction. One or more speakers offer placements below or next to the speaker, in speaking direction and below or next to the focus in the image. As the titles created for the experiments discussed in the following chapters were created before some of these films even existed, they are not based on these entire findings but rather inspired by the older examples such as *Man on Fire, Slumdog Millionaire,* and *Heroes.* The basic set of placement strategies summarised here, however, is very relevant for the overall strategies and workflow model proposed in Chapter 5.

The general recommendations for the creation of integrated titles developed in §3.5 demand intuitiveness, usefulness and satisfaction from titles. While it is difficult to rate the intuitiveness of the mostly small amount of titles, the other two demands can be rated quite easily. Concerning usefulness, the translations seemed mostly suitable and readable. The eyestrain was reduced in most cases due to small distances in between consecutive titles and most titles were placed close to the action and speakers. Concerning satisfaction (based on pleasant layout and comprehensible design concept), all titles appeared to be placed within the safe area, used suitable typefaces and legible colour combinations and saturation. Shortcomings included very few incidents of unintended simultaneity, the use of the rather weak top-centre position, collisions with relevant image areas, and a too long distance to the main focus. While the SDH titles were mostly consistent concerning the placement strategies, some films with integrated titles lacked consistency concerning both placement and design and could therefore inflict irritation and reduced entertainment. As consistency is relevant for all three demanded characteristics of integrated titles, this can be seen as the most important lacking feature and the most serious shortcoming. If shortcomings are avoided and the general recommendations developed in §3.5, §4.1.3, and §4.2.4 are followed, it is to be assumed that the individual placement and design of integrated titles leads to better reception and increased entertainment value of the respective film. Based on the so far presented theoretical framework, a basic workflow had to be developed to create the integrated titles for the reception study. This workflow and its application is presented in the following chapter.

# 5 A proposed workflow

After the analysis of existing subtitling guidelines, their shortcomings, the graphical translation of text elements, and the summary of common placement strategies, the impression hardened that strict norms or guidelines for integrated titles would not be the right solution for such an individual and artistic medium like film.[1] The many possibilities to work creatively with text elements, typography, and image composition as well as extensive discussions with filmmakers and subtitle professionals also played an important part in this decision. Therefore, a concept for modular guidelines and recommendations for the creation of integrated titles was created that could be combined based on individual requirements. The following steps were identified as essential for the workflow:

- Translation process

- Analysis

- Operationalisation

- Application

The translation process includes the first draft as well as corrections and adjustments throughout the whole process. However, the major part of the translation process should be complete before starting with the other steps – the analysis of the film material, decision on strategies that will be used, and the application of both. These steps are illustrated in the following chart (Figure 5.1).

Except for the translation process that is described and discussed in detail in many other places as well as in §1.2.2, the other three modules and the connected tasks are presented in the following sections.

---

[1]Parts of this chapter are also published in the book chapter "A proposed workflow for the creation of integrated titles based on eye tracking data" in the book "Seeing into screens: Eye tracking and the moving image" (2017, Bloomsbury).

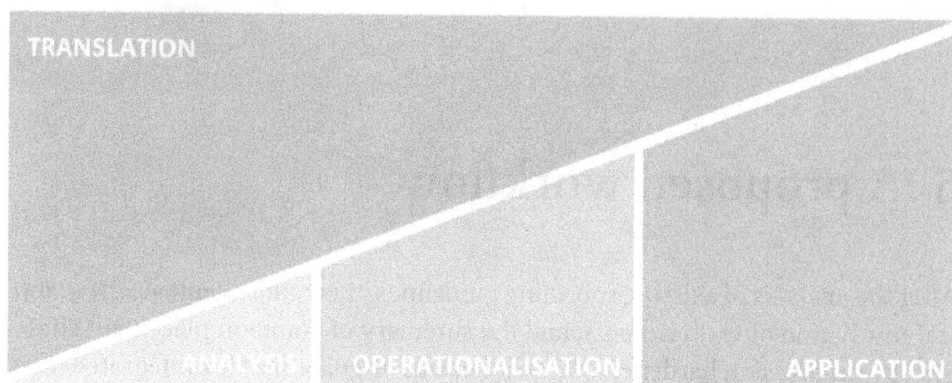

Figure 5.1: Relevant steps for the creation of integrated titles

## 5.1 Analysis

The analysis of the film material should include the image composition and the filmmaker's intentions (see §3.3), a definition of the overall complexity of the film and individual scenes (as this influences the use of placement strategies, effects, and layout), and an understanding of the typographic identity of the film. Additionally, a look at the target group is important.

The question whether the target group is made up of a hearing or a deaf audience and whether it uses a spoken language or sign language as first language can easily influence placement and layout strategies. The following possible purposes of subtitles should be taken into account:

- Interlingual translation

- Intralingual translation

- Intralingual translation for the prelingually deaf

- Intralingual translation for the postlingually deaf and hard-of-hearing

Especially the differenciation between a hearing and a hard-of-hearing or deaf audience as well as the differences within the hearing-impaired group should be taken into account – this includes the difference between being born deaf or having become deaf postlingually:

> People who are born hearing and become deaf late in life, are "physically deaf", but "culturally hearing". They grew up speaking a spoken language, using the telephone, the TV, the radio. They think, speak, read, write and

base their opinions on the world they knew before they became deaf. They rarely learn a signed language. People who are born into the Deaf Community, and whose first native language is a signed language, not a spoken one, are "culturally Deaf". Most of them are physically deaf as well. Some of them are born deaf or became deaf at a very young age. Some of them are hearing people born into all-deaf families, and even though they can hear, even though they speak a spoken language, their first language was a signed language, not a spoken language. They base their view of the world from the Deaf perspective. They are "physically hearing" but "culturally-deaf". (Sutten 2016)

It can be assumed that hearing-impaired audiences are more interested in additional layout effects such as the colour-based indication of speakers. Furthermore, it is likely for prelingually deaf audiences to demonstrate a lower reading pace (Dyer et al. 2003: 215ff.).[2]

Together with the translation, an analysis of content and situations should take place. The pace of speech acts, music and sound, and the existence, number, and layout of text elements can influence the space and time available for the integrated titles. As these aspects are tightly connected to the image and as discussed in §3.3 on the influence of film studies on the creation of integrated titles, a basic understanding of image composition rules should be present. Aspects of filmmaking such as angles, lenses, depth perception, cuts, etc. help to understand how a shot works, what format it is, and what content is presented in what way. Only if the image composition and image systems that are at work are understood, can primary and secondary areas be defined and a good position for a title be found. As concluded in §3.5, a basic understanding of the following aspects as well as of film studies and the filmmaker's intentions should help to interpret atmosphere and tone:

- Shot compositions

- Tools and rules

- Emotion + Story (e.g. for layout, but also timing and content translation)

- Rhythm (e.g. for title timing)

- Eye-trace (title placement)

---

[2]Cf. https://www.valdosta.edu/student/disability/documents/captioning-key.pdf [2016–08–12].

- Use of three-dimensional space (speaker identification, indication of speaking direction, atmosphere)

- Image systems (titles should follow a continuative system that provides recognition value and supports the film without becoming the main focus)

Being a combination of these and further aspects mentioned in §3.3, films and individual scenes can be assigned various levels of difficulty concerning the placement of integrated titles. These levels of difficulty are based on a number of characteristics that can either complicate the title placement or make it easier:

- *Static scenes (easier) vs. more active scenes (harder)*: In a static scene with little movement (concerning both camera and elements in the image), the title placement is almost as easy as when designing a poster.[3] It is less likely for the background – and therefore, the contrast – of a title to change abruptly or an important element to move behind the title. With increasing movement in the scene or of the camera, placement becomes more difficult.

- *No visible speaker vs. one or more visible speakers*: As faces and gaze directions are salient features and strong eye catchers, a larger number of visible persons – especially speakers – increases the difficulty of title placement. Speakers are a primary area of the image that should not be covered by a title – at least not the face or other parts of the body that are obviously the main focus in the scene. With a single visible speaker, there's usually enough secondary space for title placement and movement can still be integrated or at least balanced. With an increasing number of visible speakers, less and less secondary image area is left for the titles. Close-ups, especially of the face, pose an additional challenge.

- *Speaker inside the frame vs. speaker outside the frame*: This characteristic is comparable to the number of visible speakers. However, with a speaker outside the frame, it is still possible to indicate his or her position in relation to the frame.

- *No cuts during speech act vs. cuts during speech act*: Cuts change the image and, if taking place during speech, can cause the area behind a title to cease providing sufficient contrast, or might even contain a relevant element that should not be covered.

---

[3]Cf. http://www.pro-media.org/download/VISATT-Analyse.pdf [2016–08–12] on effective text placement in poster design.

- *Secondary area is predominant vs. primary area is predominant*: The primary area usually includes speakers' faces, elements that are in the main focus due to the lens and editing, as well as elements the speaker relates to by looking at, mentioning, touching it, etc. (see §7.5.2). The remaining area can usually be defined as secondary and be covered by titles.

- *Strong contrast vs. weak contrast*: This characteristic is mostly self-explanatory. An even image can provide a strong contrast and therefore ease title placement while a chaotic or very bright image can make it difficult. The layout of the titles can be adjusted by using a strong outline or shadow.

The translation and the analysis of the image are closely linked and together make up the content analysis. The complexity and form of both are determined for the film and individual scenes: Do monologues outweigh dialogues, are there many quick-paced fights or rather formal greetings and discussions, where are the speakers in relation to other focus points, and are there many pre-existing text elements in the image? These considerations allow for first basic decisions concerning placement and layout strategies. The layout strategies are not only based on the content and complexity, however, but should also be preceded by an analysis of the typographic identity of the film. Type faces, colours, and existing placement and effect strategies should be considered and incorporated in the layout of the integrated titles (see §2.3).

## 5.2 Operationalisation

Based on the criteria developed in Chapter 2 and Chapter 3, the following characteristics are required from integrated titles:

- Intuitiveness (learnability, efficiency, and memorability)

- Usefulness

    - Suitable translation (e.g. preventing negative acoustic feedback effects)

    - Consistency (following comprehensible rules and avoid irritation, frustration or amusement when not intended)

    - Readability / legibility

    - Reduced eyestrain (small distance in between consecutive titles)

    - Close to action and close to speaker (speaker identification)

- Satisfaction, based on the combination of pleasant layout and comprehensible design concept:

    – Titles are within safe area

    – Suitable typeface

    – Legible colour combinations

    – Saturation index <85 %

    – Not obscuring speaker's mouth, other text elements or important activity

Provided with full access to existing text elements and this basic set of additional skills, the creation of integrated titles should be possible. However, especially the sources on usability demand comprehensible rule sets for titles (at least within a film). Chapter 4 therefore analysed the placement strategies of commercial integrated titles and provided the basic positions as listed in Table 5.1.

Table 5.1: Basic set of positions for integrated titles developed in Chapter 4

| Visible speakers | Placement strategy |
|---|---|
| Off-screen | Below focus |
| | Next to focus |
| | Speaking direction |
| 1 Speaker | Below speaker |
| | Next to speaker |
| | Speaking direction |
| 2+ Speakers | Below focus / speaker |
| | Next to focus / speaker |
| | In between speakers |

These positions can of course be combined with more individual positions based on the film's image composition and atmosphere. While these positions describe the actual physical position in relation to the speaker, it should be based on a specific concept, ideally developed for each film individually. Based on the so far mentioned criteria, a number of layout and placement objectives can be derived. The following list constitutes a first draft and can be expanded as needed:

- *Short distances for high(er) information processing*: As the eye movements between focus points are so fast that no information can be absorbed or processed (see §6.1), one objective can be to place titles as close as possible to main focus areas to decrease loss of information. For the present study, these main focus areas could be clearly defined based on the recorded eye movements. With integrated titles being closer to the main focus areas, the viewing behaviour of audiences watching a film with integrated titles is more likely to resemble the natural viewing behaviour of an audience that does not require a translation. This objective can therefore also be called NATURAL FOCUS.

- *No coverage of primary areas*: If the image composition is to be taken especially into account and no primary areas or elements should be covered, eye tracking data could be used here as well to define these areas. Basic knowledge of film studies and communication design principles (see §3.1 and §3.3) can also help with the analysis and interpretation of film scenes.

- *Indication of speaker and speaking direction*: The position of a title can take place in a way that makes it possible to connect the title quickly to the speaker (e.g. below a speaker). Furthermore, the position of a title can also indicate speech direction or the position of the conversation partner. This also supports a natural focus, e.g. in a conversation between two speakers with the titles placed in between them.

- *Legibility*: Good legibility and readability are usually achieved through a strong contrast and even background. A well-designed title can still be read in front of a changing background and reflects the image's colour concept rather than disturbing it (while still creating a strong enough contrast to be read easily).

- *Individual aesthetic and/or typographic concepts*: Other concepts might focus less on usability but rather on supporting a film's atmosphere, tone, or image composition. This can be reflected by the typographic identity, effects, or special placement strategies (cf. *John Wick*).

- *Accessibility*: Finally, accessibility can be the reason for the use of integrated titles in a film. This might include already mentioned objectives such as the speech direction indication but also additional ones such as noise indication or colour-based speaker identification.

When deciding what objectives should be reached through the concept for the integrated titles for a specific film, it should be clear from the beginning whether the overall concept is primarily artistic (see e.g. *Man on Fire* and *Slumdog Millionaire*) or the aim is to improve the overall legibility and information intake (as was the purpose of the present study). Additionally, concepts can include aims such as transportation or immersion that have been shown to even increase through the existence of subtitles or titles in a film.[4]

Another topic that should be taken into consideration is effects. While this has not been studied in the present experiment or the analysed films in the previous chapters, they definitely play a relevant role and present an interesting topic for a follow-up study. The following effects were present in the films with integrated titles analysed in Chapter 4:

- *Kinetic effects*: These are titles that illustrate motion, e.g. by moving over the screen or being placed consecutively in a way that indicates motion (cf. *Heroes*). Moving titles were visible multiple times e.g. in *Man on Fire* moving in and out of the frame or in *Nochnoy Dozor* following an object that is thrown towards a person.

- *Spatial effects*: Some titles are edited in a way that it seems like another element in the image is in front of it, e.g. a person walking by will cover the title when passing. This was done in *Man on Fire, John Wick, Nochnoy Dozor*, and *Fast Five*.

- *Repetitive effects*: Some titles were repeated additionally, e.g. before and after cuts or to emphasize a statement (*Man on Fire, Nochnoy Dozor*).

- *Transformative effects*: These effects cover a wide range of possibilities that seems unlimited due to today's tools and software. For example, *Man on Fire* has titles that disperse and leave focus because the speaker is crying and *Nochnoy Dozor* features titles that disperse into a blood trail to illustrate the speaker being a vampire on the hunt.

- *Display effects*: While conventional subtitles are usually displayed uniformly, this can also be adjusted. Titles can be faded in and out faster or slower to indicate speech pace or emotions, they can be displayed letter by letter or line by line, they can blur in or out, etc. (see *Man on Fire*).

---

[4]Cf. "The Impact of Subtitles on Psychological Immersion", Prof. Dr. Jan-Louis Kruger, Macquarie University, Australia, and Vaal Triangle Campus, North-West University, South Africa, "Languages & The Media" conference in Berlin [2014–11–06].

- *Typographic effects*: The layout and especially typography of a title can also convey information – font size or form (e.g. capitals) can visualise volume, specific fonts can cause certain associations, etc.

For the present study, the following effects were used, aiming to support the atmosphere and increase the information flow:

- *Fade in/out*: Slow, emotional or hesitant statements are faded in and out slowly. Sentences that are left unfinished are faded out slowly, while quick and clear or confident speech kept with the usual quick fade in and out.[5]

- *Simultaneity*: Displayed at the same time, integrated titles can indicate multiple speakers talking simultaneously.

- *Depth effect*: Several titles simulate depth as titles are briefly covered by a speaker's hand as he or she makes big gestures, or when someone moves a little bit in front of a title. Before a title was covered, it was made sure that it was completely visible long enough to be read properly.

Depending on the individual film, genre, and intentions, a wide range of effects is possible and can be used to support the film's atmosphere but also increase the entertainment value and maybe even the accessibility of the film.

## 5.3 Application

After a decision has been made on the strategies as well as the layout for the titles, it's time to place the integrated titles in the film – using the chosen layout. In order to do this, the first step should be to identify the focus points in the scene based on the analysis of the film and its image composition. This can be achieved by dividing the image visible during a speech act (or music or noise, etc.) into primary and secondary areas. The integrated titles should then be placed in the secondary areas where possible and not cover primary areas and elements. Next, the chosen layout features should be controlled – do the titles look the way planned and have the intended effect? Also, the contrast should always be strong enough to ensure legibility (unless illegibility is intended). During a final check, the need for additional information or additional effects should be analysed. Additional information might be necessary for fully accessible titles, and

---

[5]The film encyclopedia of the University of Vienna offers some definitions and examples on fading effects, see https://wiki.univie.ac.at/pages/viewpage.action?pageId=35751449 [2016–08–15].

additional effects might be required in order to support a film's specific tone and atmosphere.

Figure 5.2 gives a final overview over the proposed workflow for the creation of integrated titles.

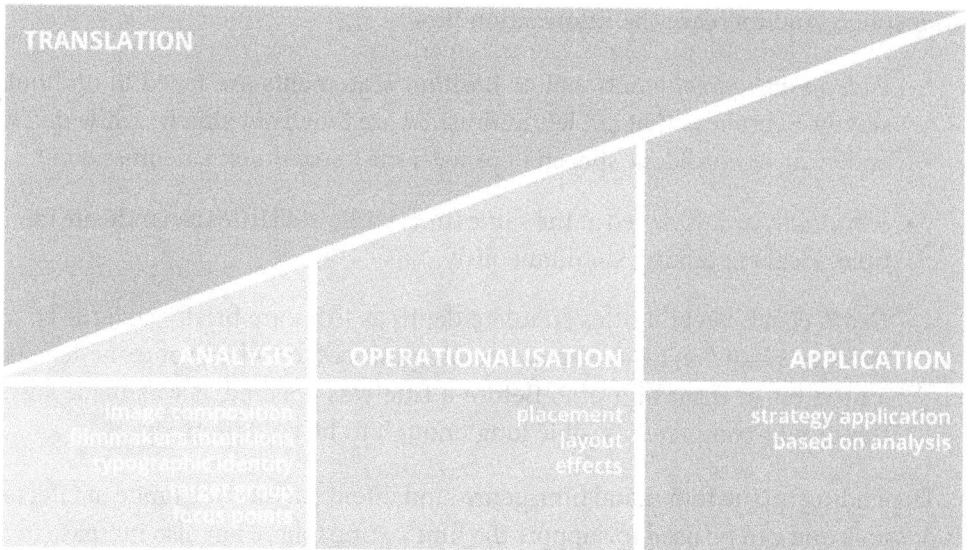

Figure 5.2: Detailed proposed workflow for the creation of integrated titles

As concepts like these should definitely be tested outside the study they were created for as well as criticised and improved again and again, there is a wide range of possible follow-up studies. The strategies and workflow have so far been tested in the course of a Bachelor thesis, a research project, and in a real-life setting. Especially the Bachelor thesis by Hevesi (2015) led to adjustments based on the student's feedback. Hevesi created integrated titles for the English short film *Carry On Only* (USA 2013) and did a small eye tracking- and questionnaire-based study with three English native participants and eight German participants dependent on subtitles. Based on the presented placement strategies, the workflow, and results from the pilot study in 2012, as well as the eye movements of the English participants, the integrated titles for *Carry On Only* were developed. They followed the film's typographic identity and made use of a few effects (spatial, typographic, and display effects). The eye tracking data revealed that during the title display, the participants spent more time on the image than on titles, they did not show any unnatural searching behaviour and the recorded eye movements did not show signs of stress. In the questionnaire, at least 75 % of the participants rated legibility, stress, time for image exploration, detail perception, and effects positively. However, most participants did not really notice the effects or cared much about them. Concerning the workflow, the need for adjustments and changes to the translation during the process was added.

For a further study on the reception of integrated titles by Kruger et al. (n.d.), integrated titles were created for the first 30 minutes of the English blockbuster film *Sherlock Holmes – A Game of Shadows* (USA 2011). As this is quite an action-packed film, it was decided to keep to the conventional position in the bottom-center area of the frame as long as there was no superior position. The titles indicate speaker and speaking direction, were placed close to main focus points, and made use of spatial and display effects (see Figure 5.3, Kruger et al. n.d.). No need for adjustments of the workflow was observed.

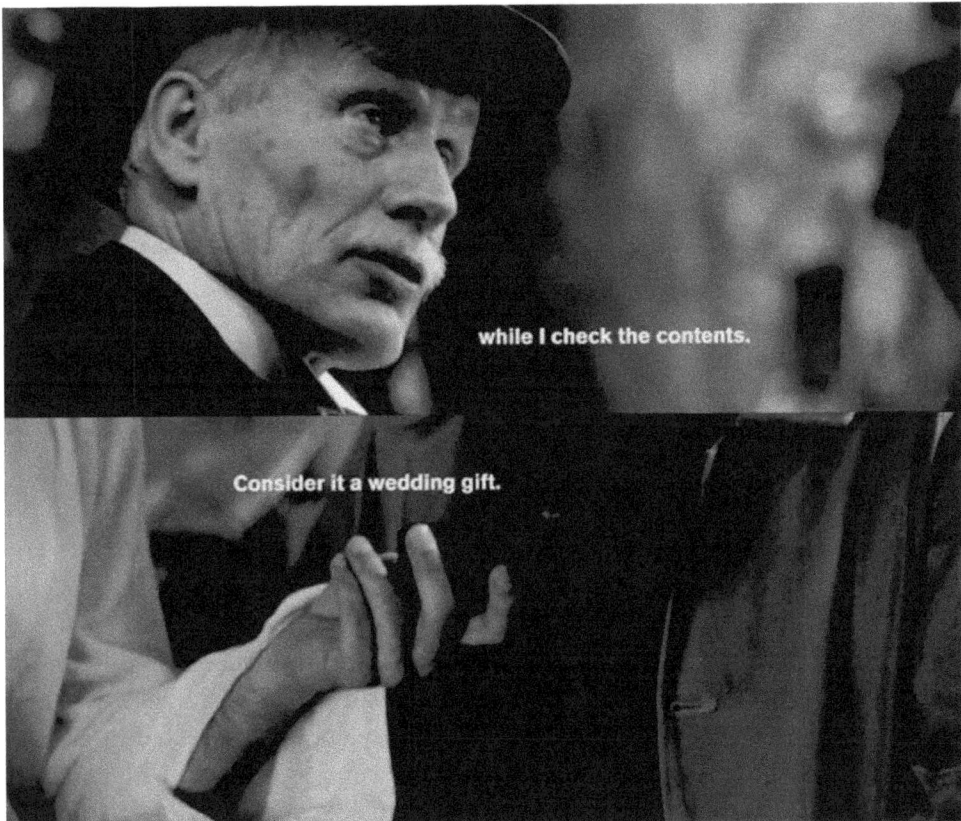

Figure 5.3: Edited scene including integrated titles for *Sherlock Holmes – Game of Shadows* (00:05:38, 00:17:17)

The most recent project that made use of the proposed placement strategies and workflow took place in cooperation with the filmmaking and production team of *Notes on Blindness* (UK 2016) and was supervised by Pablo Romero-Fresco, who advised concerning placement and accessibility. Feedback came from the filmmakers, producers, subtitle professionals (who created the SDH), and Pablo Romero-Fresco. As these integrated titles are targeted at a hearing-impaired audience, noise indication and colour-based speaker identification were added (see Figure 5.4).

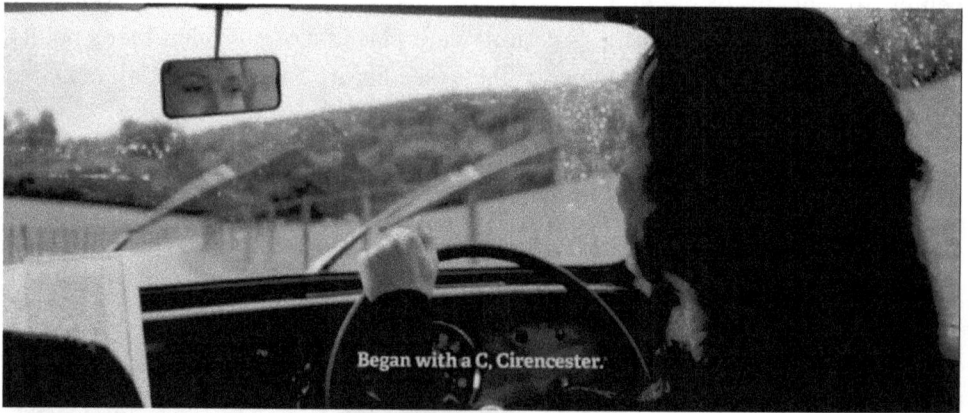

Figure 5.4: Colour-based speaker identification in *Notes on Blindness* (00:03:17)

The colours were chosen per speaker and taken from the colours that are present during scenes with that person. Another new feature was the additional indication of speaking volume and source (see Figure 5.5).

## 5.4 Summary

Based on the theoretical framework developed in the previous chapters, a basic workflow for the creation of integrated titles was drafted, being the first of its kind. Including the four steps of translation, analysis, operationalisation, and application, it gives an overview over the process behind integrated titles. The analysis should include a discussion of the image composition of the film and the filmmaker's intentions – ideally interview-based – as well as an analysis of the pre-existing text elements and the typographic identity they create. Before any decisions concerning the overall concept are made, the target group should be defined and basic focus points be identified. This should result in a concept consisting of the chosen strategies for placement, layout, and effects which are then

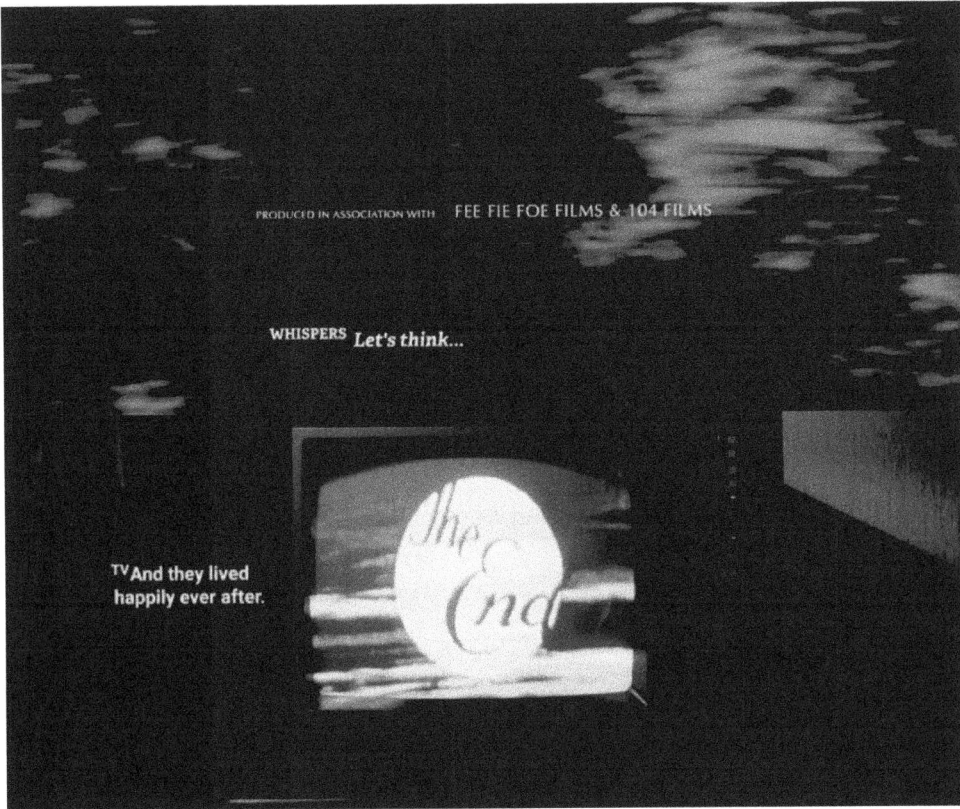

Figure 5.5: Volume and source indication in *Notes on Blindness* (00:02:53, 00:24:29)

applied in the final step. A professional tool that allows this kind of placement is *Adobe Premiere Pro*, which is presented in §7.2.2. First application tests after the pilot study in 2012 (see §7.3) such as the Bachelor's thesis by Hevesi (2015) provided feedback on the workflow and led to some adjustments that were finally applied in the first real-life and commercial project *Notes on Blindness*, which also highlighted applicability in the area of accessibility.

In order to analyse the reception of both conventional subtitles and integrated titles, eye tracking can give insight concerning reaction times, reading durations, and general eye movements across the image. As eye tracking was chosen to be the main tool of analysis of the present study, the following chapter gives a basic introduction to eye tracking and relevant eye tracking areas and studies.

# 6 Eye Tracking and subtitling: Eye tracking as a research tool

Early scientists of the 19th century were the first to be involved with eye movement analysis and associated cognitive processes. The investigation of eye movements nowadays is done by means of sophisticated eye tracking methods, research in this area has since come a long way, and, as Kruger has put it, eye tracking "provide[s] us with a window on the internal systems of the mind (cf. Marchant et al. 2009)" (Kruger n.d.). It is well-developed in several related fields such as reading and translation process research as well as psycholinguistics and was established in audiovisual translation studies "even before it had gained prominence within Translation Studies in the late 1990s" (Kruger n.d.). In analysing the processing of audiovisual text, and mainly subtitles, a wide range of different factors have to be taken into account.

The following section focuses on the relevant fundamentals of eye tracking research, including the anatomical structure of the eye and its function, eye tracking itself, its practical application in general and usability as well as audiovisual research in particular.

## 6.1 Function of the eye and eye tracking research

Even though the human eye is quite simple in its physical structure and movements (Joos et al. 2005: 1), it is not a mere sensor and by itself responsible for the exploration of the surroundings but also part of communicative interaction and indicative of cognitive processes (2005: 1). The strong eye-mind hypothesis by Just and Carpenter states that eye movements are correlates of mental processing as "there is no appreciable lag between what is being fixated and what is being processed" (1980: 331), and Holmqvist et al. see "functional links between what is fixated and cognitive processing of that item – the longer the fixation, the 'deeper' the processing" (2011: 328). While interpretation of eye movement data should take place "within the context of a given theoretical framework" (Radach & Kennedy 2004: 8), "numerous subsequent studies have shown that the spa-

tial and temporal relationship between eye movements and information processing cannot be captured by these simple principles" (Radach & Kennedy 2004: 8;
cf. Rayner 1998: 375ff.), referring to the eye-mind hypothesis and immediacy assumptions by Just and Carpenter. While this depends on the field of study, some
limitations of these assumptions should be taken into account:

- Attention of viewers might be affected by "mind wandering" or "mind
  drifting" (Hvelplund 2014: 209) as well as "thoughts may drift unintention-
  ally during reading" (2014: 209), which is a "frequent and common phe-
  nomenon [...]" (Hvelplund 2014: 219).

- Eye trackers might produce "drift" (Hvelplund 2014: 210), leading to the
  recorded eye position becoming gradually displaced.

- Posner noted that – in "simple laboratory tasks" (Schotter & Rayner 2012:
  85) – focus and attention "may be separated or dissociated" (2005: 5). Therefore, it is "[...] important to distinguish between overt changes in orienting
  that can be observed in head and eye movements, and the purely covert
  orienting that may be achieved by the central mechanism alone [...]" (2005:
  5). Schotter and Rayner also note that, while "overt attention (where the
  eyes are fixating) is tightly linked to covert attention (where the mind is
  attending)" (Schotter & Rayner 2012: 85) and the "most thorough and effective processing is reserved for that done in the fovea, some processing
  can also be accomplished for information in the parafovea and peripheral
  vision" (2012: 85).

- Additionally, Posner noted that "in many tasks, a shift of attention to the
  saccade target precedes the actual eye movement [...]" (2005: 5). Hvelplund
  reports that it is possible for the mind to be "up to 250 milliseconds ahead
  of the eye" (2014: 210; cf. O'Brien 2009: 252, Holmqvist et al. 2011: 379). Additionally to being ahead, the mind can also "lag a little behind" (Hvelplund
  2014: 211).

Taking all these limitations into consideration, Radach & Kennedy (2004: 9)
still rate "the relation between fixation positions and durations and local processing" as "strong enough to produce reliable effects when sampled over groups
of participants and items and in this sense eye movement measures provide an
extremely sensitive index of local processing load" (2004: 9; Hvelplund 2014: 211).
Overall, the eye can cover a visual field of approximately 120° vertically and
150° horizontally (Flothow 2009: 3). Light is let in through the pupil and projects

an upside down image onto the retina. The fovea centralis, also known as the central fovea or just fovea, has the highest density of receptors (cones) and allows for the sharp central vision needed to perceive visual details, for example during reading. Here, the eye achieves its highest resolution in less than 2° of our visual field (cf. Kruger n.d.). Therefore, the eye has to be constantly adjusted in order to focus on specific elements in the visual field (Holmqvist et al. 2011: 21–24). This small area of sharp central vision and the constant adjustments underline the eye-mind hypothesis by Just and Carpenter, as the position of the optical axis is relevant in order to determine the attention focus of a person (Just & Carpenter 1980; Flothow 2009: 3).

The different kinds of observed eye movements are divided into various categories. Fixations and saccades are particularly relevant for the analysis of eye movements. During fixations, a specific point in space – the fixation point – is at the centre of visual attention and the eye relatively inactive for a short period of time. During fixations, visuospatial processing (perceiving objects in space) takes place and information is taken in. The typical mean duration of a fixation is between 200 and 300 ms with the minimal fixation duration being around 100 ms (Rayner 1998: 373; Flothow 2009: 2; Holmqvist et al. 2011: 23). Usually, fixations are considerably longer, especially during reading (225–250 ms) and oral reading (275–325 ms), but also during tasks such as scene perception (260–330 ms) or visual search (180–275 ms) (Rayner 1998; Jakobsen & Hvelplund Jensen 2008).

Saccades are the movements between the fixation points, describing the movement of the eye from one fixation point to another. These fast ballistic eye movements are especially abrupt – according to Joos et al. (2003: 17), the latency is around 150 to 200 ms – and with speeds up to 1000°/s (2003: 17) and durations between 30 and 80 ms (Holmqvist et al. 2011: 23), they are so fast that the eye cannot absorb or process any information during a saccade (Flothow 2009: 4; "saccadic suppression", Volkmann et al. 1978; "saccadic omission", Chekaluk & Llewellyn 1994: 373; Schotter & Rayner 2012: 84–85). Information absorbed during fixations, however, can be partially processed during the following saccades (Holmqvist et al. 2011), usually preventing information loss and deficits. Therefore, saccades are "rapid, ballistic movements [...] that abruptly change the point of fixation" (Purves et al. 2001: 431) that can be both voluntary and reflexive and cannot be corrected during the movement. They are part of four groups of eye movements that are generally distinguished (Purves et al. 2001; Joos et al. 2005):

- Saccades

- Smooth pursuit movements

- Vergence movements

- Vestibulo-ocular movements

Smooth pursuit movements are so-called "tracking movements" (Purves et al. 2001: 431) and prevent information from leaving the central field of sharp vision (Joos et al. 2003: 1; cf. Rickheit et al. 2003). They are the reactions to movements of the body or the surroundings and stabilize the focus. They can be voluntary as a person can decide to track a moving stimulus or not (Purves et al. 2001: 431) and include the opto-kinetic nystagmus[1] and the vestibular nystagmus.[2] Vergence movements can be seen as part of the smooth pursuit movements but can also happen involuntarily (Joos et al. 2003: 4). They "align the fovea of each eye with targets located at different distances from the observer" (Purves et al. 2001: 432). The vestibulo-ocular movements compensate for head movements. Joos et al. (2003) also mention that fixations are not completely motionless themselves. Micro movements occur within fixations and include drifts, micro saccades and tremors. Drifts are the constant 'slipping' from the fixation target, and they are compensated by micro saccades. Tremors are the smallest, trembling movements of the eye with movements slightly less than one minute of arc and frequencies around 50 Hz. This 'inaccuracy' in the eye muscle control prevents exhaustion in the photoreceptors and is necessary as these receptors only react to a change in light.

So far, mainly fixations and saccades have been analysed during research. Another measure mentioned in several studies is pupil size. However, Holmqvist et al. advise caution due to the pupil's sensitivy "to not only changes in cognitive load" (2011: 393) but also to light intensity, emotions such as fear, stress, and pain as well as medicine and stimulants (2011: 393, Hvelplund 2014: 214). Therefore, this study focuses on fixations and saccades to analyse the viewer's gaze behaviour and measure visual attention. These eye movements can be recorded with an eye tracker,[3] in this case the Tobii TX300 which is introduced and discussed in §7.1.

While there are quite different methods of eye movement registration (for an overview, see Rickheit et al. 2003: 147), all of them are based on anatomi-

---

[1] An involuntary reflex to maintain a stable retinal image (Joos et al. 2003: 4) during a "replacement of the retinal image" (Joos et al. 2003: 4, author's translation).

[2] An involuntary reflex to maintain a stable fixation during head and body movement (Joos et al. 2003: 4).

[3] For a short overview on eye tracking history, refer to http://www.uxbooth.com/blog/a-brief-history-of-eye-tracking/ [2014–11–21, in German] and https://www.cs.hs-rm.de/~linn/fachsem0809/eyetracking/Eye_Tracking.pdf [2014–11–21, in German].

cal and physiological properties of the eye that are accessible by self-evaluation or through the observation of others (see Rickheit et al. 2003: 145).[4] Electro-oculography uses "carefully positioned electrodes" to measure changes "in [the] electrical potential between the front and the back of the eye" (Technical Challenges 2014) caused by the eye position and is widely used, e.g. in fMRI setups. It works relatively to the head position but is prone to artifacts and not suitable for infants or other viewers that might not be able to control or suppress their head movements. Other systems are based on infrared limbal reflections, canthus tracking and scleral coil techniques. Eye trackers making use of one or two Purkinje images were very accurate and could even record micro saccades, but were also expensive and are now widely replaced by video-based eye trackers. These video systems are based on cameras that film one or both eyes and image processing software that determines the position of a "salient feature" (Technical Challenges 2014) such as pupil and corneal reflections of infrared light (Duchowski 2007: 54; cf. Hvelplund 2014: 205). These "two points of reference on the eye are needed to separate eye movements from head movements" (Duchowski 2007: 60) and most head-mounted and desk-mounted video-based eye trackers achieve the necessary data by subtracting the corneal reflection created by (near) infrared light sources from the pupil position, i.e. its centre. Two techniques are used to create the reflection, called dark-pupil and bright-pupil, depending on the placement of the illumination source. If the illumination source is placed within the optical axis of the camera, the light is reflected off the retina and the pupil appears to be bright – similar to the red eye effect during photography. If the illumination source is placed somewhere else, the light reflected off the retina is directed away from the camera and the pupil appears dark, thus creating the dark-pupil effect.

Eye tracking systems that are based on Purkinje images (or reflexes) summarise at least four reflections of objects that are created due to the eye's structure. Normally, the first and the fourth image are analysed and can be seen as "small white dots in close proximity to the (dark) pupil" (Curtis 2015):

> These two images move similarly under translation of the eye, that is, they move through the same distance and in the same direction as the eye. During rotation of the eye, the separation between the two images changes proportionally with the sine of the angle of rotation. Thus angular eye position

---

[4]For a description of the early efforts and history of eye tracking, see this presentation: https://www.uniklinik-freiburg.de/fileadmin/mediapool/07_kliniken/psy_psykuj/pdf/lehre/ESSEM_2014/ESSEM_2014_--_Lecture_slides_--_Hutton_-_Technical_challenges.pdf [2015–12–08].

can be obtained from the relative positions of the two images (disregarding their absolute position), free of error induced by translation. (KU Leuven 2016: para. 4)

These eye tracking systems are calibrated by "measuring user gazing at properly positioned grid points (usually 5 or 9)" (KU Leuven 2016: para. 4). Their accuracy is "typically measured in degrees of visual angle" (Hvelplund 2014: 205), with other relevant factors being the "degree of invasiveness" (2014: 205) and sampling rate. Remote (or desktop) eye trackers can be seen as less invasive than other systems and are "generally the preferred type in translation research" (Hvelplund 2014: 205; cf. O'Brien 2009: 263). Studies relevant for this experiment are those on eye movements in reading, scene perception, usability, and, subsequently, subtitling.

## 6.2 Eye movements in reading

Radach and Kennedy claim that much of the knowledge of eye movements has been "established in the context of reading research" (2004: 5), which can be seen as quite a specific field of study. Hvelplund states that "visual exposure to letters automatically activates a processing stream that cannot be interrupted intentionally, unless looking away from those letters" (2014: 209; cf. Valdés et al. 2005: 279). While the beginnings of eye tracking research can be traced back to Huey in 1908, and the mid-1970s are seen as the starting point of modern eye tracking research (cf. Rayner & McConkie 1976; Just & Carpenter 1980; Rayner & Pollatsek 1989), Frenck-Mestre and Pynte (1997) published what Keating calls the "first published eye-tracking study" (2014: 69) of "reading behavior of adult second language (L2) learners" (2014: 69). Eye tracking offered possibilities of "detecting subtle differences between native and non-native language processing" (Keating 2014: 70) in real-time. Further relevant studies and overviews were published by Rayner (1998) and Radach et al. (2004). Rayner and colleagues showed that "fixation duration and saccade lengths in reading do not correlate with those measures in scene perception and search" (Rayner 2009: 1459) and offers especially insights into "how readers respond to processing difficulties" (Keating 2014: 87).

As Radach and Kennedy state, "fixations [in reading] are positioned in a very systematic, word-based, fashion" (2004: 5). Eye tracking data can therefore show whether a word is fixated or not, where it is fixated, amplitudes of "incoming and outgoing saccades" (Radach & Kennedy 2004: 6), their direction (progressive or regressive) as well as interword and intraword movements of saccades (Radach

& Kennedy 2004: 6). An overview of "word-based spatial eye movement measures" and "word-based temporal eye movement parameters" can be found in Radach/Kennedy (2004: 6f.) as well as information on fixation patterns in passes, i.e. first and second pass gaze durations (Radach & Kennedy 2004: 7). Depending on their function, fixation probability of words differs strongly – while "content words are fixated about 85 % of the time, [...] function words are fixated about 35 % of the time" (Rayner 1998: 375; cf. Rayner 2009: 1461). Additionally, fixation probability rises with increasing word length (Rayner & McConkie 1976; Rayner et al. 1996; Rayner 2009).

Referred to by Rayner and Pollatsek as direct control of eye movements (1989), "information acquired during a given fixation can influence the duration of that fixation as well as the amplitude of the outgoing saccade" (Radach & Kennedy 2004: 5). Fixation duration is said to increase with perceived difficulty (Hvelplund 2014: 211; cf. Rayner & Duffy 1986), decreasing frequency and predictability of words (Hvelplund 2014: 211), and increasing complexity and difficulty of words (Hvelplund 2014: 211; cf. Rayner & Pollatsek 1989, Rayner & Duffy 1986). Furthermore, "lexical and/or syntactic ambiguity [...] affect fixation duration" (Jakobsen & Hvelplund Jensen 2008: 103).[5] Typical fixation durations are associated with various eye movement behaviours such as silent reading, oral reading, scene perception, and visual search (Rayner 2009: 1460; Rayner 1998: 375), and differing reading purposes such as for comprehension or for translation influence eye movements and gaze times (Jakobsen & Hvelplund Jensen 2008: 120; cf. Hvelplund 2014: 212).

As information is only taken in during fixations, the term "perceptual span" (Keating 2014: 72) describes the "amount of useful information that a reader can extract from a text on a given fixation" (2014: 72). The spread of the perceptual span is asymmetric as more information to the right of the fixation is perceived than to the left (2014: 72). For English readers, research states that about 14–15 characters to the right and 3–4 characters to the left are noticed. However, only words up to 7–8 characters to the right can be identified (2014: 72). This is, of course, different for other writing systems such as Hebrew or Chinese (Rayner 2009: 1462; Keating 2014: 73). Part of the amount of useful information a reader can extract can also be what is referred to as a "parafoveal preview benefit" (Keat-

---

[5] As skipping and refixations occur regularly during reading, alternative measures of fixation time have been developed. These include "first-fixation duration (the duration of the first fixation on a word), single-fixation duration (those cases where only a single fixation is made on a word), and gaze duration (the sum of all fixations on a word prior to moving to another word). All of the measures are contingent on the word being fixated on a first-pass forward fixation." (Rayner 2009: 1461)

ing 2014: 74f.), i.e. information about the upcoming word. If that kind of information is perceived, words visible during previous fixations are read faster (Keating 2014: 74f.; cf. Rayner 1998, Rayner 2009: 1466f.).

Research indicates that saccades are usually "aimed at the centre of the selected target word" (Radach & Kennedy 2004: 10), which seems optimal for word processing. Their length is on average nine characters and in between one and 20 characters (Keating 2014: 71). Mature readers initiate about 85–90 % forward (progressive) saccades and 10–15 % backward (regressive) saccades (Rayner 1998: 375, 387; Rayner 2009: 1460; Keating 2014: 71). These backwards directed saccades, also called regressions (Keating 2014: 71) are due to comprehension difficulties or errors in saccade programming (Keating 2014: 71) with visible differences between good and poor readers (Rayner 1998: 375). Additionally, backwards directed saccades can be "return sweeps [...] to move the eyes from the end of one line of text to the beginning of the next line of text" (Keating 2014: 72). However, progressive saccades form the vast majority of saccades and usually land on the following word or that after (N+1 or N+2), with regressions predominantly landing on words N-1 or N-2 (Radach & Kennedy 2004: 10; Rayner 2009: 1461ff.). Further relevant aspects are "saccade latency" (Rayner 1998: 372) that describes the time "it takes to initiate an eye movement" (1998: 372) and the skipping of words, i.e. words not being fixated. This happens from errors in saccade programming or "when a word is visible and identifiable in the parafovea" (Keating 2014: 74). The probability for being skipped is below 20 % for content words and about 60 to 80 % for function words (Carpenter & Just 1983), with word length being relevant (cf. Rayner & McConkie 1976; Keating 2014). Most of the mentioned values are

> very much influenced by text difficulty, reading skill, and characteristics of the writing system. Thus, as text gets more difficult, fixations get longer, saccades get shorter, and more regressions are made [...]. Also, typographical variables like font difficulty can influence eye movements; more difficult to encode fonts yield longer fixations, shorter saccades, and more regressions [...]. (Rayner 2009: 1460)

Dependent variables and further measures are listed by Jakobsen and Hvelplund Jensen (2008: 107), Hvelplund (2014: 215), and Rayner (1998, 2009). The analysis of cognitive processes in reading is based on fixation times and regressions (Keating 2014: 75). As mentioned before, processing difficulty leads to longer reading times and "may induce regressions to words previously read" (Keating 2014: 75). The overall word identification process is affected by various factors such as "frequency, word familiarity, age of acquisition [and] number of meanings" (Keating 2014: 77).

Concerning scene perception, Rayner states that fixations are longer and saccades are larger than in reading (2009: 1476). Not every part of a scene is fixated but mostly the "informative parts" (2009: 1476) and the perceptual span covers "about half of the total scene" (2009: 1476). Various characteristics of objects within a scene affect "the ease with which an object is identified" (Rayner 2009: 1477), such as frequency, orientation, and "how well camouflaged it is" (2009: 1477). Further information on preview benefit and eye movement control in scene perception can be found in Rayner (1998: 398ff.; 2009: 1477ff.). Rayner also mentions a study by Carroll et al. (1992) on cartoons that reports "longer fixation durations on the cartoon (...) than on the caption" (Rayner 1998: 392), no consistent movement back and forth between elements, and dominance of the caption over the picture. Additionally, research on how people look at advertisements by Pieters & Wedel (2008) and on how viewers alternate their visual attention between information sources (Rayner et al. 2001) might offer further insight on static combinations of image and text.

The visual processing of the moving image in film can be quite similar. While there are many studies on general image processing, Lautenbacher (2012) makes a case of specific elements capturing the human's gaze like no other: "The attention capturing strength of certain visual elements seems to be so strongly linked to human communicational behaviour that they could almost be considered bottom-up factors, even though they are not of an intrinsic pictorial nature" (2012: 140) – this seems to especially be the case with "human faces and their gaze directions in pictures" (2012: 140) as they are "very powerful gaze catchers" (Lautenbacher 2012: 141–142; cf. Birmingham et al. 2008) and salient features. As subtitles mainly appear during dialogues that are strongly connected to faces, this strong attraction to the human face in images and the "coercive force of the viewed human gaze" (Lautenbacher 2012: 144) tell us that conventional subtitles are not placed ideally. On the other hand, the response time has been found to be shorter "when the target appears at the gazed-at location than when it appears at the non-gazed-at location" (Birmingham et al. 2008: 986). However, viewers usually look at "areas that [...] support human communication (e.g. mouth, eyes, and gaze direction" (Lautenbacher 2012: 145). Without a given task "the default point of observation will be the human face and the gaze directions it suggests, thus putting the human face somewhere between a bottom-up visual saliency and a top-down search object" (Lautenbacher 2012: 145–146). Therefore, if observing the human face is seen as a "communicational reaction" (2012: 145–146), Lautenbacher sees a possibility of successfully integrating "significance and social attention triggered by human face and text" (2012: 145–146) and concludes that a "global, integrated approach to the translation of audiovisual documents" (Lautenbacher 2012: 153) is needed. As Gottlieb states, it is "hardly surprising [that] this additive nature of subtitling – in which the near-empty visual verbal channel is suddenly 'flooded' with subtitled lines – changes the working strategies of the translator as well as viewers' strategies of perception" (2012: 39). Whether the eye tracking of subtitles can simply be seen as a combination of reading and image processing or should be treated as a separate field with unique characteristics and challenges will be discussed in the following chapter.

## 6.3 Eye tracking and subtitling

Perceiving and processing subtitles is very different to reading static texts or looking at static scenes. The combination of eye tracking and dynamic content such as film creates challenges such as the high probability of moving fixated elements (cf. Huff et al. 2010) and deviating reading strategies:

> [...] any text that appears in film (e.g. subtitles), is on screen for a limited period of time, forcing the reader to adopt reading strategies that differ slightly from those in the reading of static text where the reader is much more in control of the pace of reading. (Kruger n.d.; cf. Kruger & Steyn 2014)

Film viewers have to "read at a pace imposed by the movie" (Schotter & Rayner 2012: 83) and keep shifting their gazes between image and subtitle (2012: 83). The goal of performing eye tracking on subtitles is to create an understanding of, on the one hand, what is perceived in the image, the fixation duration on relevant elements in the scene, and on the other hand, the processing of audiovisual text, how fast and thoroughly the audiences read the subtitles and what parts they fixate longer, how they split their visual attention between image and film, and – of course – the overall impact of the subtitles on the audience's comprehension of the film (cf. Fox 2012, Kruger n.d.). Concerning perception, Lautenbacher summarises it this way:

> Because of the simultaneity of these visual elements, the question is whether this combination of pictures and text creates a contradiction in the perception process or not. More specifically, with subtitled films, the question is how this combination affects the reception of films, and what implications this might have for subtitling strategies. (2012: 135)

When faced with the question whether the presence of subtitles might "over-shadow important semiotic pictorial elements for meaning construction or die-gesis in film" (Lautenbacher 2012: 149), subtitles should be seen as part of the many elements films consist of and that build the "overall meaning of an audio-visual document" (Lautenbacher 2012: 150). In Belgium, d'Ydewalle and his col-leagues conducted some of the first and during recent years most relevant eye tracking studies on subtitling. The first studies focused on attention allocation (e.g. d'Ydewalle et al. 1985) and how it overlaps with sound, image and text (see d'Ydewalle & Gielen 1992). While these studies laid the foundations of today's eye tracking research on subtitles and indicated "a human propensity to read what is on the screen to be read" (Lautenbacher 2012: 148, cf. "Automatic Reading Be-haviour", d'Ydewalle et al. 1991), the study conducted in 2007 by d'Ydewalle and De Bruycker brought "eye tracking research in AVT to the next level" (Kruger n.d.) – it illustrated that automatic processing of subtitles does indeed take place and that two-line subtitles were processed more thoroughly and being skipped less. Recent years have produced a wide variety of studies focused on aspects such as the processing of linguistic features or suitable presentation rates. Ghia (2012) found significantly more deflections in the presence of non-literal transla-tion, therefore showing the impact of the translation quality on subtitle reading, and Moran (2012) discussed the effects of linguistic variation on the reception of subtitles. Jensema and colleagues focused on changes in eye-movement patterns and researched the impact of presentation rate on deaf viewers (2000a), finding that hearing viewers spent between 10 and 31.8 % on subtitles and deaf viewers up to 84 % (2000b, 2000a). Szarkowska and colleagues found similar values while studying the impact of verbatim, standard and edited subtitles (2011). While there was little difference for hearing participants, deaf viewers' attention allocation was very different in between these conditions: They spent just under 70 % on ver-batim subtitles, 60 % on standard subtitles, and 50 % on what they called 'edited subtitles'. The hard-of-hearing spent 60 % on verbatim and under 50 % on edited subtitles.

Romero-Fresco (2015) finally deviates from the strict separation of image and subtitle processing and focuses on the overall viewing speed opposed to "presen-tation speed or reading speed" (Kruger n.d.). He defines viewing speed as "the speed at which a given viewer watches a piece of audiovisual material, which in the case of subtitling includes accessing the subtitle, the accompanying im-ages and the sound" (2015: 337). His extensive eye tracking study showed that presentation speed is closely connected to the split attention between image and subtitle reading. While viewers spent about 60 % of the time on the image at a speed of 120 wpm (words per minute), increasing the speed to up to 200 wmps, viewers spent less and less time on the image with finally only exploring the image 20 % of the time a subtitle was visible. This is of course closely connected to the decreasing time available to read the subtitle and offers good indicators of what makes a suitable presentation speed.

Studies as the one by Romero-Fresco show that there are not only differences in the reading behaviour of static text and subtitles but also in the way it is measured. Therefore, the following section will provide a basic overview of suitable eye tracking measures for the analysis of subtitle reception.

### 6.3.1 Measuring eye movements in AVT

Based on recent eye tracking research on audiovisual translation (d'Ydewalle et al. 1991; d'Ydewalle & De Bruycker 2007; Moran 2012; Caffrey 2009; Ghia 2012; Kruger & Steyn 2014), a number of values and measurements of eye tracking in audiovisual translation can be identified. Kruger lists the following as most useful:

- *Mean fixation duration*: This measure provides a useful index of the processing effort, but should be used only to compare similar activities (e.g. reading of different types of subtitles and not reading to scene perception).

- *Dwell time*: This provides a measure of the total time viewers spent looking at a particular area of interest, including both fixations and saccades.

- *Number of fixations per word*: This is particularly useful when an attempt is made to measure the extent to which subtitles were processed, although a more nuanced measure would take into account refixations and regressions.

- *Average forward saccade length*: Like the number of fixations per word, this measure makes it possible to determine whether viewers performed regular reading.

- *Glance count*: This measure gives an indication of the number of times viewers shifted between different areas on the screen (e.g. image and subtitle)

- *Number of skipped subtitles:* This is a fairly rough indication of how many subtitles were not even noticed by viewers, but should be considered together with other measures (Kruger n.d.).

Further interesting measures are the latency time, or 'reaction time' or 're-sponse time', the "time between the appearance of the subtitle and the first fix-ation on the subtitle" (Kruger n.d.), the saccade amplitude or saccade length, re-gressions and revisits, fixation counts and total fixation duration.

## 6.3.2 Relevant studies

While there is a noticeable number of eye tracking studies on subtitling in gen-eral,[6] there are only a few studies on alternative subtitling strategies similar to integrated titles. In the following, four studies will be presented. The studies by Künzli & Ehrensberger-Dow (2011) and Caffrey (2009) are relevant due to their structure and use of both eye tracking and questionnaire data to investigate inno-vative subtitling strategies. The other two studies by Armstrong & Brooks (2014) and Brown et al. (2015) are relevant due to their focus on what they call "dynamic subtitles", a concept similar to integrated titles.

Künzli and Ehrenberger-Dow looked at the "reception capacity and audience response" (2011: 187) of 27 participants that watched four film excerpts with ei-ther standard subtitling or "innovative subtitling" (2011: 187). These innovative subtitles (or surtitles) comprised "additional information regarding language and culture-specific elements in the original soundtrack" (2011: 187) and were inves-tigated by means of simultaneous eye tracking and consecutive questionnaires. The reception was analysed based on mean fixation durations and percentage of gaze time in specific areas. The questionnaire focused on film content, its per-ception and the participant's satisfaction. While they did not find significant dif-ferences in between the two modes (possibly due to the very specific participant group of young students), the experiment design provides a good basis for similar studies.

Caffrey (2009) investigated the impact of pop-up glosses similar to the sur-titles in Künzli and Ehrensberger-Dow. They are mostly used in the translation of Japanese anime and originate from fansubbing. Based on eye tracking mea-sures such as skipped subtitles, gaze time, mean fixation duration, word fixation probability, and pupil size, he reported "a higher number of skipped subtitles, and a lower percentage gaze time in the subtitle area, lower mean fixation dura-tion, and lower word fixation probability" (Kruger n.d.). The questionnaire data suggested an increase of the processing effort and the perceived subtitle speed.

In their 2014 TVX conference paper, Armstrong & Brooks (2014) discussed the enhancement of subtitles through "integrating them with the moving image, and

---

[6]For an overview, see Perego (2012).

enabling choice in subtitle size and style" (2014). Besides discussions of the placement, ways of feature avoidance, and the relevance of the screen size, Armstrong and Brooks developed a "positional subtitle editor in HTML5 and JavaScript that reads popular subtitle formats and allows them to be positioned and saved" (2014) in BBC's own format. While this is also possible with editors such as *Aegisub*,[7] the editor includes a simple image analysis that scores "areas of the image based on how much they change, and whether they contain an important feature such as a face or on-screen graphics" (2014). Additionally, their subtitle format includes the bounding box of the subtitle and therefore allows for easy cross-referencing with and visualisation of the corresponding eye tracking data.

Their study included four 90 seconds clips from three episodes of the BBC drama series *Sherlock*. Five versions were created that combined French audio with traditional and dynamic subtitles, English audio with traditional and dynamic subtitles, and one unaltered version without subtitles as a baseline for comparison. Using a Tobii X-120, they recorded the gaze behaviour of 24 English native speakers who did not understand French and were not habitual subtitles users. They created 420 areas of interest for the subtitles and found that "people spent less time reading subtitles, and more time looking at the drama when using dynamic subtitles" (Armstrong & Brooks 2014, cf. Brown et al. 2015).

In a follow-up article, Brown et al. designed two more experiments on the "dynamically positioned subtitles" (2015) presented in the 2014 article, one of them with hearing-impaired users. They compared the baseline of viewers without subtitles with the gaze behaviour of viewers with dynamic subtitles and found it to be closer to the baseline for dynamic subtitles. They used a 1:50 minutes clip from *Sherlock* (S01E01) with 34 subtitles and presented it to 26 participants that were habitual subtitle users (on a daily basis) and eight participants that would watch it without subtitles and were no habitual subtitle users. As factors for the placement of the dynamic subtitles, they named "the character speaking the line; the background; and; the position of the previous and subsequent subtitles" (Brown et al. 2015). For four subtitles, they tested alternative positions and re-authored these and two more. The subtitles were displayed in the sans-serif typeface Helvetica Neue in 32 pixels, white, and with a slim black outline. They kept the timing of the traditional subtitles.

Based on their research on user experience (UX) design, they propose a new framework for subtitle evaluation that takes into consideration visual attention, aesthetics, involvement, familiarity, perceived usefulness, perceived usability, and endurability (Brown et al. 2015). The measurement of the gaze pattern based on

---

[7]Cf. http://www.aegisub.org [2016–08–07].

dwell time was inconclusive between the traditional and dynamic subtitle conditions. Their interview-based qualitative analysis, however, revealed that five participants disliked the dynamic titles, eight participants were "broadly positive" and twelve "very keen on the idea" (Brown et al. 2015):

> The majority of people who watched dynamic subtitles enjoyed the experience, and wanted to try them further. A number of participants were very keen, and would have liked to convert to dynamic subtitles immediately. (Brown et al. 2015)

Participants wished for speaker identification, readability and subtitles not obscuring the action. Brown et al. concluded that participants felt more immersed and missed less (2015). They found gaze patterns more similar to the baseline without subtitles and those participants who disliked the dynamic titles stated that they did not really rely on subtitles anyway. The most enthusiastic participants were those who rely "on subtitles as an access service" (Brown et al. 2015), therefore Brown et al. concluded that it would be "desirable for viewers to have the option to revert to traditional subtitles if they, or their viewing companions preferred" (2015).

## 6.4 Eye tracking and usability research

As mentioned in §3.2 and as there are no specific usability guidelines for subtitles, Mosconi and Porta recommend to generally apply web accessibility and usability rules to them (Mosconi & Porta 2012). Similarly, there's little eye tracking research in the area of subtitle usability or layout. And while eye tracking has been present in cognitive studies for quite some time, it is still comparably new in the area of usability research. Schiessl et al. see the limitations of "conventional methods [...] to those processes which are part of conscious reflection and conscious control" (2003: 2) while eye tracking can "provide detail data about the users' visual attention on user interface elements" (Manhartsberger & Zellhofer 2005: 141; cf. Schiessl et al. 2003: 2) and as "source of information about user behaviour" (2003: 2). It can "provide insight into users' decision making while searching and navigating interfaces" (Goldberg et al. 2002: 3) and allows understanding of "visual and display-based information processing and the factors that may impact upon the usability of system interfaces" (Poole & Ball 2005: 1). As eye tracking can "unveil response biases of subjects due to an artificial testing environment" (Schiessl et al. 2003: 9), its use often "results in a higher validity of usability data" (2003: 9). Limitations and shortcomings are discussed in Jacob & Karn (2003).

The main focus of eye tracking studies in usability research is the allocation of visual attention and "amount of processing" (Jacob & Karn 2003) an item receives, usually in order to improve interfaces, processes, human-computer interaction (HCI), and real-time eye tracking for disabled users (for a discussion of eye tracking as an input device, see e.g. Jacob & Karn 2003, Kaur et al. 2003, Poole & Ball 2005: 8ff.) in both "commercial and academic practice" (Ehmke & Wilson 2007: 1). Especially websites and software programmes are being analysed in eye tracking-based usability research and the demand "is flourishing and it is becoming more common to include eye-tracking in the range of techniques used for this purpose" (Ehmke & Wilson 2007: 2). Researchers analyse visualisations of eye tracking data to "identify confusion on the part of the user, reading or scanning behaviours, or simply [...] areas that users are not looking at" (Ehmke & Wilson 2007: 2). Studies such as Goldberg et al. (2002) indicate a "connection between eye-tracking patterns and users' decision making processes" (Ehmke & Wilson 2007: 2). Common topics are the distinction between reading or scanning text elements (Manhartsberger & Zellhofer 2005: 147f.), wording problems as users will "rather ignore a link they do not understand, than finding out what is behind that link" (2005: 149), the definition and testing of layout and web standards (2005: 150), affordance, i.e. the degree of "an object's sensory characteristics intuitively [implying] its functionality and use" (2005: 150), and "wrong eye catchers and vampire effects" (2005: 151) that "draw away and consume the users attention completely" (2005: 151).

In using eye tracking, researchers try to relate eye movement patterns to specific usability problems. Ehmke and Wilson give an overview of common usability problems such as "expected information missing" (2007: 9), "ineffective presentation" (2007: 9) or "unclear input format" (2007: 9) that can be based on single eye movement measures or a combination of patterns, i.e. correlating "a high number of fixations across the page and navigation, followed by fixations on one element only" (2007: 9) to the usability problem of "ineffective presentation through unclear item grouping" (2007: 9). The following measures and possible interpretations are mentioned in Ehmke and Wilson (2007: 2), based on Poole and Ball (2005: 4ff.) and Jacob and Karn (2003: 582):

- *Overall number of fixations*: This measure is "thought to be negatively correlated with search efficiency [...]" (Jacob & Karn 2003: 585) and is usually strongly connected to the task duration (2003: 585).

- *Gaze (%) on each AOI*: The "proportion of time looking at a particular display element (of interest to the design team) could reflect the importance of that element" (Jacob & Karn 2003: 585).

- *Overall fixation duration mean*: Long fixations can indicate interest or confusion (Ehmke & Wilson 2007: 2) or "a participant's difficulty extracting information from a display [...]" (Jacob & Karn 2003: 585).

- *Number of fixations on each AOI*: Used by Cowen et al. (2002) in connection to the "standard task performance measure (time)" (McCarthy et al. 2003: 404). It is also said to be "strongly correlated with task duration, and this measure has been used as a proxy for measures of task performance [...]" (McCarthy et al. 2003: 404).

- *Gaze duration mean on each AOI*: This can reflect the "difficulty of information extraction" (McCarthy et al. 2003: 409; cf. Fitts et al. 1950) and is "longer if participant experiences difficulty" (Jacob & Karn 2003: 585). Gaze frequency can reflect the "importance of that area of the display" (2003: 585).

- *Overall fixation rate*

- *Scanpath*: An analysis of the scanpath can indicate the "efficiency of the arrangement of elements in the user interface" Jacob & Karn 2003: 585). Goldberg and Kotval (1999) defined an optimal scanpath as a "straight line to a desired target, with relatively short fixation duration at the target" (Poole & Ball 2005: 6). The scanpath length can indicate "less efficient searching (perhaps due to a sub-optimal layout)" (2005: 6) and the "transition probability between AOIs" (Ehmke & Wilson 2007: 4) can "indicate efficiency of the arrangement of elements in the user interface" (2007: 4).

Jacob and Karn also mention the "number of gazes on each area of interest" (2003: 582), the "number of involuntary and number of voluntary fixations" (Ehmke & Wilson 2007: 585), the "percentage of participants fixating an area of interest" (2007: 585) as this "can serve as a simple indicator of the attention-getting properties of an interface element" (2007: 586), and the "time to first fixation on target area of interest" as a "useful measure when a specific search target exists" (2007: 586). Goldberg and Kotval (1999) also name the following measures: Number of fixations, (total) fixation duration, average fixation duration; fixation/saccade ration, fixation spatial density (as a "global measure of the total amount of processing performed on each page" (Cowen et al. 2002), and saccade amplitude (as "larger saccades can indicate more meaningful cues, as attention is drawn from a distance" [Ehmke & Wilson 2007: 2]). Finally, McCarthy et al. (2003) added "glance frequency", defined as "one or more successive fixations to the same screen object" (2003).

Further possibly interesting aspects of eye movement behaviour mentioned by Ehmke and Wilson (2007: 2) are backtracking saccades that can indicate confusion, participants not looking at specific elements, scanning and searching behaviour instead of reading behaviour, specific patterns such as a back and forth between two elements, the first and last area or element users look at, and interaction such as clicking or following links. This behaviour should be "discussed with users afterwards" (Ehmke & Wilson 2007: 2) or the study extended with "retrospective protocols [...] to explain their decisions and thoughts", e.g. in form of post-experience eye-tracked protocols (PEEP, cf. Ball et al. 2006).

Concerning the relevance for the present topic, the study by McCarthy et al. (2003) is especially interesting: They analysed the conflicting advice on the best position for navigation menus on websites,[8] as these either follow user expectations or are based on "results from user testing with alternative layouts" (2003: 401). Their results show that "users rapidly adapt to an unexpected screen layout" (2003: 401) and concluded that "designers should not be inhibited in applying design recommendations that violate layout conventions as long as consistency is maintained within a site" (2003: 401). While Nielsen (1999) found that menu labels that follow user expectations lead to an 80 % success rate in product search and only 9 % if not (McCarthy et al. 2003: 401) and also IBM design guidelines (2003) recommend placement in expected areas – in the case of navigation menus, in the upper left area of a site. McCarthy et al. see web search as a combination of expectations that "exert a top-down influence" (2003: 402; cf. Goldberg et al. 2002) and the display that "exerts a bottom-up influence" (2003: 402; cf. Goldberg et al. 2002), influenced by e.g. "layering, separation, colours and contrast" (2003: 402, cf. Tufte 1990) as well as "motion or animation" (2003: 402; cf. Hillstrom & Yantis 1994). McCarthy et al. tested for a difference in simple and complex websites and found differences in task duration (2003: 407), confirming their hypotheses that "performance will be better with the left menu" (2003: 407), meaning the menu being placed in the expected area. However, this only applied to the "first page visit" (2003: 407). The users' expectations are "rapidly updated to reflect the layout of the current page" (2003: 407) and "showed a significant decrease in task

---

[8]Concerning web search, relevant studies include the Stanford-Poynter study (Lewenstein et al. 2017; cf. McCarthy et al. 2003: 403), Cowen et al. (2002), and Goldberg et al. (2002).

completion time after the first page visit" (2003: 409). They see the advantage of "sites that conform to expectations" (2003: 412) as "short-lived" (2003: 412), which shows that "violating the expectation or convention of the left menu bar has little long-term effect on task performance" (2003: 412). They noted a "rapid adaption to the unexpected layout" (2003: 413), which led to their conclusion that mainly the "internal consistency of a site [...] is important" (2003: 413). As the integrated titles analysed in the present study also violate placement and layout conventions as well as user expectations, their usability is a relevant issue, reflected in the applied eye movement measures and the reported enjoyment and entertainment value by the viewers.

## 6.5 Summary

Eye tracking research and reading studies have shown that "visual exposure to letters automatically activates a processing stream that cannot be interrupted intentionally" (Hvelplund 2014: 209; cf. Valdés et al. 2005: 279) and that fixations and their analysis in reading take place word-based. Typographical variables can influence eye movements (Rayner 2009: 1460) and salient features in images are highly relevant, revealing human faces and gaze directions as strong gaze catchers (Lautenbacher 2012: 141f.). Subtitled film, however, has to be treated as a separate, very specific field of both scene perception and reading: Text is only visible a limited period of time and the reading speed is imposed by the film (Schotter & Rayner 2012: 83). Additionally, gaze shifting between image and subtitles sets audiovisual products apart from static text or scene perception. Researchers look at what is perceived, the fixation duration on specific elements, the split attention between image and subtitle, text processing, and image processing. In that combination, statements on the overall perception, comprehension, and enjoyment of subtitled film can be made and basic usability problems be discussed.

To gain further basic insight into the perception of integrated titles, the impact of position and layout of integrated titles will be investigated. Simultaneous eye tracking will be used to analyse the perception and cognitive processing, analysing mean fixation duration, dwell time (in AOIs), and reaction time. Additionally, a post-hoc questionnaire will focus on enjoyment, satisfaction, the aesthetic experience of the participants and the usability of the integrated titles. The aim is to determine whether there are differences in the perception and enjoyment of integrated titles compared to conventional subtitles.

# 7 Method and experiment design

The aim of the present study is to analyse and discuss the impact of integrated titles on both the audience's perception and aesthetic experience. While eye tracking research and the traditional set of guidelines for subtitles have been established in audiovisual translation for quite a while now, the structure of the study and its combination of both translation studies and communication design is innovative and unprecedented. Based on the complete analysis of the impact of the graphical translation of text elements in film and English integrated titles that are only rarely retained in the German translation of films, a first workflow for the creation of integrated titles was drafted and tested in order to create the film material compared and discussed in this study. This chapter gives an overview of the experiment setup, the preliminary pilot study carried out in 2012, the resulting hypotheses, and the main study. As visual attention can be measured by examining the participant's gaze behaviour, expressed in fixations and saccades, the eye tracker is the most relevant part of the experiment setup and both the system and software used will be presented in the following.

## 7.1 Eye tracking setup

Both the pilot study and the main experiment were conducted with the Tobii TX300, a video-based eye tracking system that uses Purkinje images.[1] Its high sampling rate of 300 Hz theoretically allows for precise data and despite the high resolution of the screen (1920 x 1080 pixels), head movements did not constitute a major issue. The system collects gaze samples, calculates and represents them as saccades and fixations, and also measures pupil size and reports data on eyelid movements. It consists of the eye tracking element and a removable 23'' TFT screen, which can be used separately or in combination, as was done in the two studies. The system is accompanied by the software package *Tobii Studio*. Two different versions (each up-to-date at the time of the respective study) were used in the pilot study and the main experiment and caused different challenges. Both these challenges and the overall features of the software programme are presented in §7.2.3.

---

[1] Cf. http://www.tobiipro.com/product-listing/tobii-pro-tx300/ [2016–04–12].

## 7.2 Software

Besides a number of commonplace software programs such as *Microsoft Excel* for the organisation of the film corpus lists and basic calculations and the *R* suite[2] for "data manipulation, calculation and graphical display" (R Project 2016), three additional major tools were used in this study. *Subtitle Workshop* was used in order to manage the conventional English subtitles provided by the filmmaker as well as to create the conventional German subtitles. *Premiere Pro* was used to create the integrated titles, associated effects and to export the required video files. Finally, *Tobii Studio* was used for data collection with the eye tracker, AOI (area of interest) creation, and basic data analysis and export.

### 7.2.1 Subtitle Workshop: A traditional freeware subtitling tool

*Subtitle Workshop* is freeware software created by the Uruguayan company Uru-works[3] and is used to create subtitle files. Especially amateurs and non-professionals use freeware like this, while professional subtitle agencies generally use their own software or a commercial product. *Subtitle Workshop* consists of several modules that can be activated individually. These include a preview window and the subtitle window. Additionally, a second subtitle window can be activated for translation, making it possible to see both source and target subtitle at the same time. The in and out times can be selected either through the preview window or manually. The subtitle files can then be saved in a wide range of file formats, such as the popular subrip format (.srt)[4] that is highly compatible and allows integration into videos, DVDs, BDs or upload to YouTube. While *Subtitle Workshop* is suitable for creating basic subtitle files and therefore sufficient for creating the conventional subtitle files used in the studies, other freeware software such as *Aegisub* allows for a wider range of data formats and additional features such as individual placement in the image. No issues arose during work with *Subtitle Workshop* and the handling was easy and productive.

However, while software such as *Aegisub* allows individual positions of titles and a range of colour and format features, sophisticated effects can still best be achieved with professional video editing software. Therefore, *Adobe Premiere Pro* was used to create the integrated titles for both the pilot and the main study.

---

[2]Cf. https://www.r-project.org/about.html [2016–08–08].
[3]Cf. http://www.uruworks.net/description.html [2016–08–09].
[4]Explanations of various subtitle formats can be found here: http://www.afterdawn.com/guides/archive/subtitle_formats_explained.cfm [2016–04–18].

### 7.2.2 Adobe Premiere Pro

*Adobe Premiere Pro* is a commercial video editing and cutting software from the American software company Adobe Systems. For the pilot study, the then up-to-date version CS6, released in May 2012, was used. The main study made use of the latest versions *Premiere Pro* CC and *Premiere Pro* CC 2015. As *Premiere Pro* is part of Adobe's 'Creative Suite', it shares many features with other products of the suite (such as *Photoshop* and *After Effects*) and therefore allows for an easier data exchange between these programs – e.g. graphic elements created in *Photoshop* can be imported into *Premiere Pro*.

*Premiere Pro* offers various tools for cutting and editing video material. For the pilot study, scenes had to be cut out of the film material used and combined into one file. For both the pilot study and main experiments, the integrated titles were created using the title tool in *Premiere Pro*. It makes it possible to place titles within the whole image and use effects on them such as masks (if parts of the title should be 'covered'), kinetic motion effects, or 3D effects. After creating the titles, they can be added to the video's timeline and the exact point in time they are to be displayed can be chosen. The project can then be exported and saved in most common video formats.

### 7.2.3 Tobii Studio

For the present study, the software offered by the manufacturer of the eye tracker, *Tobii Studio*, was used. It makes it possible to design and execute the experiment and then offers various tools for both data visualisation and analysis. As visualisation "gives a very good first impression" (Hvelplund 2014: 215), most eye tracking systems offer some kind of software that does visualisation (Hvelplund 2014: 212). *Tobii Studio* can display the current fixation point in a video of the materials looked at by participants, add a static scan path with numbered fixations to a still image of the material, indicate fixation duration visually, indicate individual participants, and present saccades as lines between fixation points. As visible from Figure 7.1, the eye movement data of one or more participants can be visualised in heat maps, gaze plots, or bee swarms (several animated fixation points indicate the various participants at the same time).

While it was used extensively during the pilot study, it mostly just provided an overview during the main experiment. However, the automatic cluster recognition tool was used to identify relevant focus areas in the image and compare visual attention distribution between the different modes. AOIs were used statistically to calculate fixation duration on the subtitle or title area and the overall

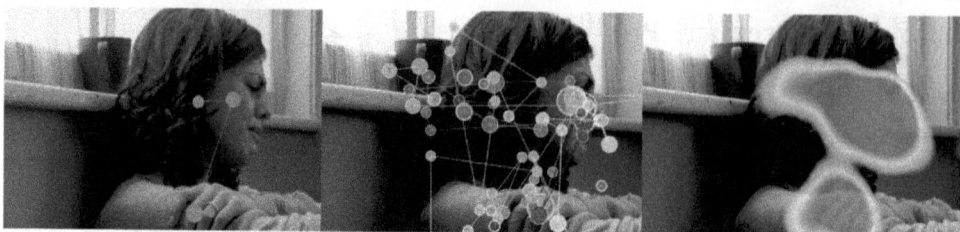

Figure 7.1: Visualisation of eye tracking data by *Tobii Studio* (scan path, accumulated scan path, heat map; *Being Human* S01E01, UK 2008–2013)

image as well as reaction times (see §8.1). The AOIs in the studies were created by hand and can be given shapes such as squares or circles but also freely drawn shapes. Issues mainly occurred during the pilot study and will be discussed in the following chapter.

## 7.3 Pilot study

The pilot study for this experiment was conducted in June and July 2012 at FTSK Germersheim, Johannes Gutenberg University Mainz.[5] While it included a substantial number of participants, only little statistical data could be retrieved due to faulty raw data and significant limitations of the software used. The aim was to not only test the equipment and software but also the process of creating integrated titles – at this point without any specific set of rules besides the goal of placing titles in a way that would allow easier speaker identification and provide an indication of the speaking direction – and verify the basic validity of the first set of general hypotheses:

- Compared to viewers of conventional titles, the viewers of integrated titles will be able to spend more time exploring the image instead of reading the title.

- The saccades of the viewers of integrated titles will be shorter compared to the saccades of viewers of conventional titles.

- The overall gaze behaviour of viewers of integrated titles will be closer to that of English natives who are not distracted by titles.

- The viewers of integrated titles will report a better aesthetic experience.

---

[5]In the course of the Master's thesis "Integrated Titles – An Alternative to Traditional Subtitles" (Fox 2012).

The equipment included the identical eye tracker Tobii TX300 and the then latest version of *Tobii Studio*. Additionally, the questionnaire on the aesthetic experience and subjective information intake for this study was to be tested.

The participants for the pilot study came from the student body – both undergraduate and graduate students – and staff of FTSK. A total of 52 participants volunteered for the pilot study, 16 of them were English native speakers and 36 were German native speakers. The German native speakers stated that – in their subjective opinion and habit – they needed German subtitles to watch English film material. As the use of subtitles is a personal and subjective decision, the English language proficiency was not tested.

The pilot study used the first episode of the first season of *Being Human* as source material. BBC describes *Being Human* as a "supernatural drama" and "dramedy",[6] referring to its mixture of fantasy, horror, drama and comedy. The first episode was broadcast in December 2008 on *BBC Three*. *Being Human* tells the story of Annie, George and Mitchell, who strive for a normal 'life'. Over 100 years old, Mitchell is the oldest of the unlikely group of friends and a vampire who renounced drinking blood 50 years ago, but still fights his thirst for blood every day. George was bitten by a werewolf and has had to fight his own inner monster ever since. Mitchell and George meet and decide to fight their demons together. Soon, they rent a little house and meet the former resident Annie, a ghost who is not done with life. Together, they want to become part of human society again. In doing so, everyone encounters his or her own very personal limits. Even though the total of five season was very successful in the UK, it never reached the German market – neither dubbed nor with subtitles. However, the American remake, produced by the BBC America, was broadcast on the German private channel *ProSieben*.[7]

The study was split into three steps: In the first step, the 16 English natives watched the whole episode in its original version (OV; without any subtitles or other edits), while the eye movements were recorded. One recording had to be excluded due to a loss of signal, wherefore only 15 recordings could be used in the analysis. The gaze plots and heat maps for each scene containing spoken content showed the main focus points or areas in these scenes that were later used as a basis for the comparison with the traditional subtitles (TS) and the integrated titles (IT).

---

[6]Cf. http://www.bbc.co.uk/programmes/b00hqlc4 [2016–04–05]

[7]Cf. http://www.serienjunkies.de/news/prosiebensat1-sichert-usversion-being-human-33444.
html [2016–04–05].

The second step included the creation of the German subtitles[8] and the eye tracking recordings with 15 German native speakers. They watched the episode in the TS condition and all recordings could be used in the analysis. The participants watched the whole episode with the German subtitles. These recordings were then analysed and compared to the recordings of the OV condition. Due to problems arising with the amount of data and clean scene selection, the decision was made to classify all suitable scenes according to their level of complexity (cf. Fox 2012). Four levels were defined and one scene per level was chosen as well as one additional scene of the lowest level as these scenes of lower complexity account for most of the analysed episode. The duration per scene was about 1 to 2 minutes. In the third step, the integrated titles were created, based on the main focus points and areas identified in the analysis of the OV recordings. Further placement strategies were the following:

- Place titles close to focus of the native participant group

- Indicate speaker

- Indicate speaking direction

- Produce sufficient contrast

- Do no cover relevant image areas or elements

A total of 21 German natives watched the IT condition while their eye movements were recorded. Of these recordings, 15 were suitable for analysis. After that, the participants were asked to fill in a questionnaire and 17 of the participants agreed. The following statements had to be rated in the questionnaire:

1. I could easily read all titles.

2. I received all necessary information through the titles.

3. I would like to watch a whole film with integrated titles.

4. I would prefer integrated titles over traditional subtitles.

5. If you prefer dubbing over subtitles (if not, please continue to question 6): I would prefer integrated titles over dubbing.

---

[8]In cooperation with Matthias Balzer. Permission for use of the episode was given by both the BBC and the production studio Touchpaper.

6. I had more time to explore the image with integrated titles (compared to traditional subtitles).

7. The integrated titles did not cover any relevant areas or elements in the image.

8. The integrated titles did not distract me from the image.

9. Due to the integrated titles, I perceived more details in the image.

10. Please rate your overall aesthetic experience with the integrated titles (1: very good; 4: very bad).

The participants had to rate the statements on their comprehension, usability of the titles, and enjoyment, using a Likert scale with the option 1 (completely agree) to 4 (completely disagree). The questionnaire was the only part of the pilot study that was sufficient for statistical analysis (see Figure 7.2).

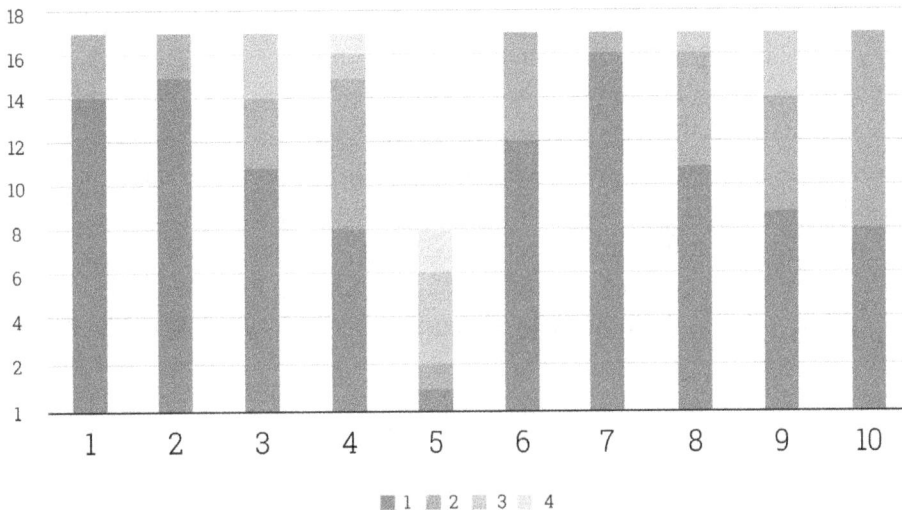

Figure 7.2: Questionnaire evaluation with the scores of 1 (completely agree) to 4 (completely disagree).

The pilot study showed that scenes of the lowest level of complexity create little difference between conventional subtitles and integrated titles concerning the split attention[9] and main attention distribution. However, the more movement and content complexity increase, the more the participants of conventional subtitles focused on the subtitle area and only infrequently paid attention to the actual image. This became visible from the analysis of the gaze plots and heat maps. The integrated titles, on the other hand, and regardless of scene complexity, created a balanced focus with participants sometimes even paying more attention to the image than the titles. The questionnaire evaluation showed that the majority of the IT participants rated their aesthetic experience and information gain as good, also in comparison with conventional subtitles. This strengthens the hypothesis that aesthetics play an active part in how film is perceived and processed.

Several issues were encountered during the pilot study. One of the main issues was the large amount of data produced by the first two sets of recordings. These recordings were about 50 minutes each. Due to incomprehensible issues in *Tobii Studio*, scenes smaller than 10 seconds could not be selected in a clean way. Start and end times often changed after selection, even if done by hand. Therefore, none of the features of *Tobii Studio* that offer automatic processing and creation of data could be used. Due to this software error, these often too long and temporally displaced scenes – of which there were several hundred – had to be corrected later by hand. This allowed basic analysis of the then produced heat maps and gaze plots but did not leave the time to create any statistical data on e.g. first fixations or fixation durations.

Besides these issues, the pilot study proved to be a good test of the first basic set of hypotheses. Furthermore, a first concept for the analysis of image composition and typographic identity emerged, and a first set of placement strategies (based on the accumulated eye tracking data) and effects could be tested. The following chapter will present the refined hypotheses that were then tested in the main study.

## 7.4 Hypotheses

Based on the pilot study, it was assumed that integrated titles, compared to traditional subtitles, would have an effect on the fixation duration, the time to first

---

[9]Chandler and Sweller define "split attention" as the result of the divided attention of a learner due to "multiple sources of information" (1991: 295), which can be – in the context of film material – transferred to splitting attention between image and title (and sound) as sources of information. More attention towards the image – rather than on the subtitle or title – was considered a positive effect as easier and faster information processing is more likely.

fixation in the title area, the attention distribution between image and title, the aesthetic experience of the audience, and the information intake. The following aspects of visual attention and the viewing experience of film audiences are relevant for the main study:

- *Fixation duration in the title area*: The fixation duration is measured from the first to the last fixation on a subtitle or title. The data evaluation in the pilot study indicated a decreased fixation duration compared to traditional subtitles. The participants seemed to re-read integrated titles less often and were more motivated to quickly return to the focal points in the image.

- *Saccade length*: The length (or duration) of a saccade describes the distance (or time) between one fixation point and the next. As no information is absorbed during saccadic movements, it seems likely that shorter saccades allow for a higher information intake and long saccades for a lower intake. Due to the placement closer to the focal points, integrated titles might induce shorter saccades.[10]

- *Correspondence to natural focus*: To allow for a viewing experience that is as close to that of a native viewer that watches the film without any titles, the gaze behaviour should be as similar as possible and the same main focus points should be fixated.

- *Reaction time*: This term describes the duration from when the subtitle or title fades in until the first fixation by the viewer. If this time is increased considerably by integrated titles, this could be a counterargument for individual placement. As this seems to be the main concern of critics of integrated titles, the reaction times of traditional subtitles and integrated titles should be compared and their difference discussed.

- *Aesthetic experience*: The participants for the integrated titles will be asked to fill in a questionnaire on their aesthetic experience and rate it compared to traditional subtitles.

---

[10]While this measure showed promise, the raw data concerning the saccades turned out to be unreliable and faulty, especially concerning the definition and length of saccades. It seems like proper scripts or finer software are required to analyse this type of data. It was therefore not analysed in this study.

Based on these initially defined aspects, the following hypotheses on integrated titles (IT) and traditional titles (TS) emerged:

Visual attention (based on eye tracking):

- Hypothesis 1: Fixation duration in the title area is shorter for IT than for TS.

- Hypothesis 2: IT participants spend more time fixating (exploring) the image than fixating (reading) the titles, experiencing a positive split attention.

- Hypothesis 3: The focus of the IT participants resembles the natural focus of the native viewers considerably more than the focus of the TS participants.

- Hypothesis 4: The reaction time of the IT participants is higher than that of the TS participants.

Aesthetic experience (based on questionnaire):

- Hypothesis 5: The IT participants experience a higher information intake.

- Hypothesis 6: The integrated titles are rated as more aesthetic.

In this study, these hypotheses are tested and discussed based on the collected eye tracking and questionnaire data. Each recording session started with the participant being introduced to the eye tracking lab and the eye tracker. The participant would then watch the episode without any prior knowledge of the topic or the goal of the experiment. The German native speakers who watched the version with the integrated titles would then fill in a questionnaire designed to cover subjective information flow and aesthetics of the titles.

## 7.5 Main study

Based on the insights gained from the pilot study, the main study tested the developed hypotheses. Based on the skill and rule sets developed in Chapter 3, Chapter 4, and Chapter 5, as well as the eye tracking studies discussed in §6.3.2, the main study consisted of the following steps:

1. Analysis of the image composition, typography, and content of the used film material – includes interview-based data with filmmaker Pablo Romero-Fresco and eye tracking data of participants watching the original film.

2. Translation of the English original subtitles into German.

3. Creation of two sets of titles: Conventional German subtitles following the guidelines and strategies described in §1.2, and German integrated titles based on the adjusted guidelines described in §7.5.3.1.

4. Title design and placement based on the typographic identity of the film (see §2.3) and the rules summaries in §3.5 and §4.3.

5. Data recording through eye tracking of the film with either conventional subtitles or integrated titles and a post-hoc questionnaire.

6. Data evaluation and discussion.

The following chapters will give on overview over the participants of the study, the film material, and the adjustments made to the conventional subtitling guidelines.

## 7.5.1 Participants

All in all, 45 volunteers participated in the experiment. Of these participants, 14 were native speakers of English between the age of 18 and 45 who study at the FTSK Germersheim, Johannes Gutenberg University Mainz, Germany, and watched the original version of the short documentary *Joining the Dots*. As film audiences are usually not homogeneous groups, no other characteristics besides native language and eye sight were determined. Each participant claimed to have normal or corrected-to-normal vision. Thirty-one participants were German native speakers who stated that they rely on German subtitles to understand English films. As using subtitles is a personal decision based on the viewer's self-assessment and not his or her factual knowledge of the foreign language, the actual level of the participants' English was not determined. Of these participants with German as their native language, 15 watched *Joining the Dots* with traditional subtitles in German. The other 16 German participants watched the film with the integrated titles. None of the participants had seen the documentary before.

## 7.5.2 Material

*Joining the Dots* is a short documentary by Pablo Romero-Fresco, screened for the first time in 2012.[11] The documentary shows an interview with Trevor Franklin who went blind at the age of 60. He speaks about his experiences and how he handles the disability. The main topic of the documentary is accessibility for the blind, focusing on television and theatre. In an interview with Pablo Romero-Fresco, the image system, compositions and key elements in the various scenes were defined and possible placements and designs discussed. Due to its documental character, *Joining the Dots* offers a simple image system[12] and clearly structured shot compositions. Frontal shots of the persons being interviewed are predominant (see Figure 7.3) while further scenes introduce important places in Trevor's life such as the theatre or his home. The interview situations and several other rather static scenes (see Figure 7.4) are well suited for integrated titles as the distribution of primary and secondary areas is quite clear and the secondary area offers enough space for the titles. Due to their rather static character, there is no immense risk of important elements moving behind the titles.

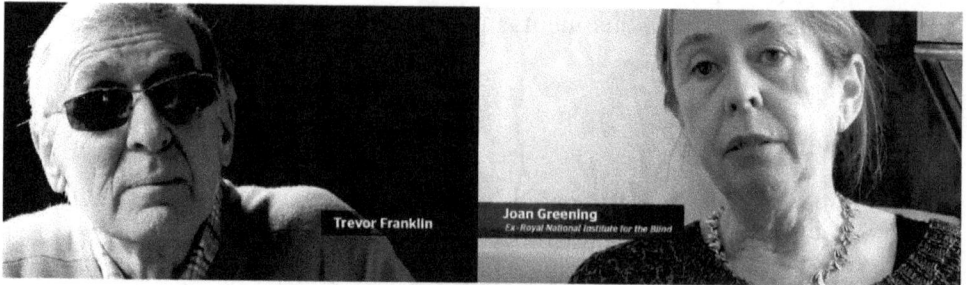

Figure 7.3: Frontal shots of the interviewees in *Joining the Dots* (00:00:52, 00:03:30)

The distribution of primary and secondary areas is based on the image composition, some technical aspects and the resulting focal points in the image. According to Mercado, "focal points refer to the center of interest in a composition, the area where the viewer's gaze will gravitate to because of the arrangement of

---

[11]For further information on *Joining the Dots*, see http://www.jostrans.org/issue20/int_romero. php [2014–10–28].

[12]For a definition of "image system" see Mercado (2010: 21): "[...] refers to the use of recurrent images and compositions in a film to add layers of meaning to a narrative. ... Because the experience of watching a film relies so much on the use of images ([...]), most films have an image system at work at some level, whether the filmmaker intends to have one or not." It is important to distinguish between the image system of a film and the individual "shot compositions" (2010: 21) of a scene.

Figure 7.4: Static scenes with evenly balanced primary and secondary areas (*Joining the Dots*, 00:01:07 and 00:01:12)

all the visual elements in the frame" (2010: 11). Thus, the combination of several technical aspects such as the used lenses that define the sharp areas in the image automatically attracts the viewer's gaze to where the director wants it to be (see §3.3 on Film Studies). These are seen as primary areas and should not be covered by titles. Other concepts that can help to define primary and secondary areas and "isolate the subject within the frame" (2010: 35) are the "rule of thirds" (2010: 7), "Hitchcock's rule" (2010: 7), "balanced/unbalanced compositions" and the overall "visual weight" (2010: 8) of elements in the shot composition. The eye tracking recordings with the English native speakers confirmed these assumptions and allowed for the distribution based on the eye tracking data. Figure 7.5 shows a heat map of the focus points of the English native participants and the corresponding definition of the primary and secondary areas.

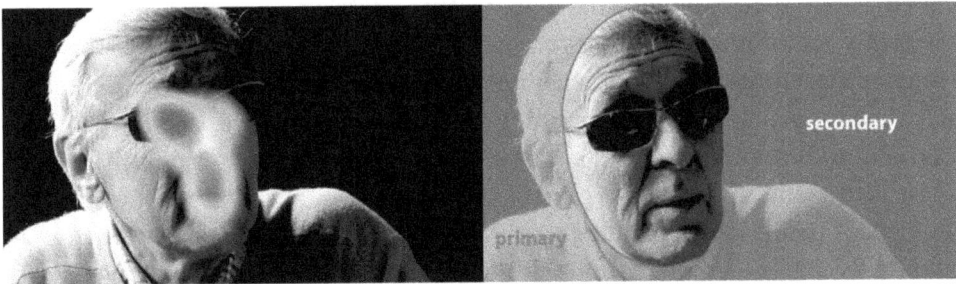

Figure 7.5: Fixation points of English natives (left) and resulting primary/secondary areas (*Joining the Dots*, 00:00:48)

Aside from these rather static image compositions, *Joining the Dots* includes some more repetitive concepts. Images with mainly blurred or fast moving elements underline the interviewee's statements, for example as Trevor speaks about the progressing loss of his sight (see Figure 7.6).

Figure 7.6: Scenes that support the overall atmosphere in *Joining the Dots* (00:00:42, 00:01:20)

The German subtitles were created according to the traditional guidelines described in §1.2. The integrated titles consisted of the same translation but were modified according to the discussions in the previous chapters.

### 7.5.3 Adjustments to the conventional subtitles

Adjustments were made regarding the conventional guidelines for subtitling, the placement of the titles, and the layout of the titles. These adjustments are presented in the following sections.

#### 7.5.3.1 Guidelines

For the integrated titles for *Joining the Dots*, the conventional guidelines presented in §1.2 were modified. The ellipses (three dots) were omitted at the end respectively beginning of sentences connecting over multiple titles due to the clear sentence structures in the documentary and the audiovisual information channels. As the participants in this study form a hearing audience, the film provides sufficient information whether a sentence was completed yet or not. Instead, ellipses at the end of a title were used to indicate hesitation or an uncompleted sentence. Commas at the end of a title were left out as the pause between two consecutive titles in combination with the auditive information was deemed sufficient. As spoken content of different speakers is not displayed in the same title in integrated titles, dashes as indication of dialogue are omitted as well – the individual positions of the titles as well as the audiovisual information should allow an identification of the speakers. Depending on the image composition and available contrast option, long one-liners and shorter two-line titles alternate. The shorter two-line titles, however, are usually more suitable due to their smaller horizontal space requirements. Furthermore, the need for italics to indicate "distant voices" (Leißner 2009: 34, author's translation; see also §1.2) was questioned, as image and plot allow an easy speaker identification for the most part of the documentary. Therefore, no italics were used to indicate a speaker outside the frame. Even though this version of *Joining the Dots* is intended for a hearing audience and the modifications are based on the assumption that the audience can connect the visible with the audible content, adjustments such as the individual placement might already provide additional information for the hearing-impaired. For a more accessible translation, useful visual elements would have to be re-evaluated and adjusted to the requirements of the respective target group.

### 7.5.3.2 Placement

As the interviews are the main element of the documentary, it was decided not to place each title individually but to rather define consistent areas for the three interviewees. Therefore, Trevor's titles are displayed in the right half of the image as he tends to look to the right. The titles for Joan Greening and Mags Silbery are displayed on the left half as they tend to look to the left. These positions were also supported by the positions of the captions with their names (see Figure 7.3) and the secondary areas in the corresponding shot compositions. For dialogues with two visible speakers in the image, the title positions would also indicate speaking direction, if possible (see Figure 7.7). Overall, all titles were place as close as possible to the main focus point in the respective scene to create small saccades between the fixations of title and image. Relevant image areas or elements were not to be covered by titles.

Figure 7.8 illustrates how the secondary areas usually allowed for a sufficient contrast. Keeping the variety of title positions to a minimum, even if the shot composition changes noticeably, might allow for more accessible adjustment, for instance for a hearing-impaired or deaf audience. For such an audience, with a possibly greater need for additional visual information, speaker-related positions allow for faster identification of the speaker, even if he or she is not visible on the screen. Colour is another possibility to make identification easier, even though it is not always easy to come up with a suitable colour concept for a film that works throughout the whole story.

Figure 7.7: Indication of speaking direction in *Joining the Dots* (00:06:01)

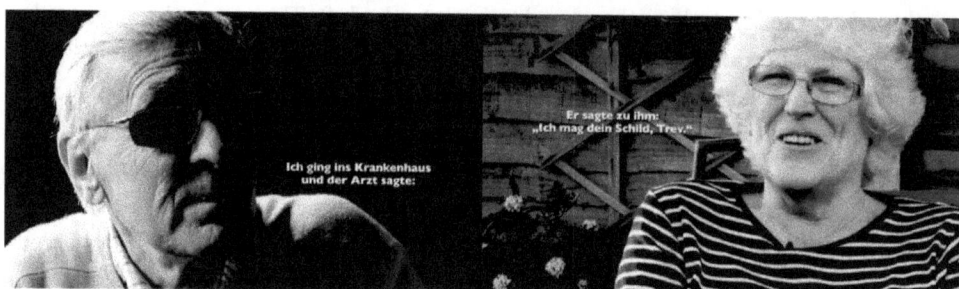

Figure 7.8: Roughly defined areas for Trevor (to the right of the speaker) and Mags (to the left of the speaker) in *Joining the Dots* (00:00:54, 00:09:40)

### 7.5.3.3 Typography

The original version of *Joining the Dots* uses two typefaces: Today's MS Office standard typeface *Calibri*[13] to display names (see Figure 7.3) and *Slab Serif*[14] for the film title, creating a simple but noticeable tone (see §2.3 on typographic film identity). The closing credits are a mixture of both typefaces. The title design

---

[13]For further information on the typeface *Calibri*, see http://www.lucasfonts.com/case-studies/calibri-consolas/ [2014–12–29].

[14]For further information on the typeface *Slab Serif*, see http://www.linotype.com/3493/introduction.html [2014–12–29].

for *Joining the Dots* was based on a detailed interview with the director Pablo Romero-Fresco and the analysis of the existing examples of integrated titles and creative solutions (see Chapter 4). After various typographic tests with typefaces and spatial effects, the typeface *Gill Sans* was chosen for the titles. The typeface was not only chosen for its appearance but also for the graphic designer behind it: Eric Gill,[15] an important English sculptor, typographer and graphic designer. The very British elements and characteristics of the documentary should also be visible in the typeface, and as "Gill Sans [is] part of the British visual heritage just like the Union Jack and the safety pin" (Archer 2007), it met this criterion. Besides the historic reference to the United Kingdom, *Gill Sans Bold* is suitable as a screen typeface due to its high legibility – the bold style's higher stroke weight ensures a good contrast and the clear design is unlikely to distract from the content. The film title itself was not to be replaced during translation but rather to be accompanied by an additional title. To underline the individuality of the project but also the manual translation act – a little reminder of the fact that a translator was at work and, at least for this project, even part of the film production –, the handwritten typeface *Dakota*[16] was chosen (see Figure 7.9).

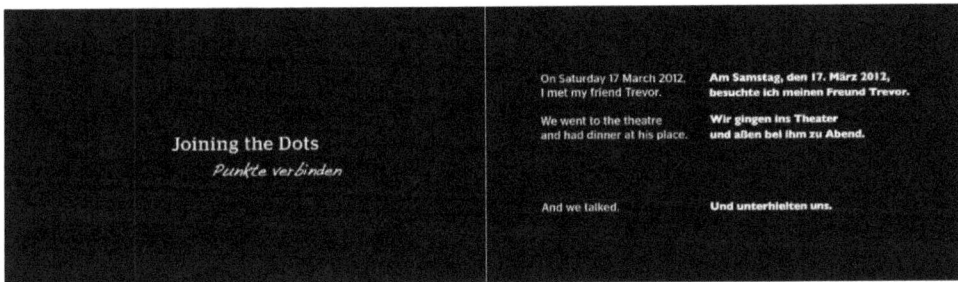

Figure 7.9: The typefaces *Dakota* (left) and *Gill Sans Bold* (right) were chosen based on the analysis of the existing typographic identity of the film (*Joining the Dots*, 00:00:10)

In addition to these layout decisions, a small number of effects were used to support the film's atmosphere and tone. Slower fade in and fade outs were used to illustrate hesitation, unfinished sentences (slow fade out at the end), and sadness. If a speaker would move minimally through the title area, a depth effect was used, meaning the speaker would partially cover the title (see Figure 7.10).

Finally, transparency was used to indicate the volume of speech (100 % transparency being normal volume and less transparency illustrating lower volume)

---

[15]For further information on Eric Gill, see http://www.ericgill.org.uk/Gill/ [2014–12–05].

[16]For further information on the typeface *Dakota*, see https://www.vletter.com/downloads/dakota-font-download-free.html [014–12–17].

Figure 7.10: Depth effect after the title was displayed for a sufficiently long time (*Joining the Dots*, 00:04:30)

or lessen a too strong contrast with the background of the title that would make the titles be more dominant than the rest of the image.

## 7.6 Summary

This chapter provided an overview over the pilot study, the resulting hypotheses, and the main study. This includes the experiment setup, participants, and used film material. Several adjustments were made to the traditional subtitles in order to create the set of integrated titles for *Joining the Dots*. Using a Tobii TX300 eye tracker, the eye movements of 45 participants were recorded watching the English short documentary *Joining the Dots* in three conditions: original (unsubtitled), subtitled, and with integrated titles. Of these participants, 14 were English native participants watching the original and 31 were German participants dependent on translation watching the film with either traditional subtitles (15 participants) or integrated titles (16 participants). The integrated titles follow a distinct set of rules concerning layout and placement, and the 16 participants watching the film with integrated titles were asked to fill in a post-hoc questionnaire on their information intake and aesthetic experience. The results of both the eye tracking recordings and the questionnaire data are presented in the following chapter.

# 8 Results and discussion

This chapter presents the statistical results from the eye tracking recordings and the post-hoc questionnaires, and goes further in discussing them regarding the previously established hypotheses. The hypotheses on visual attention were tested by analysing the eye movements of the 45 participants to determine whether integrated titles result in shorter reading time (fixation duration on the titles), more attention on the image than the title area, and a gaze behaviour more equivalent to the natural focus points of the English native speakers. Another focus was the impact of the individual placement on reaction times (time to first fixation). In the following summary of the results, "OV" is used to describe the original version the English-speaking participants watched. The traditionally subtitled version is abbreviated to "TS" (traditional subtitles) and the version with integrated titles to "IT" (integrated titles).

## 8.1 Fixation-based data

Based on the pilot study, it was assumed that by individually adjusting the formatting of a title, its font and placement, the fixation time per title would decrease compared to the traditional counterparts. These adjustments allow for faster processing (e.g. by creating a stronger contrast), and the placement closer to the natural focus motivates the audience to return to exploring the image faster.

The following statistical data is based on the eye movement recordings of the 45 participants (14 English natives and 31 German natives) of the three film versions (original, subtitled, integrated titles). The subtitled version was created with *Subtitle Workshop* and the version with integrated titles was created in *Premiere Pro*. The film version with the traditional subtitles included 132 subtitles and the version with the integrated titles included 152 titles (as dialogues, pauses, and hesitation were taken into account and corresponding titles split into several). Each scene containing a title received one AOI around the title and one AOI around the image (excluding the black frame around the film). Including film title and prologue texts, this resulted in 271 AOIs for the TS condition and 312 AOIs for the IT condition. These AOIs were each drawn by hand and the timing adjusted to perfectly reflect the display duration of each title (between one and six seconds). Additionally, 23 clusters were created for ten scenes with titles. The corresponding heat maps, clusters, and gaze plots were exported for each scene of each of the three conditions of the film containing text, amounting to 416 visualisations of eye movement data each. Based on the AOIs, a number of measures could be extracted from the data and analysed based on the previously stated hypotheses.

### 8.1.1 Hypothesis 1 – Fixation duration

*"Fixation duration in the title area is shorter for IT than for TS."*

The first hypothesis states that the integrated titles have an effect on the fixation duration on the title, i.e. fixation duration will be shorter, reflecting an easier information extraction (Jacob & Karn 2003: 585; McCarthy et al. 2003: 409; cf. Fitts et al. 1950; see Chapter 6.4). The reading times of the participants were calculated by measuring the durations of the fixations and saccades in the area of the title – expressed in the average total visit duration. The reading time for each subtitle by each of the 15 German participants in the second group (in the following referred to as "TS participants") and for each title by each of the 16 German participants in the third group (the "IT participants") was recorded. As the Shapiro-Wilk test showed a deviation from a normal distribution, the two data sets – the reading times of the TS participants and the IT participants – were compared using the Wilcoxon test: $W = 1675877$, $p < 0.001$. As the error probability p is clearly below the tolerable 5 % (0.05), there is a significant difference between the two data sets. The following mean (m) and standard deviation (sd) values were calculated:

$m(\text{total\_visit\_duration\_iT}) = 1.570$ s $\quad m(\text{total\_visit\_duration\_tU}) = 1.835$ s
$sd(\text{total\_visit\_duration\_iT}) = 1.069$ s $\quad sd(\text{total\_visit\_duration\_tU}) = 1.159$ s

The difference between the two mean values is about 265 ms – a significant reduction of 14.4 % of the reading time for integrated titles compared to the average reading time for traditional subtitles (see Figure 8.1). Therefore, the participants seemed to have less difficulty extracting information from the integrated titles, possibly due to the more considerate placement and proximity to the main focus points.

To give an impression of the underlying data, the mean values of the TVD (total visit duration) per title are illustrated in Figure 8.2 for the first 30 subtitles and titles.

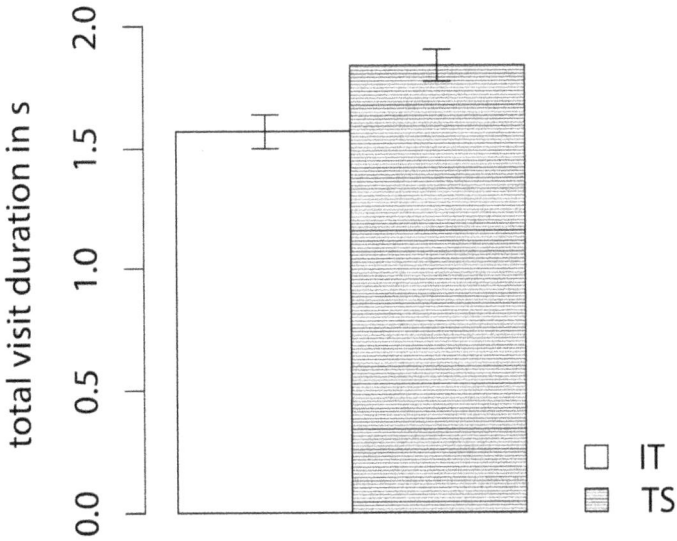

Figure 8.1: Comparison of the average total visit duration (s) of the IT and TS participants

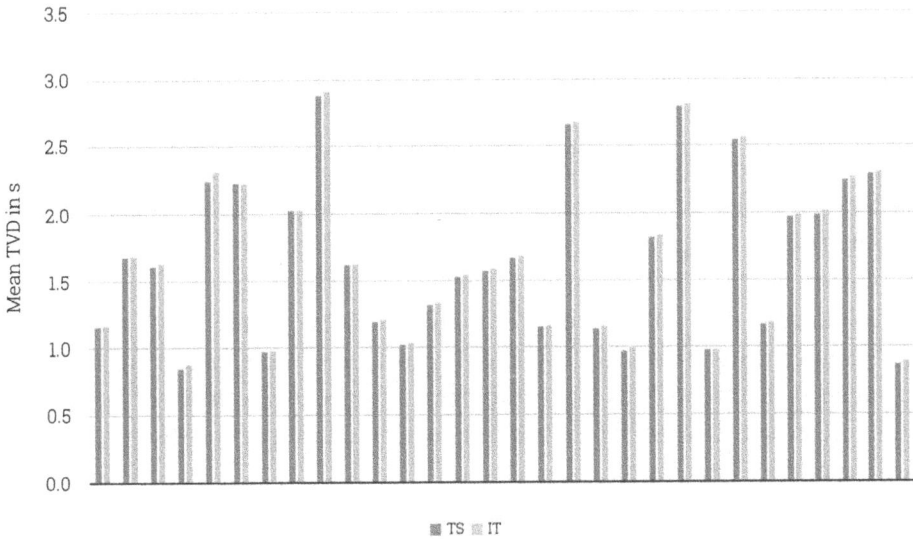

Figure 8.2: Sample of the mean TVD per title

## 8.1.2 Hypothesis 2 – Split attention

*"IT participants spend more time fixating (exploring) the image than fixating (reading) the titles, experiencing a positive split attention."*

As visible from the results concerning the first hypothesis, the IT participants spent less time focusing the titles compared to the TS participants. Based on this assumption, the second hypothesis states that the participants with integrated titles spend more time exploring the image than looking at the title. This measurement of visual attention was defined as split attention between image and title area. To test this hypothesis, the average total visit duration (TVD) of both the entire image and the title area during the stimulus, meaning the time between the title fading in and out, was measured. For all four data sets (TVD of the image TS/IT and TVD of the title area TS/IT), the Shapiro-Wilk test showed a deviation from normal data distribution. The Wilcoxon test then showed significant differences between the corresponding data sets:

(1)  wilcox.test(TVD_IT_IMAGE, TVD_IT_TITLE):  W = 4400522, p < 0.001
     wilcox.test(TVD_TS_IMAGE, TVD_TS_TITLE):  W = 2769346, p < 0.001
     wilcox.test(TVD_TS_IMAGE, TVD_IT_IMAGE):  W = 2616334, p < 0.001
     wilcox.test(TVD_TS_TITLE, TVD_IT_TITLE):  W = 2217703, p < 0.001

m(TVD_IT_IMAGE) = 3.306 s    m(TVD_IT_TITLE) = 1.570 s
m(TVD_TS_IMAGE) = 3.555 s[1]  m(TVD_TS_TITLE) = 1.835 s

The results show that on average the TS participants focused on the subtitle area for 51.6 % of the title display duration, on average 1.835 s of 3.555 s. For integrated titles, the participants focused on the title area for around 47.5 % of the time (on average 1.57 s of 3.306 s; see Figure 8.3).

This indicates that integrated titles motivate the audience to return to the actual focal point in the image faster and spend more time exploring the image while the title is visible. This is also supported by the low number of participants who fixated the title area before the title was faded in (see the discussion of the fourth hypothesis in §8.1.4).

---

[1] The duration of the average TVD on the image differs between the two conditions because some participants would leave the image AOI, e.g. looking away from the screen or the video that was surrounded by a black frame.

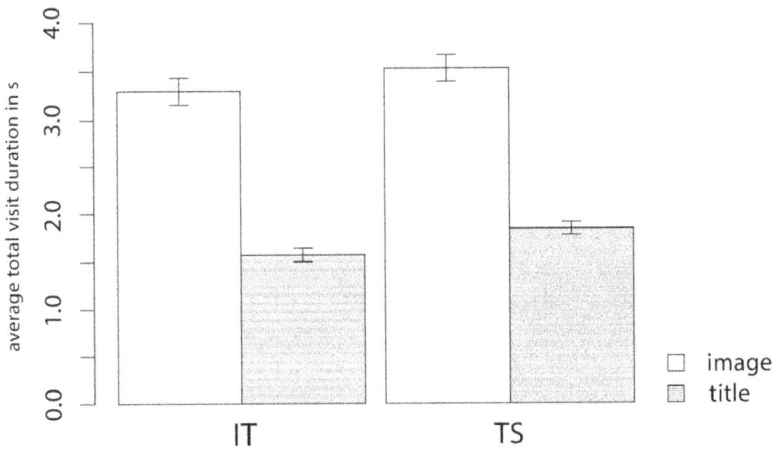

Figure 8.3: Comparison of split attention in IT and TS participants

### 8.1.3 Hypothesis 3 – Natural focus

*"The focus of the IT participants resembles the natural focus of the native viewers considerably more than the focus of the TS participants."*

The third hypothesis states that IT participants are more likely to display a more natural gaze behaviour, based on the natural focus points of the English participants, than the TS participants. The hypothesis was tested by means of a random sample of ten titles and the therein defined 23 relevant areas of attention. These areas were defined through automatically generated cluster area and the gaze behaviour of the TS and IT participants was compared to that of the 14 English native speakers. The automatically generated clusters, areas of accumulated fixations created by *Tobii Studio*, were defined as the natural focus points if more than 50 % of the participants fixated it at least once (see Figure 8.4).

These clusters were created for ten random scenes[2] and considered only when they were fixated by at least half of the corresponding participant group. Four clusters were not evaluated as they could not be interpreted clearly (marked in red in the following table) while 23 clusters were evaluated (see Table 8.1). During this sample, the natural focus points – the clusters which at least 50 % of participants viewed – were fixated by an average 87.87 % of the OV participants. Clusters at the same spot or very close were fixated by an average 75.3 % of the

---

[2]Excluding scenes in which a subtitle (TS) was divided into several titles (IT) and scenes that consisted exclusively of a title in front of a black background. The first few scenes only consisted of the film title and prologue and were therefore skipped.

Figure 8.4: Comparison of the automatically created clusters OV/TS/IT (*Joining the Dots*, UK 2012)

TS participants and 83.3 % of the IT participants. Thus, the integrated titles increased the mean number of participants that fixated the natural focus points of the English natives by 10.6 %. Additionally, the sample showed that, on average, 88.1 % of the TS participants fixated the subtitle while about 98.2 % of the IT participants fixated the integrated titles – an increase of 11.5 %.

At the first glance, however, five elements show a higher fixation percentage of the TS participants than the IT participants. These five entries (014–1, 024–1, 044–2, 094–1, and 094–2) take place in four scenes. In Scene 014, the reason is easy to find: The subtitle is much closer to the relevant element and the integrated titled, even though being placed with more consideration of the image composition, is just too far away (see Figure 8.5).

Table 8.1: Overview of the fixation percentages of the analysed cluster areas

| Cluster | Fixated Element / Area | OV | TS | IT |
|---------|------------------------|-----|-----|-----|
| 014–1 | Finger tips on white cane | 100 % | 93 % | 88 % |
| 014–2 | Sub(title) | NA[a] | 80 % | 100 % |
| 024–1 | Heads | 100 % | 100 % | 94 % |
| 024–2 | Sub(title) | NA | 87 % | 100 % |
| 034–1 | Eye/face left | 100 % | 73 % | 75 % |
| 034–2 | Eye right | 71 % | unclear | 38 % |
| 034–3 | Sub(title) | NA | 100 % | 100 % |
| 044–1 | Head left | 100 % | 80 % | 94 % |
| 044–2 | Heads right | 64 % | 93 % | 69 % |
| 044–3 | Sub(title) | NA | 100 % | 100 % |
| 054–1 | Face | 100 % | 80 % | 100 % |
| 054–2 | Sub(title) | NA | 80 % | 100 % |
| 064–1 | Eyes | 93 % | 87 % | 100 % |
| 064–2 | Mouth | 50 % | 53 % | 100 % |
| 064–3 | Sub(title) | NA | 80 % | 94 % |
| 076–1 | Face | 100 % | 87 % | 100 % |
| 076–2 | Sub(title) | NA | 87 % | 100 % |
| 084–1 | Stage right | 100 % | unclear | 56 % |
| 084–2 | Stage left | 79 % | unclear | unclear |
| 084–3 | Sub(title) | NA | 87 % | 100 % |
| 094–1 | Hands | 100 % | 93 % | 69 % |
| 094–2 | Face right | 100 % | 53 % | 44 % |
| 094–3 | Sub(title) | NA | 87 % | 94 % |
| 104–1 | Trevor's face | 64 % | 47 % | 75 % |
| 104–2 | Sheep head | 79 % | 47 % | unclear |
| 104–3 | Hands | 71 % | 40 % | 75 % |
| 104–4 | Sub(title) | NA | 93 % | 94 % |

[a]As the original version does not include any subtitles, there are no reportable values for the OV version.

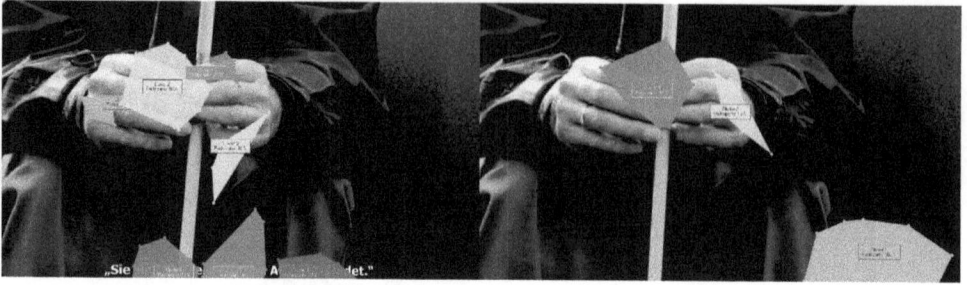

Figure 8.5: Comparison of the automatic clusters in Scene 014 (TS on the left, IT on the right)

Despite this suboptimal placement of the integrated title, the average combined attention percentage of title and element is still higher for the IT participants (94 % for IT and 86.5 % for TS). The same goes for the combined average attention percentage in Scene 024 (97 % for IT and 93.5 % for TS). For Scene 044, the reason for the lower attention percentage is quite elusive (81.5 % combined average attention for all three elements for IT and 86.5 % for TS) as the titles are in almost identical positions. Based on the low amount of integrated titles and subtitles in general placed in the top area of the image (see Chapter 4), the differences in Scene 094 could have been caused by the position being too unexpected for the viewers (see Figure 8.6).

Figure 8.6: Comparison of the automatic clusters in Scene 094 (TS on the left, IT on the right)

This shows that there is still plenty of room for improvement concerning the placement of integrated titles and further research could, for example, look at the effects of horizontal and vertical displacement compared to the traditional subtitle position.

All in all, a higher percentage of the IT participants in this random sample focused both on the natural focus points of the OV participants and the displayed titles. This indicates that integrated titles allow for a more natural focus for the audience and at the same time seem to motivate the viewer to fixate a higher percentage of the titles and extract information both faster and more effectively.

### 8.1.4 Hypothesis 4 – Reaction time

*"The reaction time of the IT participants is higher than that of the TS participants."*

The hypothesis of integrated titles increasing the reaction time is based on the assumption that an audience that is used to subtitles has already learned to switch focus to the bottom area as soon as someone in the film starts speaking. For integrated titles, one can assume that the title area is not focused until the fade-in effect initiates the eye movement (cf. "involuntary attention", Prinzmetal et al. 2005: 74). To test this hypothesis, AOIs were defined for each subtitle and title. They allow measurements of the reaction time, meaning the duration between when the title fades in and the first fixation in the corresponding AOI ("time to first fixation", TFF). The data of the 15 TS and the 16 IT participants were compared and, as the Shapiro-Wilk test was significant for both data sets, the Wilcoxon test was applied: $W = 2281026$, $p < 0.001$. The reaction time of the IT participants (74 ms) was on average 28.9 % higher (17 ms) than for the TS participants (57 ms, see Figure 8.7).

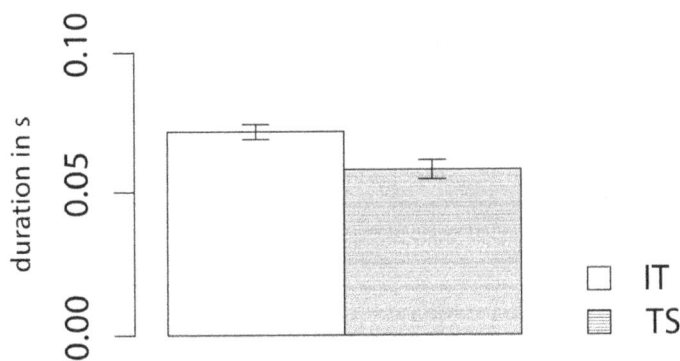

Figure 8.7: Mean reaction time

Due to the very short time frame in which the titles are visible, the difference in the TVD and split attention seemed quite small. Therefore, the explorative behaviour right before the stimulus should be examined in addition to the reaction times. A reaction time of 0 means that a participant had already focused on the area before the title was displayed. This value would be expected to only occur rarely, e.g. between consecutive titles containing long sentences.

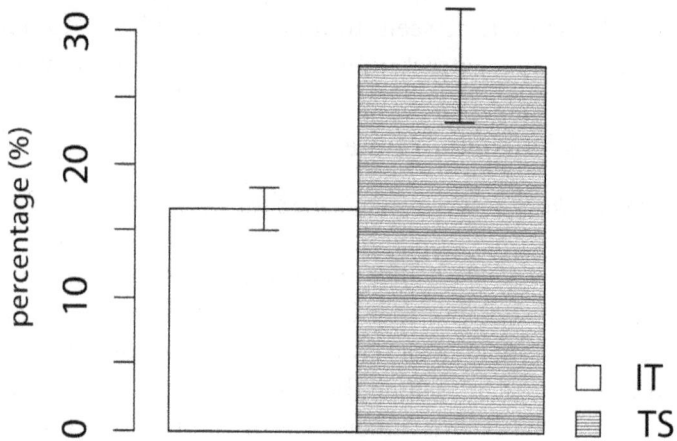

Figure 8.8: Average percentage of 0 values of TS and IT participants in TFF

Figure 8.8 shows the average percentage of 0 values in the TFF per participant per group. For each IT participants, the value 0 occurred on average 23.1 times and 33.4 times for each TS participants; this corresponds to 16.5 % of all reaction times for the IT participants and about 27.5 % for the TS participants. Therefore, the TS participants focused on the title area before the stimulus significantly more often while the IT participants remained focused on the image for a longer time. Omitting the 0 values, the increase of the reaction time was about 25.9 % (instead of 28.9 %) – from 69 ms for TS participants to 87 ms for the IT participants (see Figure 8.9).

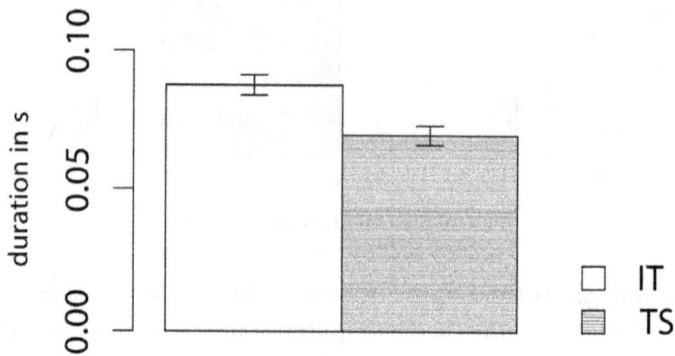

Figure 8.9: Mean reaction time without the 0 values

An increased reaction time, however, cannot strictly be interpreted as a negative effect: While a shorter reaction time might be associated with less cognitive load for the viewer or a higher level of stress, a longer reaction time might also be synonymous with the longer image exploration demonstrated by the IT participants or an overall more relaxed viewing.

## 8.2 Questionnaire data – Hypotheses 5 and 6

In addition to recording the eye movements and analysing the attention and re-action of the participants, a questionnaire on the aesthetic experience was also part of the study. As eye movements cannot tell us very much about the subjective feelings of a participant, all participants with integrated titles were asked to rank several statements after watching *Joining the Dots*.[3]

The questionnaire was divided into a general part with statements on information intake and a second part focusing on the aesthetic experience. The participants could rank the statements on a scale from 1 ("agree strongly") to 4 ("disagree strongly"), as illustrated in Figure 8.10:

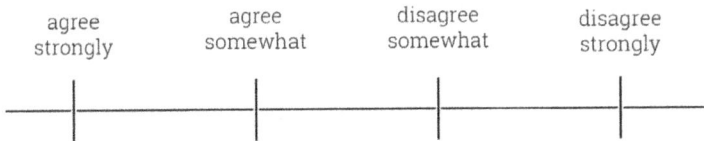

Figure 8.10: Four-point semantic differential Likert scale

Due to the even number of statements, the participants are forced to make a basic decision. For a clearer presentation of the results, the first and second ranks are interpreted as "agreement" and the third and fourth rank as "disagreement". All 16 participants with integrated titles rated all statements anonymously. The following statements[4] were to be rated:

---

[3]The questionnaire was designed following the recommendations on http://www.wpgs.de/content/blogcategory/87/355/ [2015–01–06, in German].

[4]It cannot be ruled out that a less positive wording of the statements would have influenced the overall agreement.

1. I could easily read all integrated titles.

2. I received all necessary information through the integrated titles.

3. I would like to watch an entire film with integrated titles.

4. I would prefer integrated titles to traditional subtitles.

5. I could spend more time exploring the image compared to traditional titles.

6. Due to the integrated titles, I was aware of more details in the image.

7. The integrated titles did not cover important elements in the image.

8. The integrated titles distracted me less from the image compared to traditional subtitles.

Figure 8.11 shows that more than half of the participants agreed or completely agreed with the statements. While still scoring more than 80 % agreement, statement 6 on improved detail perception was agreed with the least. In addition to the statements, the participants were asked to rate their aesthetic experience ("How would you rank your overall aesthetic experience with the integrated titles?").

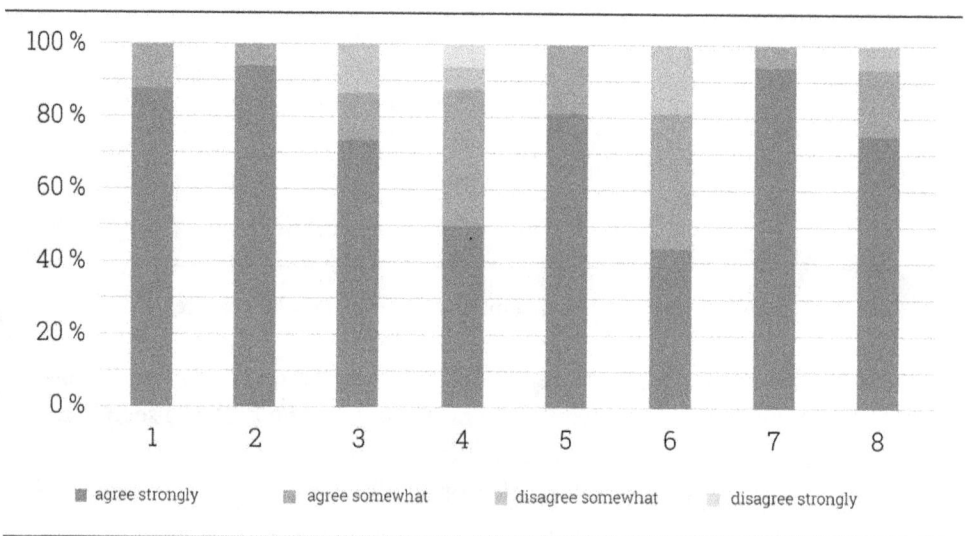

Figure 8.11: Agreement of the participants towards the statements

Concerning the fifth hypothesis on the higher information intake (*"The IT participants experience a higher information intake."*), two groups of the statements should be considered. The first group of statements shows that the integrated titles did not, from the participant's point of view, decrease the information intake (statements 1, 2, and 7), the second group indicates easier or possibly increased information extraction (statements 5 and 6). Table 8.2 gives a more detailed overview of these statements and shows that, except for the statement on participants being able to perceive more details, participants agreed strongly, confirming the hypothesis. Even though the cluster analysis in the previous chapter indicates that the IT participants exhibited a focus closer to the natural focus of the English native speakers and therefore being more likely to perceive more relevant details in the image, the participants did not have this impression and accordingly rated this statement less enthusiastically.

Table 8.2: Agreement to statements indicating a higher information intake

| Statement | Agree strongly | Agree somewhat | Disagree somewhat | Disagree strongly |
|---|---|---|---|---|
| 1: could read all titles | 14 | 2 | - | - |
| 2: all necessary information received | 15 | 1 | - | - |
| 5: more time for image exploration | 13 | 3 | - | - |
| 6: more details perceived | 7 | 6 | 3 | - |
| 8: no coverage of relevant areas | 15 | 1 | - | - |

Additionally, the participants were asked whether they generally prefer subtitling (8 participants) or dubbing (8 participants). Those who chose dubbing were asked to rate how likely they would prefer integrated titles to dubbing (see Figure 8.12). Half of the participants rated it rather likely and the other half rather unlikely. Combined with the fourth statement on preferring IT over TS, 87.5 % of the participants would prefer integrated titles over traditional subtitles and 50 % of those in favour of dubbing would also switch to integrated titles if given the possibility.

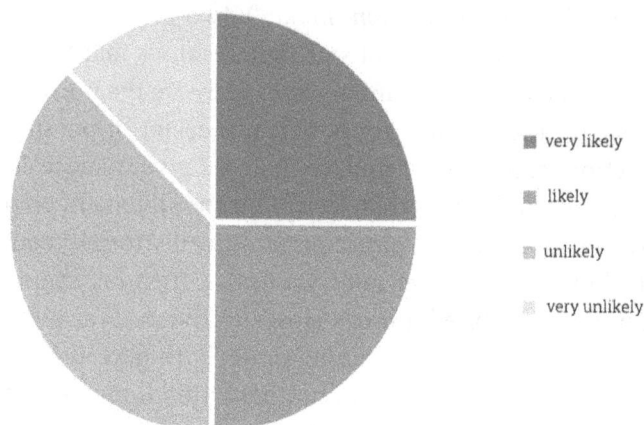

Figure 8.12: Likelihood of participants choosing integrated titles over dubbing

Finally, the participants were asked to rate their overall aesthetic experience with integrated titles compared to traditional subtitles. Nine out of the 16 participants ranked it 'very good', seven rated it as 'good'. None of the participants ranked it 'satisfactory' or 'unsatisfactory'. This confirms the sixth hypothesis (*"The integrated titles are rated as more aesthetic."*).

All in all, the hypotheses on the aesthetic experience and information intake stated an increase for both aspects for the IT participants. The evaluation of the questionnaires resulted in an overall positive rating of their aesthetic experience by the German participants – especially when the integrated titles were compared to traditional subtitles. This positive feedback supports the hypothesis that differences in design and placement of titles are perceived by the audience, and considerate placement can have positive impact on the reception and information gain. Half of the participants who normally prefer dubbing, however, did not seem to see a possible alternative in the integrated titles. Participants used to traditional subtitles on the other hand rated integrated titles as an improvement and a feasible alternative they would like to use in the future.

## 8.3 Summary

This chapter gave an overview of the results of the eye tracking study and the questionnaire handed out to the IT participants. All eye tracking results were significant and the questionnaire data yielded a useful insight into the subjective information gain and aesthetic experience of the participants. As stated in the first hypothesis, the fixation duration decreased by 14.4 % for integrated titles compared to traditional subtitles. At the same time, the second hypothesis was confirmed as the viewers of integrated titles spend more time exploring the image. Additionally, the IT participants exhibited a focus more similar to that of the OV participants, as stated in the third hypothesis. Here, small shortcomings of the integrated titles were easily revealed through a direct comparison to the traditional subtitles while still being overall more efficient. As presumed, the reaction time from title display to first fixation in the title area increased on average by about 25.9 % or 69 ms.

The analysis of the questionnaire data revealed that the majority of the participants enjoyed the integrated titles and, compared to their experiences with traditional subtitles, perceived a higher information intake and increased entertainment value.

# 9 Conclusion

The empirical study and results reported in the previous chapter provide answers to the questions developed throughout the thesis. In this concluding chapter, the theoretical foundations for the study, the results of the eye tracking recordings and the questionnaire, the proposed set of basic placement strategies, and the proposed workflow are revisited. The limitations of the study are discussed and follow-up studies and topics for future research suggested.

## 9.1 Summary

First of all, an overview of audiovisual translation with a focus in subtitling was given. The various kinds of subtitles were introduced and common challenges and shortcomings discussed – such as the paradox of aiming for invisibility. This includes the need for viewers to split their visual attention between the processing of the image and reading the titles as well as other challenges. Conventional guidelines and traditional solutions for subtitles helped to define the gap integrated titles might be able to fill. Most of these guidelines handle time and space constraints and content translation. Problems with contrast, collisions with other text elements or relevant image areas, as well as interference with the overall image composition seem to be widely accepted as unpleasant, but unavoidable features of subtitles (Chapter 2).

In a holistic approach, all kinds of text elements that can occur in films were analysed and discussed in order to define what graphical translation strategies are already used and what could be applied in integrated titles. Out of a corpus of 100 recent and influential films, 52 were analysed to give an overview of graphical translation strategies and their frequency. Additionally, typographic identity was introduced as an overall concept emerging from the combination of the used typefaces, colours, and effects throughout a film. As subtitling proved to be the main strategy in translating text elements such as captions and displays, it has to be taken into account that this translation strategy can cause interferences with the shot composition, the typographic identity of the film, the focus of the audience, and – in the worst case – collisions with other relevant text elements or image areas (§2.6).

In search of an alternative subtitling concept that can avoid, or at least decrease these negative effects, more adaptive concepts were presented. Some guidelines for SDH seem already quite thoughtful, including colour-coded speaker identification and sometimes horizontal displacement. Terms such as "abusive subtitles" (Nornes 1999), "hybrid subtitles" (Díaz Cintas & Muñoz Sánchez 2006), "speaker-following subtitles" (Park et al. 2008), "aesthetic subtitles" (Foerster 2010), "creative subtitles" (McClarty 2012), and "dynamic subtitles" (Armstrong & Brooks 2014) show the wide range of possible alternative concepts and approaches. It was decided to used the term "integrated titles" in order to include all these concepts, but also hint on the main focus to 'integrate' the titles into the film's image concept and layout.

As the creation of the integrated titles should not be purely based on translation studies, film studies, communication design, usability studies, and computer sciences were included. Film studies offer a basis on image composition and story telling, communication design helps to define aesthetics and creativity, usability studies offer knowledge on user experience and interface design, and computer sciences can help with automation and software design. This combination of fields of study led to the creation of a set of required skills (basically the understandment of filmmaker's intentions and the layout and design of a film), and desirable characteristics of good integrated titles – intuitiveness, usefulness, and satisfaction. While the design and typographic identity of titles can be quite individual depending on the film, consistency is demanded in all mentioned characteristics. Therefore, the placement strategies should be consistent and comprehensible (Chapter 3).

To form a basis for the placement strategies for integrated titles, two groups of commercially used integrated titles in films were analysed: Titles for the hearing-impaired audience with only horizontal variation ('partially integrated titles'), and integrated titles targeted mainly at hearing audiences with the subcategories 'partial translation' and 'complete translation'. The overview on the origins of the various integrated titles showed that the interference of professionals from the film business without any background in translation and subtitling brought this new course, and the analysis of the frequency of placement strategies and shortcomings demonstrated that the positions differ much less between films than suspected: noise transcriptions are placed below their source or indicate a source's position outside the frame. The same goes for a combined title of noise transcription and dialogue. Titles for off-screen speakers are placed below a focus or focal point, next to it or in indication of speaking direction. One or more speakers offer placements below or next to the speaker, in speaking direction and below or next to the focus in the image. *John Wick* was the only film where the integrated titles were recreated with the same positions and layout – in all other films, the titles were either deleted in the German image track, replaced by conventional subtitles, or accompanied by additional subtitles. While they exhibited a few incidents of unintended simultaneity, made at times use of the weak top-centre position, collided with other relevant elements or areas, and were sometimes placed too far from the main focus, the main shortcoming was inconsistency (Chapter 4).

Based on this theoretical framework and the two major analyses, the first workflow for the creation of integrated titles and a set of basic placement strategies were developed and presented. It combines on one side the translation process, including corrections and changes throughout the whole process, and on the other side the steps required for the creation of integrated titles: the analysis of the overall image concept and intention of the film, the operationalisation of placement and layout strategies, and the final application (Chapter 5).

As the main study makes use of eye tracking, an overview of relevant eye movements and functions was given as well as recent eye tracking research in general, on reading behavior, and subtitling. A number of studies were presented that influenced the design of the present study and the phrasing of the research questions (Chapter 6).

Based on the experiences gained from the pilot study in 2012, the main study made use of a Tobii TX300 eye tracker and Adobe Premiere Pro was used to create the integrated titles. The first step was to analyse the film – this included an interview with the filmmaker, Pablo Romero-Fresco. The film was then translated into German and both traditional subtitles and the integrated titles were created, including layout and placement. Of the 45 participants, 31 were German native speakers and 14 English native speakers. The English native speakers watched the original version of the film material *Joining the Dots*, providing information on the undistracted natural focus without subtitles. This gaze data did not only help in the placement of the integrated titles but could also later be compared to the gaze behavior of the German participants. Of these, 15 saw it with traditional subtitles and 16 German participants watched the film with the integrated titles. The participants who watched the version with the integrated titles were then asked to fill in a questionnaire on their experience (Chapter 7).

The results of the main study are based on a number of eye movement measures and the short questionnaire. Concerning the eye movements, the mean fixation duration in the title area and image, the correspondence to the natural focus of the natives, and the time to first fixation (reaction time) were analysed.

All hypotheses were confirmed: The fixation duration on the integrated titles decreased by about 14.4 % compared to traditional subtitles, and IT participants focused on the title area on average 47.5 % compared to 51.6 % for the TS participants. The IT participants seemed to be more motivated to focus on the image and to leave the title area directly after the reading process. Only about 16.5 % of all recorded times to first fixation were 0, indication that the IT participants were less likely to focus on the title area before the title display (compared to 28.7 % for the TS participants). This also shows that the split attention of the IT participants was stronger towards the image, resulting in more time for exploration and detail perception. Based on a random sample, the focus points of the German natives were compared to those of the English natives. The IT participants were not only more likely to fixate the same areas (83.3 % compared to 75.3 % for TS participants) but also fixated on average almost all titles (98.2 % compare to 88.1 % for the TS participants). Thus, the focus of the IT participants resembled the natural focus of the English natives stronger. As suspected, the reaction time between title display and first fixation increased – from about 57 ms on average for the TS participants to on average 74 ms for the IT participants. This, however, can also be interpreted as a result of the longer image exploration and stronger split attention towards the image. Further possible approaches of interpretation that should be included in future studies are the effects of search efficiency, processing effort, visual attention, stress level, and cognitive load.

The IT participants rated the integrated titles, compared to their previous experiences with subtitles, as more aesthetic, and they experienced a stronger information intake. This supports the hypotheses that the placement and adjusted layout can have a positive effect on the audience and increase the information intake and detail perception. The majority of participants stated that they would like to use integrated titles in the future.

All in all, the evaluation of the eye tracking data shows that integrated titles can decrease the reading time and motivate the viewer to return to the natural focus points faster. The title area seems to be less likely to be fixated before the title actually fades in, and a random sample of ten scenes indicated that the focus of an audience using integrated titles is more likely to archive the natural gaze behaviour of the native participants. The reaction time, however, increased visibly.

Practical implications from this study arise for all areas of film translation. Film producers should be aware of the effects traditional subtitles can have on the film's perception – especially in the light of top-grossing and award-winning Hollywood films making more profit in their translated versions than at home.

The presented strategies and the proposed workflow offer new possibilities for filmmakers to have their work translated more respect- and artfully for the target audience. The number of recent projects on the creation of integrated titles, e.g. the integrated titles for the hearing-impaired audience for *Notes on Blindness*, already show that the model is applicable in real-life settings.

## 9.2 Limitations

A number of limitations of the present study was already mentioned during the previous chapters or at least hinted at. The two film corpora used were far from perfect: The film corpus on text element translation did not include information on the analysed image track as this information is hard to come by – not even the client support of *Amazon Prime* or *Netflix* could clearly state the available image tracks for their films. As the example in §2.6 concerning *The Incredibles* showed, there can be quite some differences between the (original) English image track and the German image track. Furthermore, only 52 films of the 100 films in the corpus were analysed for this first study. A full analysis will provide more reliable data and a more comprehensive overview of the graphical translation of text elements in film. The corpus on integrated titles for both hearing-impaired and hearing audiences can also hardly be seen as complete. As with the other corpus, there is no reliable information available on BDs that include horizontally placed titles for hearing-impaired audiences and there are no lists available on films that include integrated titles as translation of an additional language. Therefore, this corpus can also offer an approximation of current placement strategies in English films.

Concerning the main study, a number of small limitations have to be taken into account. The film material is quite specific being a rather static documentary with little action or motion. It should therefore not be seen as representative for all kinds of films and genres. The participants were mainly university students and are therefore also a highly specific group – results with more heterogeneous groups could be different. The questionnaire was only designed for and handed out to the IT participants, therefore not offering any comparable results to the TS participants. Additionally, it was phrased very positively and thus possibly influenced the answers of the participants. For future studies, a questionnaire should be designed in a way that it can be handed out to both groups and question the participants concerning more specific topics such as enjoyment, transportation, and usability.

The main limitations in this study, however, were caused by the used software and lacking programming skills to analyse the recorded eye tracking data any other way. While *Tobii Studio* definitely improved compared to the pilot study and scene selection was possible – also with an immense expenditure of time – some measures could not be collected in a useful way and had therefore to be left out in the analysis. Mainly, this affected the analysis of saccade length, as the data just was not completely clear on this topic and an unclear scene selection had a too strong influence on it.

Concerning the creation of the integrated titles, software issues were also the main limitation. *Premiere Pro* is, so far, just not intended to create integrated titles. While there are plug-ins and tools to import traditional subtitle files such as .srt, these cannot be edited as much as titles created by hand. Therefore, each title has to be created by hand, including copying the content, the start time, the end time of the title, colours, fonts, and effects. As long as there is no automation of at least the copying process from traditional subtitle file to individual titles in *Premiere Pro*, the creation of integrated titles remains a massively time consuming process compared to the creation of traditional subtitles.

While the workflow was tested in real-life settings, no objective study of the process or the strategies has been undertaken yet.

## 9.3 Outlook

The insights into graphical aspects and effects as well as the results of this study are applicable to a range of other areas and future studies. First of all, the corpus on the graphical translation of text elements can be analysed completely and the information on available image tracks added. This would offer not only a better overview of the handling of text elements but also reveal differences in translation and provide a broader basis for future research. Combined with the concept of typographic identity, adjustments and improvements to current processes can be motivated. Additionally, a corpus on television series could reflect a more contemporary picture of translation, design, and layout of text elements (see *Sherlock* or *House of Cards* [USA 2013-]).

Acknowledging today's possibilities in the areas of machine translation, post-editing, and automatic placement, combinations of these modes can be researched and both the graphical and translation process analysed. The basis for first studies could be the proposed workflow, the presented automation algorithms, and machine translation specialised on subtitle contents.

As mentioned in §9.2, the film genre of the used material was quite specific. Further studies can investigate whether there are genres that are especially suitable (or especially unsuitable) for integrated titles. The use of integrated titles in *Sherlock Holmes – A Game of Shadows* in Kruger et al. (n.d.) indicated that even quick-paced scenes and dialogues can be handled with integrated titles.

Concerning the data analysis of eye movements when watching a film with integrated titles, there are more interesting measures future studies can investigate: the time frame after the title display, and the overall eye movements during whole scenes (before, during, and after the title display) pose interesting research opportunities. A differentiation between consecutive titles and stand-alone titles, the analysis of the individual placement, saccade length between main focus and title area as well as revisits and layout aspects such as typeface, contrast, and effects also offer more than enough interesting topics not only for eye tracking studies.

Furthermore, the accessibility of integrated titles targeted at hearing-impaired audiences poses an interesting topic. Titles such as those created for *Notes on Blindness* can be analysed regarding possible improvement, the audience's enjoyment, and information intake. This includes for example the speaker identification through colour that could be analysed based on AOIs on title and speaker as well as questionnaires. Noise indication and hints on volume and general indication of noise sources could also deliver interesting eye tracking data.

All in all, these first placement strategies and workflow, possibly together with suitable software, can become a basic tool set for subtitle professionals and filmmakers that want to create integrated titles. This process might as well become part of the film production again instead of taking place outside and far away from the initial decision makers. The goal is to motivate a more respectful handling of both the film and the translation while considering aspects such as image composition, content, and typographic identity. This would allow for the titles to actually become a part of the film's identity instead of interfering with it, providing a more authentic and accessible, and possibly more enjoyable, film experience for everyone.

# 10 Appendices

## 10.1 APPENDIX A – Film Corpus Text Elements

| Nr. | Original Title | Release | Ranking | Analysed |
|-----|---------------|---------|---------|----------|
| 1 | The Lord of the Rings: The Fellowship of the Ring | 2001 | 92.25 | y |
| 2 | The Lord of the Ring: The Return of the King | 2005 | 89.5 | y |
| 3 | Avatar | 2009 | 86 | y |
| 4 | Finding Nemo | 2003 | 82.75 | y |
| 5 | The Lord of the Rings: The Two Towers | 2002 | 77.75 | y |
| 6 | Harry Potter and the Sorcerer's Stone | 2001 | 71 | y |
| 7 | Harry Potter and the Goblet of Fire | 2005 | 69.75 | y |
| 8 | The Incredibles | 2004 | 65 | y |
| 9 | Star Wars: Episode III - Revenge of the Sith | 2005 | 62 | y |
| 10 | The Dark Knight | 2008 | 59.75 | n |
| 11 | Pirates of the Caribbean: The Curse of the Black Pearl | 2003 | 59.25 | y |
| 12 | Harry Potter and the Prisoner of Azkaban | 2004 | 57.5 | y |
| 13 | Harry Potter and the Half-Blood Prince | 2009 | 55.5 | y |
| 14 | Ratatouille | 2007 | 52.75 | y |
| 15 | Harry Potter and the Order of the Phoenix | 2007 | 52.5 | y |
| 16 | Up | 2009 | 50.25 | y |
| 17 | Pirates of the Caribbean: Dead Man's Chest | 2006 | 49.5 | y |
| 18 | Star Wars: Episode II - Attack of the Clones | 2002 | 48.5 | y |
| 19 | Harry Potter and the Chamber of Secrets | 2002 | 48 | y |

| 20 | Star Trek | 2009 | 47.5 | y |
|----|-----------|------|------|---|
| 21 | Spider-Man | 2002 | 47 | y |
| 22 | The Chronicles of Narnia: The Lion, the Witch and the Wardrobe | 2005 | 42.25 | y |
| 23 | Pirates of the Caribbean: At World's End | 2007 | 41.75 | y |
| 24 | Shrek | 2001 | 41.5 | y |
| 25 | Shrek 2 | 2004 | 41.25 | n |
| 26 | WALL·E | 2008 | 41 | y |
| 27 | Spider-Man 2 | 2004 | 40.75 | n |
| 28 | Casino Royale | 2008 | 39.25 | y |
| 29 | The Departed | 2006 | 38.25 | y |
| 30 | How the Grinch Stole Christmas | 2000 | 38 | n |
| 31 | Gladiator | 2000 | 37.5 | y |
| 32 | Troy | 2004 | 37 | n |
| 33 | No Country for Old Men | 2007 | 36.5 | n |
| 34 | Monsters, Inc. | 2001 | 35.25 | y |
| 35 | Iron Man | 2008 | 34 | y |
| 36 | The Matrix: Reloaded | 2003 | 33.25 | y |
| 37 | Shrek the Third | 2007 | 32.75 | y |
| 38 | 300 | 2006 | 30.75 | y |
| 39 | Eternal Sunshine of the Spotless Mind | 2004 | 30.5 | n |
| 40 | Ice Age: The Meltdown | 2006 | 30 | n |
| 41 | Ice Age: Dawn of the Dinosaurs | 2009 | 30 | y |
| 42 | The Bourne Ultimatum | 2007 | 29.75 | n |
| 43 | Cast Away | 2000 | 29.75 | n |
| 44 | The Twilight Saga: New Moon | 2009 | 29.5 | y |
| 45 | The Da Vinci Code | 2006 | 29.25 | n |
| 46 | There Will Be Blood | 2007 | 29 | n |

| 47 | Twilight | 2008 | 28.5 | y |
|----|----------|------|------|---|
| 48 | Batman Begins | 2005 | 28 | y |
| 49 | Madagascar | 2005 | 27.75 | n |
| 50 | X-Men: The Last Stand | 2006 | 27.5 | y |
| 51 | Elf | 2003 | 26.25 | n |
| 52 | Pride & Prejudice | 2005 | 26.25 | y |
| 53 | Spider-Man 3 | 2007 | 26.25 | n |
| 54 | The Hangover | 2009 | 26 | y |
| 55 | Transformers | 2007 | 25.75 | y |
| 56 | The Simpsons Movie | 2007 | 25.25 | n |
| 57 | Love Actually | 2003 | 25 | n |
| 58 | What Women Want | 2000 | 25 | n |
| 59 | Ice Age | 2002 | 24.75 | y |
| 60 | Mission: Impossible II | 2000 | 24.75 | n |
| 61 | Hancock | 2008 | 24.25 | n |
| 62 | Sideways | 2004 | 24 | n |
| 63 | Transformers: Revenge of the Fallen | 2009 | 23.75 | y |
| 64 | The Fast and the Furious | 2001 | 23 | y |
| 65 | Mean Girls | 2004 | 22.75 | n |
| 66 | The Queen | 2006 | 22.75 | n |
| 67 | Pearl Harbor | 2001 | 22.75 | n |
| 68 | Men in Black II | 2002 | 22.5 | n |
| 69 | Anchorman: The Legend of Ron Burgundy | 2004 | 22.25 | n |
| 70 | Madagascar: Escape 2 Africa | 2008 | 22.25 | n |
| 71 | Inglorious Basterds | 2009 | 22 | n |
| 72 | Almost Famous | 2000 | 22 | n |
| 73 | Gosford Park | 2001 | 21.75 | y |

| 74 | X-Men Origins: Wolverine | 2009 | 21.5 | y |
|---|---|---|---|---|
| 75 | United 93 | 2006 | 21.5 | n |
| 76 | Indiana Jones and the Kingdom of the Crystal Skull | 2008 | 21.5 | n |
| 77 | Lost in Translation | 2003 | 21.25 | y |
| 78 | Bruce Almighty | 2003 | 21.25 | n |
| 79 | Meet the Fockers | 2004 | 21.25 | n |
| 80 | Quantum of Solace | 2008 | 21 | n |
| 81 | Borat | 2006 | 20.75 | n |
| 82 | The Notebook | 2004 | 20.5 | y |
| 83 | Kung Fu Panda | 2008 | 20.5 | y |
| 84 | The Mummy Returns | 2001 | 20.25 | n |
| 85 | Donnie Darko | 2001 | 20 | y |
| 86 | Letters from Iwo Jima | 2006 | 20 | n |
| 87 | Fast & Furious | 2009 | 19.5 | n |
| 88 | Capote | 2005 | 19.5 | y |
| 89 | Chicken Run | 2000 | 19.25 | n |
| 90 | Requiem for a Dream | 2000 | 19 | n |
| 91 | District 9 | 2009 | 19 | y |
| 92 | The Prestige | 2006 | 18.75 | y |
| 93 | Wallace & Gromit: The Curse of the Were-Rabbit | 2005 | 18.75 | n |
| 94 | Brokeback Mountain | 2005 | 18.5 | n |
| 95 | King Kong | 2005 | 18.5 | n |
| 96 | Ocean's Eleven | 2001 | 18.5 | n |
| 97 | Night at the Museum | 2006 | 18.5 | n |
| 98 | Slumdog Millionaire | 2008 | 18.25 | n |
| 99 | American Pie 2 | 2001 | 18.25 | n |
| 100 | Million Dollar Baby | 2004 | 18 | n |

## 10.2 APPENDIX B – List of Referenced Films

*300.* 2006. Directed by Zack Snyder. USA: Warner Bros., Legendary Entertainment, Virtual Studios; Warner Bros. [1]

*Annie Hall.* 1977. Directed by Woody Allen. USA: Rollins-Joffe Productions; MGM Home Entertainment.

*Apocalypse Now.* 1979. Directed by Francis Ford Coppola. USA: Zoetrope Studios; Paramount Home Entertainment.

*Austin Powers in Goldmember.* 2002. Directed by Jay Roach. USA: New Line Cinema, Gratitude International, Team Todd; Warner Home Video.

*Avatar.* 2009. Directed by James Cameron. USA/UK: Twentieth Century Fox Film Corporation, Dune Entertainment, Ingenious Film Partners; Twentieth Century Fox Home Entertainment.

*Bad Company.* 2002. Directed by Joel Schumacher. USA/CZE: Touchstone Pictures, Jerry Bruckheimer Films, Stillking Films; Buena Vista Home Entertainment.

*Batman Begins.* 2005. Directed by Christopher Nolan. USA/UK: Warner Bros., Syncopy, DC Comics; Warner Bros.

*Being Human* [Television Series]. 2008-2013. Created by Toby Whithouse. UK: Touchpaper Television; British Broadcasting Corporation.

*Brother Bear.* 2003. Directed by Aaron Blaise. USA: Walt Disney Feature Animation, Walt Disney Pictures; Buena Vista International.

*Carry On Only* [Short]. 2013. Directed by Christopher Loope. USA: no company credits.

*Casablanca.* 1942. Directed by Michael Curtiz. USA: Warner Bros.; Warner Bros.

*Die Hard.* 1988. Directed by John McTiernan. USA: Twentieth Century Fox Film Corporation, Gordon Company, Silver Pictures; Twentieth Century Fox Home Entertainment.

*District 9.* 2009. Directed by Neill Blomkamp. ZA/USA/NZ/CAN: TriStar Pictures, Block/Hanson, WingNut Films; Sony Pictures Releasing.

---

[1]Films will be listed with main director, main production companies, and main distributor. Further information can be found on http://www.imdb.com [2016-10-20]. Country codes are based on ISO 3166.

*Dvevnoy Dozor* [Day Watch]. 2006. Directed by Timur Bekmambetov. RUS: Bazelevs Production, Challen One Russia, TABBAK; Twentieth Century Fox Home Entertainment.

*Eagle Eye.* 2008. Directed by D. J. Caruso. USA: DreamWorks SKG, Goldcrest Pictures, KMP Film Invest; Paramount Home Entertainment.

*Eternal Sunshine of the Spotless Mind.* 2004. Directed by Michel Gondry. USA: Focus Features, Anonymous Content, This Is That Productions; Constantin Film.

*Ex Machina.* 2015. Directed by Alex Garland. UK: Universal Pictures International, Film4, DNA Films; Universal Pictures International.

*Fast Five.* 2011. Directed by Justin Lin. USA: Original Film, One Race Films, Dentsu; Universal Pictures.

*Fast & Furious 6.* 2013. Directed by Justin Lin. USA: Universal Pictures, Relativity Media, Original Film; Universal Pictures International.

*Fast & Furious 7.* 2015. Directed by James Wan. USA/JP: Universal Pictures, MRC, China Film Co.; Universal Pictures International.

*Finding Nemo.* 2003. Directed by Andrew Stanton. USA: Walt Disney Pictures, Pixar Animation Studios, Disney Enterprises; Buena Vista International.

*Game of Thrones* [Television Series]. 2011-. Created by David Benioff and D. B. Weiss. USA/UK: Home Box Office, Television 360, Grok! Studio; HBO Home Entertainment.

*Gone Girl.* 2014. Directed by David Fincher. USA: Twentieth Century Fox Film Corporation, Regency Enterprises, TSG Entertainment; Twentieth Century Fox Home Entertainment.

*Grand Budapest Hotel.* 2014. Directed by Wes Anderson. USA/DE/UK: Fox Searchlight Pictures, Indian Paintbrush, Studio Babelsberg; Twentieth Century Fox Home Entertainment.

*Harry Potter* [Franchise]. 2001-2011. UK/USA: Warner Bros.; Warner Bros.

*Heroes* [Television Series]. 2006-2010. Created by Tim Kring. USA: Tailwind Productions; Universal Pictures.

*Heroes Reborn* [Television Series]. 2015-2016. Created by Tim Kring. USA: Tailwind Productions, Imperative Entertainment, Universal Television; Universal Pictures.

*Hot Fuzz.* 2007. Directed by Edgar Wright. UK/FR/USA: Universal Pictures, StudioCanal, Working Title Films; Universal Pictures.

*House of Cards* [Television Series]. 2013-. Created by Beau Willimon. USA: Media Rights Capital, Panic Pictures (II), Trigger Street Productions; Sony Pictures Home Entertainment.

*Ice Age.* 2002. Directed by Chris Wedge and Carlos Saldanha. USA: Twentieth Century Fox Film Corporation, Blue Sky Studios, Twentieth Century Fox Animation; Twentieth Century Fox Home Entertainment.

*In Bruges.* 2008. Directed by Martin McDonagh. UK/USA: Blueprint Pictures, Focus Features; Scion Films; Universum Film.

*Iron Man.* 2008. Directed by Jon Favreau. USA: Paramount Pictures, Marvel Enterprises, Marvel Studios; Concorde Home Entertainment.

*Jaws.* 1975. Directed by Steven Spielberg. USA: Zanuck/Brown Productions, Universal Pictures; Universal Pictures.

*John Wick.* 2014. Directed by Chad Stahelski and David Lynch. USA: 87Eleven; Lionsgate Entertainment.

*Joining the Dots* [Short]. 2012. Directed by Pablo Romero-Fresco. UK: no company credits.

*La Antena.* 2007. Directed by Esteban Sapir. AR: LadobleA; Capelight Pictures.

*Lilo & Stitch.* 2002. Directed by Dean DeBlois and Chris Sanders. USA: Walt Disney Pictures, Walt Disney Feature Animation; Buena Vista International.

*Limitless.* 2011. Directed by Neil Burger. USA: Relativity Media, Virgin Produced, Rogue; Twentieth Century Fox Home Entertainment.

*M.* 1951. Directed by Joseph Losey. USA: Superior Pictures; Darker Images Video.

*Man on Fire.* 2004. Directed by Tony Scott. USA/UK: Warner Bros. International; Twentieth Century Fox.

*Montreal Stories.* CAN 1991. Various directors. CAN: Atlantis Films, Cinémaginaire, National Film Board of Canada.

*Monty Python and the Holy Grail.* 1975. Directed by Terry Gilliam and Terry Jones. UK: Michael White Productions, National Film Trustee Company, Python (Monty) Pictures; Sony Pictures Home Entertainment.

*Nochnoy Dozor* [Night Watch]. 2004. Directed by Timur Bekmambetov. RUS: Channel One; Twentieth Century Fox.

*Non-Stop.* 2014. Directed by Jaume Collet-Serra. UK/FR/USA/CAN: StudioCanal, Anton Capital Entertainment, Silver Pictures; StudioCanal.

*Notes on Blindness.* 2016. Directed by Peter Middleton and James Spinney. UK: Arte France, Creative England, Impact Partners; ARTE.

*Pirates of the Carribean: The Curse of the Black Pearl.* 2003. Directed by Gore Verbinski. USA: Walt Disney Pictures, Jerry Bruckheimer Films; Buena Vista International.

*Pirates of the Carribean: Dead Man's Chest.* 2006. Directed by Gore Verbinski. USA: Walt Disney Pictures, Jerry Bruckheimer Films, Second Mate Productions; Buena Vista International.

*Pirates of the Carribean: At World's End.* 2007. Directed by Gore Verbinski. USA: Walt Disney Pictures, Jerry Bruckheimer Films, Second Mate Productions; Buena Vista International.

*Pride & Prejudice.* 2005. Directed by Joe Wright. FR/UK/USA: Focus Features, Universal Pictures, StudioCanal; Universal Studios Home Entertainment.

*Psycho.* 1960. Directed by Alfred Hitchcock. USA: Shamley Productions; Universal Pictures.

*Ronin.* 1998. Directed by John Frankenheimer. UK/FR/USA: FGM Entertainment, United Artists Corporation, United Artists; MGM Home Entertainment.

*Se7en.* 1995. Directed by David Fincher. USA: Cecchi Gori Pictures, Juno Pix, New Line Cinema; Warner Home Video.

*Seven Pounds.* 2008. Directed by Gabriele Muccino. USA: Columbia Pictures, Relativity Media, Overbrook Entertainment; Sony Pictures Home Entertainment.

*Sherlock* [Television Series]. 2010-. Created by Mark Gatiss and Steven Moffat. UK/USA: Hartswood Films, BBC Wales, Masterpiece Theatre; British Broadcasting Corporation.

*Sherlock Holmes – A Game of Shadows.* 2011. Directed by Guy Ritchie. USA: Warner Bros., Village Roadshow Pictures, Silver Pictures; Warner Home Video.

*Sin City.* 2005. Directed by Frank Miller and Robert Rodiguez. USA: Dimension Films, Troublemaker Studios; Buena Vista Home Entertainment.

*Slumdog Millionaire.* 2008. Directed by Danny Boyle and Loveleen Tandan. UK/FR/USA: Celador Films Ltd.; Twentieth Century Fox.

*Star Trek.* 2009. Directed by J. J. Abrams. USA: Paramount Pictures, Spyglass Entertainment, Bad Robot; Paramount Home Entertainment.

*Star Trek Into Darkness.* 2013. Directed by J.J. Abrams. USA: Paramount Pictures, Spyglass Entertainment, Bad Robot; Paramount Pictures.

*Star Wars* [Franchise]. 1977-. USA: various.

*Star Wars: Episode III – Revenge of the Sith.* 2005. Directed by George Lucas. USA: Lucasfilm; Twentieth Century Fox Home Entertainment.

*Stranger Than Fiction.* 2006. Directed by Marc Forster. USA: Columbia Pictures, Mandate Pictures, Three Strange Angels; Sony Pictures Home Entertainment.

*The Big Bang Theory* [Television Series]. 2007-. Created by Chuck Lorre and Bill Prady. USA: Chuck Lorre Productions, Warner Bros. Television; Warner Home Video.

*The Dancer.* 2000. Directed by Frédéric Garson. FR: EuropaCorp, TF1 Films Production; Tobis StudioCanal.

*The Departed.* 2006. Directed by Martin Scorsese. USA/HK: Warner Bros., Plan B Entertainment, Initial Entertainment Group; Warner Home Video.

*The Godfather: Part II.* 1974. Directed by Fracis Ford Coppola. USA: Paramount Pictures, The Coppola Company; Paramount Home Entertainment.

*The Incredibles.* 2004. Directed by Brad Bird. USA: Walt Disney Pictures, Pixar Animation Studios; Buena Vista Home Entertainment.

*The Lord of the Rings* [Franchise]. 2001-2003. Directed by Peter Jackson. NZ/USA: New Line Cinema, WingNut Films, The Saul Zaentz Company; Warner Home Video.

*The Lord of the Rings: The Fellowship of the Ring.* 2001. Directed by Peter Jackson. NZ/USA: New Line Cinema, WingNut Films, The Saul Zaentz Company; Warner Home Video.

*The Lord of the Rings – The Two Towers.* 2002. Directed by Peter Jackson. NZ/USA: New Line Cinema, Wingnut Films, The Saul Zaentz Company; Warner Home Video.

*The Matrix* [Franchise]. 1999-2003. Directed by Lana and Lilly Wachowski. USA: Warner Bros., Roadshow Pictures; Warner Bros.

*The Rundown.* 2003. Directed by Peter Berg. USA: Columbia Pictures Corporation, Universal Pictures, WWE Studios; Columbia TriStar Home Entertainment.

*The Twilight Saga: New Moon.* 2009. Directed by Chris Weitz. USA: Temple Hill Entertainment, Maverick Films, Imprint Entertainment; Concorde Home Entertainment.

*Train of Life.* 1998. Directed by Radu Mihaileanu. FR/BE/NL/ISR/ROU: Belfilms, Canal+, Centre National de la Cinématographie; Sunfilm Entertainment.

*Trainspotting.* 1996. Directed by Danny Boyle. UK: Channel Four Films; Figment Films, The Noel Gay Motion Picture Company; Prokino Filmverleih.

*Vivre Sa Vie.* 1962. Directed by Jean-Luc Godard. FR: Les Films de la Pléiade, Pathé Consortium Cinéma; Panthéon Distribution.

# References

Abreu, Rafael. 2014. The revival of Keanu Reeves with John Wick. http://fiusm. com/2014/11/18/the-revival-of-keanu-reeves-with-john-wick/, accessed 2016-10-08.

Althen, Michael. 2006. *Die Wunderwelten des Saul Bass [The wonderous worlds of Saul Bass]*. http://www.faz.net/aktuell/feuilleton/glosse-feuilleton-die-wunderwelten-des-saul-bass-1327162.html, accessed 2016-06-10.

Archer, Ben. 2007. *Eric Gill got it wrong; A re-evaluation of Gill Sans*. https://www. typotheque.com/articles/re-evaluation_of_gill_sans, accessed 2016-10-12.

Armstrong, Mike & Matthew Brooks. 2014. *Enhancing subtitles*. Brussels. http://www.bbc.co.uk/rd/blog/2014-10-tvx2014-short-paper-enhancing-subtitles, accessed 2016-08-01.

Armstrong, Stephen, Colm Caffrey & Marian Flanagan. 2006. Translating DVD subtitles from English-German and English-Japanese using example-based machine translation. In *MuTra 2006 - Audiovisual translation scenarios: Conference proceedings*. Copenhagen. http://www.euroconferences.info/proceedings/2006_Proceedings/2006_Armstrong_Stephen_et_al.pdf, accessed 2016-08-01.

Ball, Linden J., Nicola Eger, Robert Stevens & Jon Dodd. 2006. Applying the PEEP method in usability testing. *Interfaces* (67). 15–19.

Bayram, Servet & Duygu M. Bayraktar. 2012. Using eye tracking to study on attention and recall in multimedia learning environments: The effects of design in learning. *World Journal on Educational Technology* 4(2). 81–98.

Beckman, Rachel. 2008. An out-of-character role for subtitles. *Washington Post*. http://www.washingtonpost.com/wp-dyn/content/article/2008/11/14/AR2008111400700.html, accessed 2016-10-08.

Benjamin, Walter. 1972. *Gesammelte Schriften Band IV*. Rolf Tiedemann & Hermann Schweppenhäuser (eds.). Frankfurt am Main: Suhrkamp.

Bianchi, Francesca & Tiziana Ciabattoni. 2007. Captions and subtitles in EFL learning: An investigative study in a comprehensive computer environment. In Anthony Baldry, Maria Pavesi, Carol Taylor-Torsello & Christopher Taylor (eds.), *From didactas to ecolingua. An ongoing research project on translation and corpus linguistics*, 69–90. Trieste: Edizione Università di Trieste.

Birmingham, Elina, Walter F. Bischof & Alan Kingston. 2008. Social attention and real-world scenes: The roles of action, competition and social content. *The Quarterly Journal of Experimental Psychology* 61(7). 986–998.

Blu-ray Disc Association. 2015. *White paper Blu-ray Disc (TM) format.* http://blu-raydisc.com/Assets/Downloadablefile/White_Paper_General_4th_20150817_clean.pdf, accessed 2016-06-05.

Bouchehri, Regina. 2008. *Filmtitel im interkulturellen Transfer.* Berlin: Frank & Timme GmbH.

Bradley, Steven. 2016. *Vanseo Design.* http://vanseodesign.com, accessed 2016-08-01.

Brown, Andy, Rhia Jones & Mike Crabb. 2015. *Dynamic subtitles: The user experience.* Brussels.

Caffrey, Colm. 2009. *Relevant abuse? Investigating the effects of an abusive subtitling procedure on the perception of TV anime using eye tracker and questionnaire.* Dublin: Dublin City University Doctoral dissertation.

Carpenter, Patricia A. & Marcel Adam Just. 1983. What your eyes do while your mind is reading. In Keith Rayner (ed.), *Eye movements in reading: Perceptual and language processes*, 275–307. New York: Academic Press.

Carroll, Patrick J., Jason R. Young & Michael S. Guertin. 1992. Visual analysis of cartoons: A view from the far side. In Keith Rayner (ed.), *Eye movements and visual cognition: Scene perception and reading*, 444–461. New York: Springer-Verlag.

Chandler, Paul & Paul Sweller. 1991. Cognitive load theory and the format of instruction. *Cognition and Instruction* 8(4). 293–332.

Chaume, Frederic. 2004. Film studies and translation studies: Two disciplines at stake in audiovisual translation. *Meta* 49(1). 12–24.

Chekaluk, Eugene & Keith R. Llewellyn. 1994. Masking effects in saccadic eye movements. In Géry d'Ydewalle & Johan Van Rensbergen (eds.), *Visual and oculomotor functions – Advances in eye movement research*, 45–54. Amsterdam: Elsevier.

Cherim, Mike. 2007. *Usability in design.* Beast Blog. http://green-beast.com/blog/?p=169, accessed 2016-10-07.

Chion, Michel. 1993. *La audiovisión.* Barcelona: Paidós.

Chun, Bong-Kyung, Dong-Sung Ryu, Won-Il Hwang & Hwan-Gue Cho. 2006. An automated procedure for word balloon placement in cinema comics. *Lecture Notes in Computer Science: Advances in Visual Computing.* 576–585.

Cowen, Laura, Linden J. Ball & Judy Delin. 2002. An eye-movement analysis of web-page usability. In Xristine Faulkner, Janet Finlay & Françoise Détienne (eds.), *People and computers XVI – Memorable yet invisible: Proceedings of HCI 2002*. London, United Kingdom: Springer-Verlag.

Curtis, Adam. 2015. *Eye-based interaction in graphical systems: Theory & practice part II Eye tracking systems*. http://slideplayer.com/slide/5886977/, accessed 2016-10-07.

Danan, Martine. 2004. Captioning and subtitling: Undervalued language learning strategies. *Meta* 49(1). 67–77.

De Linde, Zoe & Neil Kay. 1999. *The semiotics of subtitling*. Manchester: St. Jerome.

De Sousa, Sheila C. M., Wilker Aziz & Lucia Specia. 2011. Assessing the post-editing effort for automatic and semi-automatic translations of DVD subtitles. In Galia Angelova, Kalina Bontcheva & Ruslan Mitkov (eds.), *Proceedings of Recent Advances in Natural Language Processing*, 97–103. Hissar.

Delabastita, Dirk. 1996. Wordplay as a translation problem: A linguistic perspective. In Harald Kittel, Armin Paul Frank, Norbert Greiner, Theo Hermans, Werner Koller, José Lambert & Fritz Paul (eds.), *Übersetzung, translation, traduction*, 600–606. Berlin: de Gruyter.

Díaz Cintas, Jorge. 2005. Back to the future in subtitling. In Heidrun Gerzymisch-Arbogast & Sandra Nauert (eds.), *MuTra 2005 – Challenges of Multidimensional Translation: Conference Proceedings*. http://www.euroconferences.info/proceedings/2005_Proceedings/2005_proceedings.html, accessed 2016-10-07.

Díaz Cintas, Jorge & Pablo Muñoz Sánchez. 2006. Fansubs: Audiovisual translation in an amateur environment. *The Journal of Specialised Translation* 6. 37–52.

Díaz Cintas, Jorge, Pilar Orero & Aline Remael. 2007. *Media for all. Subtitling for the Deaf, audio description, and sign language*. Amsterdam, New York: Rodopi.

Díaz Cintas, Jorge & Aline Remael. 2007. *Audiovisual translation: Subtitling*. Manchester: St. Jerome.

Dick, Bernard F. 2005. *Anatomy of film*. Boston, New York: Bedford, St. Martin's.

Duchowski, Andrew T. 2007. *Eye tracking methodology: Theory and practice*. London: Springer-Verlag.

d'Ydewalle, Géry & Wim De Bruycker. 2007. Eye movements of children and adults while reading television subtitles. *European Psychologist* 12(3). 196–205.

d'Ydewalle, Géry & Ingrid Gielen. 1992. Attention allocation with overlapping sound, image, and text. In Keith Rayner (ed.), *Eye movements and visual cognition* (Springer Series in Neuropsychology), 415–427. New York: Springer-Verlag.

d'Ydewalle, Géry, Caroline Praet, Karl Verfaillie & Johan Van Rensbergen. 1991. Watching subtitled television: Automatic reading behaviour. *Communication Research* 18(5). 650–660.

d'Ydewalle, Géry, Johan Van Rensbergen & Joris Pollet. 1985. Reading a message when the same message is auditorily available in another language: The case of subtitling. *Psychological Reports of Leuven University* 54.

Dyer, Annabella, Mairéad MacSweenay, Marçin Szerzerbinski, Louise Green & Ruth Campbell. 2003. Predictors of reading delay in deaf adolescents: The relative contributions of rapid automatized naming speed and phonological awareness and decoding. *Journal of Deaf Studies and Deaf Education* 8(3). 215–229.

eAccess+. 2016. *eAccess+*. http://hub.eaccesplus.eu, accessed 2016-10-07.

Egoyan, Atom & Ian Balfour (eds.). 2004. *Subtitles: On the foreignness of film.* Cambridge: MIT Press, Alphabet City.

Ehmke, Claudia & Stephanie Wilson. 2007. Identifying web usability problems from eyetracking data. In Tom Ormerod & Corina Sas (eds.), *BCS-HCI '07 Proceedings of the 21st British HCI Group Annual Conference on People and Computers: HCI...but not as we know it, vol. 1*, 119–128. Lancester: University of Lancaster.

Ehrenhauser, Sabine. 2007. *Typografische Animationen – Schrift in Bewegung: Analyse der durch Kinetic hervorgerufenen Veränderungen im Vergleich zu statischer Typografie [Typographic animation – Moving text: Analysis of kinetic typography compared to static typography]*. FH Hagenberg Doctoral dissertation. http://theses.fh-hagenberg.at/thesis/Ehrenhauser07, accessed 2016-05-15.

Felperin, Leslie. 2005. Review of 'Night Watch'. *Sight & Sound* 15(10). 79–80.

Ferrer Simó, María R. 2005. Fansubs y scanlations: La influencia del aficionado en los criterios profesionales. *Puentes* 6. 27–43.

Fishel, Mark, Yota Georgakopoulou, Sergio Penkale, Volha Petukhova, Matej Rojc, Martin Volk & Andy Way. 2012. From subtitles to parallel corpora. In *The 16th Annual Conference of the European Association for Machine Translation*, 3–6. Trento.

Fitts, Paul M., Richard E. Jones & John L. Milton. 1950. Eye movements of aircraft pilots during instrument-landing approaches. *Aeronautical Engineering Review* 9(2). 24–29.

Flanagan, Marian. 2009. Using example-based machine translation to translate DVD subtitles. In Mikel L. Forcada & Andy Way (eds.), *Proceedings of the 3rd Workshop on Example-Based Machine Translation*, 85–92. Dublin.

Flothow, Sebastian. 2009. *Eye Tracking. Ein Überblick über Geschichte, Methoden und Anwendung [Eye tracking. An overview of its history, methods, and appli-*

*cation*]. https://www.cs.hs-rm.de/~linn/fachsem0809/eyetracking/Eye_
Tracking.pdf, accessed 2012-06-26.

Foerster, Anna. 2010. Towards a creative approach in subtitling: A case study. In
Jorge Díaz Cintas, Anna Matamala & Josélia Neves (eds.), *New in-sights into au-
diovisual translation and media accessibility. Media for All 2*, 81–98. Amsterdam:
Rodopi.

Ford Williams, Gareth. 2009. *Bbc.co.uk online subtitling editorial guidelines v1.1.*
http://www.bbc.co.uk/guidelines/futuremedia/.../online_sub_editorial_
guidelines_vs1_1.pdf, accessed 2016-10-08.

Fowler, Roger. 1986. *Linguistic criticism.* Oxford: Oxford University Press.

Fox, Wendy. 2012. *Integrierte Bildtitel – Eine Alternative zur traditionallen Untertitelung [Integrated titles – An alternative to traditional subtitling].* Germersheim: FTSK Germersheim, Johannes Gutenberg University Mainz Master's
thesis.

Frenck-Mestre, Cheryl & Joël Pynte. 1997. Syntactic ambiguity resolution while
reading in second and native languages. *The Quarterly Journal of Experimental
Psychology* 50(1). 119–148.

Gallagher, Brian. 2004. Review of 'Man on Fire'. *MovieWeb.* https://movieweb.
com/movie/man-on-fire/review-REKbKKPOEMWaOT/, accessed 2016-10-08.

Gambier, Yves. 1994. La retraduction, retour et detour [retranslation, return and
detour]. *Meta* 39(3). 413–417.

Ghia, Elisa. 2012. The impact of translation strategies on subtitle reading. In Elisa
Perego (ed.), *Eye-tracking and audiovisual translation*, 155–181. Rome: Aracne.

Goldberg, Joseph H. & X. P. Kotval. 1999. Computer interface evaluation using
eye movements: Methods and constructs. *International Journal of Industrial
Ergonomics* 24(6). 631–645.

Goldberg, Joseph H., Mark J. Stimson, Marion Lewenstein, Neil Scott & Anna
M. Wichansky. 2002. Eye tracking in web search tasks: Design implications.
In *Proceedings of the Eye Tracking Research & Application Symposium*, 51–58.
New York: ACM Press.

Gottlieb, Henrik. 1998. *Subtitling.* In Mona Baker (ed.), *Routledge encyclopedia of
translation studies*, 244–248. London, New York: Routledge.

Gottlieb, Henrik. 2012. Subtitles – Readable dialogue? In Elisa Perego (ed.), *Eye
tracking in audiovisual translation*, 37–82. Rome: Aracne.

Graham, Bill. 2014. 'John Wick' filmmakers on how to direct action, DGA, Keanu
Reeves' advice, and more. *The Film Stage.* http://thefilmstage.com/features/
john-wick-filmmakers-on-how-to-direct-action-dga-keanu-reeves-advice-
and-more/, accessed 2016-06-12.

Groensteen, Thierry. 2007. *The system of comics.* Jackson, MS: University of Mississippi Press.

Gulliver, Stephen R. & George Ghinea. 2003. How level and type of deafness affect user perception of multimedia video clips. *Universal Access in the Information Society* 2(4). 374–386.

Hausberger, Florian. 2006. *Main Titles – Titelsequenzen im Film: Eine analytische Kategorisierung [Main titles – Title sequences in film: An analytical categorisation].* FH Hagenberg Diploma Thesis.

Heaton, James. 2011. *The difference between marketing and branding.* http://www.tronviggroup.com/the-difference-between-marketing-and-branding/, accessed 2016-06-05.

Herbst, Thomas. 1994. *Linguistische Aspekte der Synchronisation von Fernsehserien: Phonetik, Textlinguistik, Übersetzungstheorie [Linguistic aspects of the dubbing of television series: Phonetics, text linguistics, translation theory].* Tübingen: Max Niemeyer.

Hevesi, Julia. 2015. *Anwendung und Auswertung der modularen Richtlinien zur Erstellung integrierter Titel nach Fox anhand des Kurzfilms Carry On Only [Application and analysis of the modular guidelines for the creation of integrated titles by Fox, by means of the short film Carry On Only].* Germersheim: FTSK Germersheim, Johannes Gutenberg University Mainz Bachelor's Thesis.

Hickethier, Knut. 2007. *Film- und Fernsehanalyse [Film and television series analysis].* Stuttgart, Weimar: Metzler.

Hillstrom, Anne P. & Steven Yantis. 1994. Visual motion and attentional capture. *Perception & Psychophysics* 55(4). 399–411.

Holmqvist, Kenneth, Marcus Nystrom, Richard Andersson, Richard Dewhurst, Halska Jarodzka & Joost Van de Weijer. 2011. *Eye tracking: A comprehensive guide to methods and measures.* Oxford: Oxford University Press.

Hong, Richang, Meng Wang, Xiao-Tong Yuan, Mengdi Xu, Jianguo Jiang, Shuicheng Yan & Tat-Seng Chua. 2010. Dynamic captioning: Video accessibility enhancement for hearing impairment. In *Proceedings of the International Conference on Multimedia,* 421–430. ACM.

Hu, Yongtao, Jan Kautz, Yizhou Yu & Wenping Wang. 2013. Speaker-following video subtitles. *ACM Trans. Multimedia Com-put. Commun. Appl.* 2(3).

Huff, Markus, Frank Papenmeier, Georg Jahn & Friedrich W. Hesse. 2010. Eye movements across viewpoint changes in multiple object tracking. *Visual Cognition* 18(9). 1368–1391.

Hvelplund, Kristian Tangsgaard. 2014. Eye tracking and the translation process: Reflections on the analysis and interpretation of eye-tracking data. *Minding*

*Translation. Con la traducción en mente (MonTI Special Issue 1)*. 201–223. http: //www.e-revistes.uji.es/index.php/monti/article/view/1706.

IBM. 2003. *Web design guidelines*. http://www-3.ibm.com/ibm/easy/eou_ext.nsf/ Publish/572, accessed 2016-10-17.

IMDb-1. 2016. *La Antena.* http://www.imdb.com/title/tt0454065/?ref_=fn_al_tt_1, accessed 2016-10-10.

ITC. 1999. *Guidance on standards for subtitling.* http://stakeholders.ofcom.org. uk/binaries/broadcast/guidance/itc_stnds_subtitling_word.doc, accessed 2014-12-15.

Ivarsson, Jan. 1992. *Subtitling for the media – A handbook of an art.* Stockholm: Transedit.

Ivarsson, Jan & Mary Carroll. 1998. *Subtitling.* Simrisham: Transedit.

Jacob, Robert J. K. & Keith S. Karn. 2003. Eye tracking in human-computer interaction and usability research: Ready to deliver the promises. In Jukka Hyona, Ralph Radach & Heiner Deubel (eds.), *The mind's eyes: Cognitive and applied aspects of eye movement*, 573–605. Oxford: Elsevier Science.

Jakobsen, Arnt Lykke & Kristian Tangsgaard Hvelplund Jensen. 2008. Eye movement behaviour across four different types of reading task. In Susanne Göpferich, Arnt Lykke Jakobsen & Inger M. Mees (eds.), *Looking at eyes: Eye-Tracking studies of reading and translation processing* (Copenhagen Studies in Language 36), 103–124. Copenhagen: Samfundslitteratur.

Jauß, Hans Robert. 1991. *Ästhetische Erfahrung und literarische Hermeneutik [Aesthetic experience and literary hermeneutics].* Frankfurt am Main: Suhrkamp.

Jensema, Carl J., Sameh El Sharkawy, Ramalinga S. Danturthi, Robert Burch & David Hsu. 2000a. Eye movement patterns of captioned television viewers. *American Annals of the Deaf* 145(5). 464–468.

Jensema, Carl J., Sameh El Sharkawy, Ramalinga S. Danturthi, Robert Burch & David Hsu. 2000b. Time spent viewing captions on television programs. *American Annals of the Deaf* 145(3). 275–285.

Joos, Markus, Jens R. Helmert & Sebastian Pannasch. 2005. Blickbewegungsmessung und praktische Anwendungen [Eye movement measurement and practical applications]. TU Dresden. http://tu-dresden.de/die_tu_dresden/ fakultaeten/fakultaet_mathematik_und_naturwissenschaften/fachrichtung_ psychologie/i3/applied-cognition/publikationen/pdf/joos2005b.pdf, accessed 2014-10-04.

Joos, Markus, Matthias Rötting & Boris M. Velichkovsky. 2003. Die Bewegungen des menschlichen Auges: Fakten, Methoden, innovative Anwendungen [Movement of the human eye: Facts, methods, innovative applications]. In Gert Rickheit, Theo Herrmann & Werner Deutsch (eds.), *Psycholinguistik / Psycholinguistics. Ein internationales Handbuch / An international handbook*, 142–168. Berlin, New York: de Gruyter.

Jüngst, Heike E. 2010. *Audiovisuelles Übersetzen. Ein Lehr- und Arbeitsbuch.* Tübingen: Narr Verlag.

Just, Marcel Adam & Patricia A. Carpenter. 1980. A theory of reading: From eye fixations to comprehension. *Psychological Review* 87. 329–354.

Just, Marcel Adam & Patricia A. Carpenter. 1987. *The psychology of reading and language comprehension.* Newton, MA: Allyn & Bacon.

Karamitroglou, Fotios. 1998. A proposed set of subtitling standards in Europe. *Translation Journal* 2(2). http://www.accurapid.com/journal, accessed 2016-10-07.

Kaur, Manpreet, Marilyn Tremaine, Ning Huang, Joseph Wilder, Zoran Gacovski, Frans Flippo & Chandra S. Matravadi. 2003. Where is 'it'? Event synchronization in gaze-speech input systems. In *Proceedings of the Fifth International Conference on Multimodal Interfaces*, 151–158. New York: ACM.

Keating, Gregory D. 2014. Eye-tracking with text. In Jill Jegerski & Bill Van Patten (eds.), *Research methods in second language psycholinguistics*, 69–92. London: Taylor & Francis.

Kenworthy, Christopher. 2011. *Master shots vol 2: Shooting great dialogue scenes.* Studio City, CA: Michael Wiese Productions.

Kofoed, D. T. 2011. Decotitles, the animated discourse of Fox's recent anglophonic internationalism. *Reconstruction* 11(1). http://reconstruction.eserver.org/Issues/111/Kofoed.shtml, accessed 2016-10-10.

Krammer, Klaudia. 2001. Schriftsprachkompetenz gehörloser Erwachsener [Written language proficiency of deaf adults]. In *Veröffentlichungen des Forschungszentrums für Gebärdensprache und Hörgeschädigtenkommunikation der Universität Klagenfurt*. Klagenfurt: Foschungszentrum für Gebärdensprache und Hörgeschädigtenkommunikation. http://www.uniklu.ac.at/zgh/downloads/krammer.pdf, accessed 2016-10-08.

Kraus, Andreas. 2010. *Zur Problematik des Übersetzens im Rahmen der Live-Untertitelung [On the problem of translation during live subtitling].* Universität des Saarlandes dissertation.

Kruger, Jan-Louis. N.d. Eye tracking in audiovisual translation research. In Luis Perez-Gonzalez (ed.), *The Routledge handbook of audiovisual translation*. London: Routledge.

Kruger, Jan-Louis, Stephen Doherty, Wendy Fox & Peter de Lissa. N.d. Multimodal measurement of cognitive load during subtitle processing: Same-language subtitles for foreign language viewers. In Isabel La Cruz & Riitta Jääskeläinen (eds.), *New directions in cognitive and empirical translation process research.* London: John Benjamins.

Kruger, Jan-Louis & F. Steyn. 2014. Subtitles and eye tracking: Reading and performance. *Reading Research Quarterly* 49(1). 105–120.

KU Leuven (ed.). 2016. *Dual purkinje eyetrackers.* Leuven. http://ppw.kuleuven. be/home/english/research/lep/resources/purkinje, accessed 2016-08-04.

Künzli, Alexander & Maureen Ehrensberger-Dow. 2011. Innovative subtitling. A reception study. In Cecilia Alvstad, Adelina Hild & Elisabet Tiselius (eds.), *Methods and strategies of process research*, 187–200. Amsterdam: John Benjamins.

Kurlander, David, Tim Skelly & David Salesin. 1996. Comic chat. *Procs. SIGGRAPH.* 225–236.

Lambourne, Andrew. 2012. Climbing the production chain. In. Berlin.

Lautenbacher, Olli P. 2012. From still pictures to moving pictures – Eye tracking text and image. In Elisa Perego (ed.), *Eye tracking in audiovisual translation*, 135–155. Rome: Aracne.

Leißner, Stefanie. 2009. *Untertitelung einer Episode der BBC Sitcom "Yes Minister".* Essen: BDÜ.

Lewenstein, Marion, Gregory Edwards, Deborah Tatar & Andrew Devigal. 2017. *The stanford poynter project.* http://www.poynter.org/eyetrack2000/, accessed 2017-12-27.

Liebig, Martin. 2016. *Die gefühlte Lesbarkeit [Perceived readability].* http://www. designtagebuch.de/wiki/die-gefuehlte-lesbarkeit/, accessed 2016-10-10.

Loyd, Jeremy. 2013. *Typographic readability and legibility.* Envato tuts+. http:// webdesign . tutsplus . com / articles / typographic - readability - and - legibility -- webdesign-12211, accessed 2016-10-08.

Luyken, Georg-Michael. 1991. *Overcoming language barriers in television: Dubbing and subtitling for the european audience.* Düsseldorf: European Institute for the Media.

Manhartsberger, Martina & Norbert Zellhofer. 2005. Eye tracking in usability research: What users really see. In *Empowering software quality: How can usability engineering reach these goals? Usability symposium*, 141–152. OCG Publication.

Marchant, Paul, David Raybould, Tony Renshaw & Richard Stevens. 2009. Are you seeing what I'm seeing? An eye tracking evaluation of dynamic scenes. *Digital Creativity* 20. 153–163.

Marleau, Lucien. 1982. Les sous-titres... un mal necessaire [Subtitles... a necessary evil]. *Meta* 27(3). 271–285.

McCann, Michael J. 2005. The ethics of non translation. *Irish Translators' and Interpreters' Association's monthly ITIA Bulletin* (10).

McCarthy, John D., M. Angela Sasse & Jens Riegelsberger. 2003. Could I have the menu please? An eyetracking study of design conventions. In *Proceedings of HCI 2003*, 401–414. London: Springer-Verlag.

McClarty, Rebecca. 2012. Towards a multidisciplinary approach in creative subtitling. *Monographs in Translating and Interpreting (MonTI)* 4. 133–155.

McConkie, George W., Paul W. Kerr, Michael D. Reddix, David Zola & Arthur M. Jacobs. 1989. Eye movement control during reading: II. Frequency of refixating a word. *Perception and Psychophysics* 46. 245–253.

McCort, Kristinha. 2002. *Titles throughout time.* http://www.arnokroner.com/education/design/cg/foundation/titles_throughout_time.pdf, accessed 2016-06-12.

Media Consulting Group. 2007. *Study on dubbing and subtitling needs and practices in the European audiovisual industry (In association with Peacufulfish).* Paris, London. http://edz.bib.uni-mannheim.de/daten/edz-b/gdbk/07/ksj/study_dub_subtitle_en.pdf, accessed 2016-10-10.

Meggs, Philip B. 1997. *Six chapters in design.* Dublin: Chronicle Books.

Melero, Maite, Antoni Oliver & Toni Badia. 2006. Automatic multilingual subtitling in the etitle project. In *Proceedings of the Twenty-eighth International Conference on Translating and the Computer.* Londin: Aslib.

Mercado, Gustavo. 2010. *The filmmaker's eye. Learning (and breaking) the rules of cinematic composition.* Burlington, MA: Focal Press.

Mistry, Jaina. 2015. *Film review: John Wick.* Time Well Spent. http://timewellspent.com/2015/02/21/film/film-review-john-wick, accessed 2016-10-10.

Molerov, Dimitar. 2012. *Schriftlicher Text im Film und seine Übersetzung: Die Inserts der BBC-Serie Sherlock (2010-12). Aus der Perspektive von Untertiteltheorie, Comictheorie und Translationspraxis* [Written text in film and its translation: Inserts in the BBC television series Sherlock (2010-12). From the perspective of subtitling theory, comic theory, and translation practive]. Germersheim: FTSK Germersheim, Johannes Gutenberg University Mainz Master's Thesis.

Moran, Siobhan. 2012. The effect of linguistic variation on subtitle reception. In Elisa Perego (ed.), *Eye tracking in audiovisual translation*, 183–222. Rome: Aracne.

Mosconi, Maruo & Marco Porta. 2012. Accessibility and usability in the context of human-computer interaction. In Elisa Perego (ed.), *Eye tracking in audiovisual translation*, 105–134. Rome: Aracne.

Müller, Mathias & Martin Volk. 2013. Statistical machine translation of subtitles: From OpenSubtitles to TED. In Iryna Gurevych, Chris Biemann & Torsten Zesch (eds.), *Language processing and knowledge in the web*, 132–138. Berlin, Heidelberg: Springer-Verlag.

Murch, Walter. 2001. *In the blink of an eye: A perspective on film editing*. Los Angeles, CA: Silman-James Press.

Nagel, Silke. 2009. Das Übersetzen von Untertiteln: Prozess und Probleme der Kurzfilme 'Shooting Bookie', 'Wasp' und 'Green Bush' [The translation of subtitles: Process and problems in the short films 'Shooting Bookie', 'Wasp' and 'Green Bush']. In Silke Nagel, Susanne Hezel, Katharina Hinderer & Katrin Pieper (eds.), *Audiovisuelle Übersetzung. Filmuntertitelung in Deutschland, Portugal und Tschechien*. Frankfurt am Main: Frankfurt am Main: Lang.

NDA. 2016. *CEUD website*. http://universaldesign.ie/Technology-ICT/Digital-TV-equipment-and-services/guidelines-for-digital-tv-equipment-and-services/Language-translations/Ensure-that-subtitles-are-easy-to-read/, accessed 2016-03-25.

Nedergaard-Larsen, Birgit. 1993. Culture-bound problems in subtitling. *Perspectives: Studies in Translatology* 2. 207–242.

Neves, Josélia. 2007. Of Pride and Prejudice: The divide between subtitling and sign language interpreting on television. *The Sign Language Translator and Interpreter (SLTI)* 1(2). 251–274.

Neves, Josélia. 2009. Interlingual subtitling for the deaf and hard-of-hearing. In Jorge Díaz Cintas & Gunilla Anderman (eds.), *Audiovisual translation: Language transfer on screen*, 151–169. New York: Palgrave Macmillan.

Nielsen, Jakob. 1999. *Do interface standards stifle design creativity?* Jakob Nielsen's Alertbox. http://www.useit.com/alertbox/990822.html, accessed 2016-10-17.

Nielsen, Jakob. 2003. *Usability 101: Introduction to usability*. https://www.nngroup.com/articles/usability-101-introduction-to-usability, accessed 2016-10-08.

Nord, Christiane. 1993. *Einführung in das funktionale Übersetzen. Am Beispiel von Titeln und Überschriften. [Text functions in translation: Titles and headings as a case in point]*. Tübingen: Francke.

Nornes, Abé Mark. 1999. For an abusive subtitling. *Film Quarterly* 52(3). 17–34.

O'Brien, Sharon. 2009. Eye tracking in translation-process research: Methodological challenges and solutions. In Inger M. Mees, Fabio Alves & Susanne

Göpferich (eds.), *Methodology, technology and innovation in translation process research: A tribute to Arnt Lykke Jakobsen* (Copenhagen Studies in Language 38), 251–266. Copenhagen: Samfundslitteratur.

O'Hagan, Minako. 2009. Evolution of user-generated translation: Fansubs, translation hacking and crowdsourcing. *The Journal of Internationalisation and Localisation* 1. 94–121.

Orero, Pilar. 2006. Real-time subtitling: A Spanish overview. *Intralinea – Special Issue on Respeaking.* http://www.intralinea.org/specials/article/Real-time_subtitling_in_Spain, accessed 2016-10-24.

Orrego Carmona, David. 2015. *The reception of (non)professional subtling.* Universitat Rovira i Virgili, Spain Doctoral dissertation.

Park, Seung-Bo, Kyung-Jin Oh, Heung Nam Kim & Geun-Sik Jo. 2008. *Automatic subtitles localization through speaker identification in multimedia system.* http://ieeexplore.ieee.org/document/4573173/, accessed 2016-10-10.

Pedersen, Jan. 2005. How is culture rendered in subtitles? In *MuTra conderence proceedings.* http://www.euroconferences.info/.../2005_Pedersen_Jan.pdf, accessed 2016-10-08.

Perego, Elisa (ed.). 2012. *Eye tracking in audiovisual translation.* Rome: Aracne.

Perego, Elisa, Fabio Del Missier, Marco Porta & Mauro Mosconi. 2010. The cognitive effectiveness of subtitle processing. *Media Psychology* 13. 243–272.

Pieters, R.ik & M. Wedel. 2008. Informativeness of eye movements for visual marketing. In Michel Wedel & R. Pieters (eds.), *Visual marketing. From attention to action,* 43–71. New York: Lawrence Erlbaum.

Poole, Alex & Linden J. Ball. 2005. *Eye tracking in human-computer interaction and usability research: Current status and future prospects.* In Claude Ghaoui (ed.), *Encyclopedia of Human Computer Interaction.* Idea Group.

Posner, Michael I. 2005. Orienting of attention. *Journal of Experimental Psychology* 32. 3–25.

Preiser, Siegfried. 1976. *Kreativitätsforschung [Creativity research].* Darmstadt: Wissenschaftliche Buchgesellschaft.

Prinzmetal, William, Samuel Park & Christin McCool. 2005. Attention: Reaction time and accuracy reaveal different mechanisms. *Journal of Experimental Psychology: General* 134(1). 73–92.

Purves, Dale, George J. Augustine, David Fitzpatrick, Lawrence C. Katz, Anthony-Samuel LaMantia, James O. McNamara & S. Mark Williams (eds.). 2001. *Neuroscience.* Sunderland: Sinauer Associates, Inc.

Quitsch, Julian. 2010. *Der Film vor dem Film [The film before the film].* Halle: Burg Glebichstein Hochschule für Kunst und Design Diploma Thesis.

R Project. 2016. *About.* https://www.r-project.org/about.html, accessed 2016-08-08.

Radach, Ralph, Albrecht W. Inhoff & Dieter Heller. 2004. Orthographic regularity gradually modulates saccade amplitudes in reading. *European Journal of Cognitive Psychology* 16. 27–51.

Radach, Ralph & Alan Kennedy. 2004. Theoretical perspectives on eye movements in reading: Past controversies, current issues, and an agenda for future research. *European Journal of Cognitive Psychology* 16(1). 3–26.

Rawsthorn, Alice. 2007. The director Timur Bekmambetov turns film subtitling into an art. *The New York Times.* http://www.nytimes.com/2007/05/25/style/25iht-design28.1.5866427.html?_r=0, accessed 2016-10-08.

Rayner, Keith. 1975. The perceptual span and peripheral cues in reading. *Cognitive Psychology* 7. 65–81.

Rayner, Keith. 1998. Eye movements and attention in reading, scene perception, and visual search. *Psychological Bulletin* 124. 372–422.

Rayner, Keith. 2009. Eye movements and attention in reading, scene perception, and visual search. *Journal of Experimental Psychology* 62(8). 1457–1506.

Rayner, Keith & S. D. Duffy. 1986. Lexical complexity and fixation times in reading: Effects of word frequency, verb complexity and lexical ambiguity. *Memory and Cognition* 14. 191–201.

Rayner, Keith & George W. McConkie. 1976. What guides a reader's eye movements? *Vision Research* 16(8). 829–837.

Rayner, Keith & Alexander Pollatsek. 1989. *The psychology of reading.* Englewood Cliffs, NJ: Prentice Hall.

Rayner, Keith, Caren M. Rotello, Andrew J. Stewart, Jessica Keir & Susan A. Duffy. 2001. Integrating text and pictorial information: Eye movements when looking at print advertisements. *Journal of Experimental Psychology: Applied* 7. 219–226.

Rayner, Keith, Sara C. Sereno & Gary E. Raney. 1996. Eye movement control in reading: A comparison of two types of models. *Journal of Experimental Psychology–Human Perception and Performance* 22(5). 1188–1200.

Reiß, Katharina & Hans J. Vermeer. 1984. *Grundlegung einer allgemeinen Translationstheorie [Towards a general theory of translation action].* Tübingen: Max Niemeyer.

Remael, Aline. 2007. Sampling subtitling for the deaf and the hard-of-hearing in Europe. In Jorge Díaz Cintas, Pilar Orero & Aline Remael (eds.), *Sampling subtitling for the deaf and the hard-of-hearing in europe*, 23–52. Amsterdam: Rodopi.

Remael, Aline, Annick de Houwer & Reinhild Vandekerckhove. 2008. Intralingual open subtitling in Flanders: Audiovisual translation, linguistic variation and audience needs. *Journal of Specialised Translation* 10. 76–105.

Rickheit, Gert, Theo Herrmann & Werner Deutsch. 2003. *Psycholinguistik: Ein internationales Handbuch [Psycholinguistics: An international handbook]*. Berlin: de Gruyter.

Robinson, Tasha. 2014. "John Wick". *The Dissolve.* https : / / thedissolve . com / reviews/1168-john-wick/, accessed 2016-10-08.

Romero-Fresco, Pablo. 2013. Accessible filmmaking: Joining the Dots between audiovisual translation, accessibility and filmmaking. *Journal of Specialised Translation* 20. 201–223.

Romero-Fresco, Pablo. 2015. *The reception of subtitles for the deaf and hard-of-hearing in Europe.* Bern: Peter Lang.

Rosen, Steven. 2006. "Night Watch" freaks the BOT; "CSA" score well in New York. *IndieWIRE.* http://www.indiewire.com/2006/02/night-watch-freaks-the-bot-csa-scores-well-in-new-york-77119, accessed 2016-10-10.

Rozema, Patricia. 2004. Little life lines in "Desperanto". In Atom Egoyan & Ian Balfour (eds.), *Subtitles: On the foreigness of film,* 65–67. Cambridge, MA: MIT Press, Alphabet City.

Schiessl, Michael, Sabrina Duda, Aandreas Thölke & Rico Fischer. 2003. Eye tracking and its application in usability and media research. *MMI Interaktiv – Eye Tracking* 1(6). 41–50.

Schotter, Elizabeth R. & Keith Rayner. 2012. Eye movements in reading. Implications for reading subtitles. *Eye Tracking in Audiovisual Translation.* 83–104.

Schreitmüller, Andreas. 1994. *Filmtitel [film titles].* Münster: University of Constance Doctoral dissertation.

Screenfont. 2016. http://www.screenfont.ca, accessed 2016-07-01.

Secară, Alina. 2016. Cn U read ths? The reception of txt language in subtitling. In Dorothy Kenny (ed.), *IATIS yearbook, human issues in translation technology.* London, New York: Routledge.

Seifferth, Veronika. 2009. *Die deutsche Synchronisation amerikanischer Fernsehserien [The German dubbing of American television series].* Trier: Wissenschaftlicher Verlag Trier.

Shneiderman, Ben. 1998. *Designing the user interface: Strategies for effective human-computer interaction.* Boston, MA: Addison-Wesley Longman.

Sinha, Amresh. 2004. The use and abuse of subtitles. In Atom Egoyan & Ian Balfour (eds.), *Subtitles: On the foreigness of film,* 65–67. Cambridge, MA: MIT Press, Alphabet City.

Stein, Morris I. 1953. Creativity and culture. *The Journal of Psychology* 36. 311–322.

Stolze, Radegundis. 1997. *Übersetzungstheorien. Eine Einführung [Translation theory. An introduction]*. 2nd edn. Tübingen: Gunter Narr Verlag Tübingen.

Subtitling International UK. 1994. *Subtitling for TV and video – A short manual*. London: Subtitling International (UK) Ltd.

Sutten, Valerie. 2016. *Physical versus cultural deafness*. SignWriting. http://www.signwriting.org/about/questions/quest024.html, accessed 2016-10-12.

Szarkowska, Agnieszka. 2009. The audiovisual landscape in Poland at the dawn of the 21st century. In Angelika Goldstein & Biljana Golubović (eds.), *Foreign language movies – Dubbing vs. subtitling*, 185–201. Hamburg: Verlag Dr. Kovač.

Szarkowska, Agnieszka, Izabela Krijtz, Zuzanna Kłyszejko & Anna Wieczorek. 2011. Verbatim, standard, or edited? Reading patterns of different captioning styles among deaf, hard of hearing, and hearing viewers. *American Annals of the Deaf* 156(4). 363–378.

Technical Challenges. 2014. https://www.uniklinik-freiburg.de/fileadmin/mediapool/07_kliniken/psy_psykuj/pdf/lehre/ESSEM_2014/ESSEM_2014_--_Lecture_slides_--_Hutton_-_Technical_challenges.pdf, accessed 2016-03-25.

TFDVD Research Labs. 2005. *TFDVD implements 'seamless branching'*. http://www.dvdverification.com/public/85.cfm, accessed 2016-06-05.

Thompson, Peter. 2000. *Subtitles*. http://www.chicagomediaworks.com/files/subtitles.pdf, accessed 2016-10-08.

Törnqvist, Egil. 1995. Fixed pictures, changing words. Subtitling and dubbing the film "Babettes Gæstebud". *TijdSchrift voor Skandinavistick* 16(1). 47–64.

Tufte, Edward R. 1990. *Envisioning information*. Cheshire, CT: Graphics Press.

Valdés, Berenice, Andrés Catena & Paloma Marí-Beffa. 2005. Automatic and controlled semantic processing: A masked prime-task effect. *Consciousness and Cognition* 14. 278–295.

Veiga, Maria José. 2009. The translation of audiovisual humour in just a few words. In Jorge Díaz Cintas (ed.), *New trends in audiovisual translation – Topics in translation*, 162–179. Bristol: Multilingual Matters.

Vit, Armin. 2005. *Subtítulos en acción (Subtitles in action)*. http://www.underconsideration.com/speakup/archives/002231.html, accessed 2016-10-08.

Volk, Martin. 2008. The automatic translation of film subtitles. A machine translation success story? In Joakim Nivre, Mats Dahllöf & Beáta Megyesi (eds.), *Resourceful language technology: Festschrift in honor of Anna Sågvall Hein*. Uppsala: Uppsala University.

# References

Volk, Martin, R. Sennrich, C. Hardmeiner & F. Tidström. 2010. Machine translation of TV subtitles for large scale production. In, 53–62. Denver, USA.

Volkmann, Frances C., Lorrin A. Riggs & Keith D. White. 1978. Central and peripheral determinants of saccadic suppression. In John W. Senders, Dennis F. Fisher & Richard A. Monty (eds.), *Eye movements and the higher psychological functions*, 35–54. Hillsdale, NJ: Lawrence Erlbaum.

Weinberger, Anja. 2010. *Corporate Identity: Großer Auftritt für kleine Unternehmen [Corporate identity: Big performance for small companies]*. Munich: Stiebner Verlag GmbH.

Zabalbeascoa, Patrick. 1996. Translating jokes for dubbed television situation comedies. *Translator* 2(2). 235–257.

# Name index

# Subject index